MEXICO

T R A V   B U G S
TRAVEL GUIDES

Publisher:	Aileen Lau
Project Editor:	Catherine Khoo
Assisting Editor:	Vanita Jayaram
	Emma Tan
DTP Design & Layout:	Sares Kanapathy
	Sarina Afandie
	Michelle Ng
Production:	Brian Wyreweden
Illustrations:	June Tham
Cover Artwork:	Susan Harmer
Maps:	Hong Li

First Edition, 1994

© Sun Tree Publishing Limited

For all enquiries concerning Editorial, Production, Rights and Marketing:

Sun Tree Publishing Singapore Pte Ltd
205, Henderson Road #03-01
Henderson Industrial Park
Singapore 0315
Tel: (65) 276 4700
Fax: (65) 276 4727

ISBN: 981-00-4282-5
Printed in Singapore

Titles published/in progress:
Alaska – American Southwest – Australia – Bali – California – Canada – Caribbean – China –England – Florida – France – Germany – Greece – Hawaii – Italy – India – Indonesia – Ireland – Japan – Kenya – Malaysia – Mexico – Nepal – New England – New York – Pacific Northwest USA – Singapore – Spain – Thailand – Turkey – Vietnam

MEXICO

Text by
Tan Chung Lee
Keith Mundy

Project Editor
Catherine Khoo

CONTENTS

C O N T E N T S

C O N T E N T S

CONTENTS

WHAT TO DO

EASY REFERENCE

MAPS

From ancient times to the present day

the color and vigor of nature is reflected in Mexico's colorful blossoms.

and the revolutionary

The artistic, the sublime

as portrayed in Mexico's culture of paintings and murals.

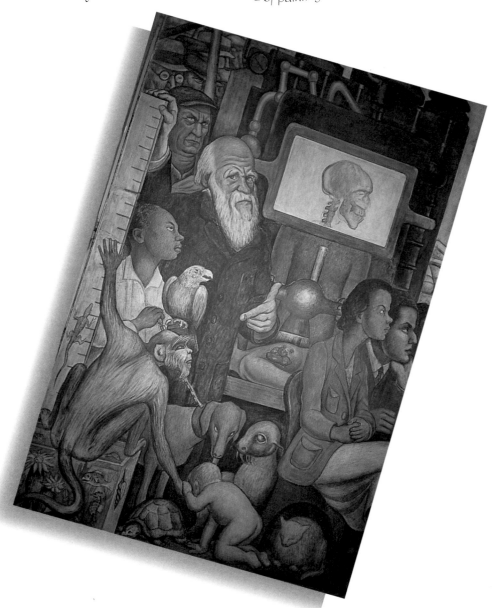

Bold and beautiful, proud and picturesque,

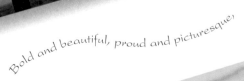

Mexico, the land of the sombrero, tequila, marimbas and mariachis.

Color. Fiery passion. Fervor. Magnificent Mexico exudes all of this and more. Just like the kind of mural the bold artful strokes of Diego Rivera would have produced, Mexico is a vivid tableau of amazing diversity, in terms of its climate, geography, culture, people and myriad attractions. Land of myths, the *mariachi*, the macho male, and of perennial pyramids whose builders worshipped the sun, Mexico is anything but dull.

There's plenty to see and do: you can go on a ramble through charming colonial towns to marvel at their elegant mansions and splendid churches.

Or step back in time to discover ancient cities and ceremonial centers; dive underwater to explore spectacular coral gardens, or take to the high seas for some thrilling game fishing tee off at a magnificent golf course, or sit back to watch an exciting bullfight.

Mexico is also a land of incredible photo opportunities. Competing for the cam-

Welcome to the land of myths, mariachis, macho males and dark-haired beauties.

Introduction

1

A view of the Caribbean sea and bone-white sands.

era's eye are grand mountainous landscapes and panoramic coastal views; colorful markets and exquisite handicrafts; vibrant, costumed dancers at festivals and exotically attired Indians in remote villages.

Nation of Steep Contrasts

It is a nation of steep contrasts. The warm cobalt – blue waters of the Pacific wash the idyllic beaches of Mexico's resort-studded western coastline, which draws millions of foreign visitors a year. In the east, the emerald-colored Caribbean Sea fringes the bone-white sandy shores of Mexico's thumb-shaped Yucatan Peninsula, whose unlikely com-

bination of fun-in-the-sun glitzy resorts and steamy jade-green jungles pockmarked with ancient Maya temples, makes it one of the country's most popular tourist destinations.

Between the two coasts lies a different Mexico: a central plateau averaging 1,524 m (5,000 ft) high and forming the heartland of the nation. It is the agricultural belt of Mexico yielding grain, fruit and vegetables to sustain its 82 million population; it was also the birthplace for the struggle of independence and the home of the majority of its people.

Like crinkled onion paper, the plateau rises to peak at three of the nation's snow-capped and highest summits over 5,182 m (17,000 ft), Pico de Orizaba, Popocatepetl and Iztaccihuatl.

The mesmerizing color and exuberance of Mexico's festivals!

Zesty Fiestas

The latter two, are in a romantic legend that is the stuff of Mexican folklore. What's more, many of such legends are the focus of the zesty fiestas that Mexicans celebrate each year. The Mexicans are an exuberant fun-loving people who have an ear for music, a penchant for dance and artistic hands that produce some of the world's most stunning handicrafts. Imbued with such a lively spirit, it is little wonder that fiestas are celebrated with so much gusto for they give Mexicans the perfect excuse to make merry and to indulge in eating, which is almost a national pastime.

Ah...the fiestas Mexicanas cel-ebrate, sometimes last for days. Join the people in the streets as they celebrate; it may be standing room only but it's the best way to truly capture the Mexican spirit.

An Enigmatic People

Mexicans are also an enigmatic lot. A family-doting and deeply religious individual, who crosses himself whenever he passes a church, the Mexican male, for instance, often thinks nothing of taking on a mistress after marriage. You may come across Mexicans who are surly and who may disparagingly call anyone remotely resembling a *norte-americano* a *gringo* (or a *gringa* if she's a

Spear-fishing in the abundant waters off Mexico.

woman); yet, you will also meet Mexicans who are warm and welcoming to visitors. They will personally walk with you to your destination if you are lost; they are curious to know where you come from and they are delighted if you speak some Spanish.

Manana Syndrome

There will be times, though, when you will be exasperated by the *manana* syndrome and by the Mexican habit of turning up late for appointments and sometimes not at all!

Mexicans move to a different rhythm: service in places like restaurants and bus stations is unhurried; if nothing can be achieved today, the attitude is, don't worry, there's always tomorrow (*manana*).

It is also difficult to typify the Mexican. As in other parts of the world, each day in the urban centers of Mexico, executives in suits ride in chauffeured limousines or drive in their own sedans to offices and factories while millions of others, both men and women, ride on buses and trains to report for work. Yet, elsewhere in outlying areas in Mexico, a different world also exists. Whole villages of Indians who are descended from Mexico's ancient civilizations carry on much as their ancestors did. These native Indians, wear traditional costumes and speak their own language. By farming in the fields, weaving textiles and

Pyramids are major tourist attractions.

fashioning crafts by hand, they are following a pattern of life that has been largely unbroken from the days of the Maya, the Olmecs or the Aztecs.

It is this diversity and unpredictability that make Mexico such a fascinating place to visit. Unless you have plenty of time, it is impossible to see all of Mexico at once; it's too big and the distances too great. Decide what you wish to see and concentrate your travels in one area, returning to explore the other parts of the country on future trips. And one thing's for sure, Mexico is one country you will want to keep coming back to. Through our essays, illustrations and helpful nuggets of information, we will guide you to the best places to go, and advise you on what to see and do, in short, we will open up the magical world that is Mexico, for you to enjoy. *Bienvenido y buen viaje!*

Fast Facts

Area: 761,601 sq miles
Population: 81.25 million
Capital: Mexico City, D.F.
Language: Spanish with Indian languages spoken in remote areas
Government: Republic (31 states and a federal district)
Economy: Agriculture, tourism and petroleum
People: Mestizos (mixed ancestry), Indians, Europeans
Religion: Predominantly Catholic (95 per cent)
Currency: Mexican peso
National flower: Dahlia
National bird: Golden eagle
National colors: Red, green and white
Highest point: Pico de Orizaba at 5,700 m (18,701 ft) high.

Mexico has one of the most profound cultural traditions in the world, comparable to Italy, Egypt, India or China. Like Egypt especially – another pyramid builder – its ancient traditions were suddenly superseded by an invading culture which radically transformed it, –. the Spanish Conquest was decisive in the case of Mexico. Today its culture is overwhelmingly of European origin, but with a strong and ever present undercurrent from the pre-Columbian past. The civilisations that have contributed to Mexico go back several thousand years, far before Columbus' 1492 voyage of discovery which brought the American continent to the knowledge of the Old World for the first time.

Imposing Toltec warrior columns.

History

7

The civilisations of pre-Columbian America evolved in total isolation. From their ancient dawn until the Spanish Conquest, they never once came

Colonial depiction of the AD 1325 founding of Tenochtitlan.

into contact with other cultures or continents. The American continent became populated in the paleolithic age by hunters who had crossed the Bering Strait from Asia to Alaska either over a land bridge or over ice, up to 40,000 years ago. These Asian peoples, erroneously labelled "Indians" by the Spanish, gradually spread southwards until they had settled all the way to Cape Horn by 11,000 years ago. In Central America and the Andes civilisations began to rise 3,000 years ago. The American civilisations evolved quite independently from their Old World counterparts.

The result was original and paradoxical, offering both enormous deficiencies and astounding discoveries. The pre-Columbians had no knowledge of the wheel, the plough or the potter's wheel; they had no domestic animals except dogs, turkeys, bees and llamas (in Peru). Nonetheless they elaborated a system of writing and perfected astonishingly accurate calendars. Metallurgy was used only to produce sacred vessels for religious ceremonies and gold and silver ornaments, yet the pre-Columbians created vast political organisations and their societies were governed by powerful religious structures.

Agrarian Economies

These civilisations developed in two main areas: in today's central and southern Mexico and Guatemala, and in the

Benito Juarez

Monument to Benito Juarez in Oaxaca.

The change that came over Mexico in the 19th century can be seen most clearly in the origins of its three most celebrated leaders: Miguel Hidalgo the *creole* revolutionary, Benito Juarez the Indian reformer, and Porfirio Diaz the *mestizo* dictator.

All three were from social groups previously excluded from power under Spanish rule. Of the three there can be no doubt who was the most progressive and the best loved: Juarez.

Benito Juarez was born a Zapotec Indian in a village of Oaxaca, and orphaned at the age of three. At 12, speaking no Spanish, he walked 75 km to Oaxaca City to seek work. Taken in by a friar, the boy became a household servant and was provided with an education. Destined for the priesthood, he became a lawyer instead. His mind was incisive, his manner orderly, his morality strict. Patient and determined, he became a professor of law, gave his services free of charge to the poor, and rose to be Governor of Oaxaca from 1847 to 1852.

Taking to national politics as an advocate of liberal reform and opponent of Santa Anna, he was imprisoned and exiled in New Orleans, later to return and take part in Santa Anna's ousting. He became Minister of Justice and in 1857 drew up the Juarez Law, which took away privileges of the church and the army and sought to establish a more democratic state with a liberal constitution. Since Juarez was able to distinguish Christian ideals from church power politics and was desirous of promoting individual liberty, this law included the separation of church and state, nationalisation of church lands and the guarantee of religious freedom. The conservatives vehemently contested it and steely Juarez took over as president. The War of the Reforms ensued in 1858, savage and uncompromising.

When unpaid debts prompted the French to invade and occupy Mexico, Juarez fought them whilst the conservatives welcomed them. The country split once more – between imperialists and republicans. Juarez was on the run most of the time; gradually, his shabby black coach came to symbolise the patriotic heart of Mexico, forever in pursuit of republican freedoms.

The tide turned in Juarez's favor in 1864. After Emperor Maximilian's brief reign, Juarez returned to power and set about further curtailing conservative power through abolishing the great *haciendas*, a mammoth task which was far from done by the time of his death, by a heart attack, in 1872.

Juarez was the people's hero, but he had not advanced them very far against the status quo, and his great rival Porfirio Diaz, also from a humble Oaxaca background, was to worsen their plight. Still Juarez made a notable mark, and it is from his rule that many people date the true birth of the Mexican nation and republic, for he reshaped the constitution to benefit all Mexicans and not just the old power structure inherited from the Spanish.

Giant head in the Olmec-La Venta site.

central Andes in South America. They had essentially agrarian economies: the main food crops were corn, beans and squash (potatoes in the Andes), and they were familiar with the properties of medicinal substances, spices and fibers such as cotton. Their total isolation from the rest of the world is proved by the pre-1492 absence of cereals (wheat or rice), as well as by the absence of cocoa, tomatoes, tobacco, potatoes and other American plant products until the 16th century.

The roots of today's Mexico lie in

A recreation of Tlaloc, the Rain God in Teotihucan culture.

the civilisations that grew up in Mesoamerica, the historians' term for the pre-Hispanic region stretching from central Mexico down to Honduras. In these tropical climes, various peoples built a series of successive civilisations centered in different areas, of which the Mayas and the Aztecs are but the best known. All of them were characterised by massive ceremonial structures and a subservience to religious leaders.

This core culture, with its sacrifices to the gods and elaborate time-keeping practices, plainly derived from the hunters' and farmers' dependence on the vagaries of nature and their desire to predict and control them. In this they were led first by tribal shamans, later by priest-kings, and finally by warrior em-perors. All of the Mesoamerican cultures shared these peculiarities: hieroglyphic writing, books of bark paper or deerskin which were folded like screens, a complex permutation calendar, a team game played with a rubber ball in a special court, specialised markets in which cocoa beans were the currency, human sacrifice and self-mutilation, and worship of a rain god and the imperturbalbe Feathered Serpent.

The Formative Period

The Olmecs founded the first great Mesoamerican civilisation, flourishing from about 1200 to 400 BC. The Olmec heartland was on the Gulf Coast in

Guardians at the Aztec temple in Zocalo.

today's Veracruz and Tabasco states, a region of swamps, lagoons and forests. Here they erected great ceremonial centers featuring massive sculpted human heads. They possessed artistic skills, such as basalt and jade carving, so sophisticated as to indicate a long period of development, of which we know little.

The Olmecs exerted the first culturally unifying influence on Mesoamerica. Olmec myths and rituals were handed down to the Mayas, Zapotecs, Mixtecs, Toltecs and Aztecs. Their hieroglyphic writing and calendrical concepts later appeared in Maya culture. At their La Venta site stand the two fundamental monuments which characterise all subsequent civilisations – the pyramid and the ball court.

The Classic Period

Teotihuacan was the New World's first great city and the most powerful political and cultural force in Mesoamerica during the early Classic Period. Sited just northeast of modern Mexico City, in the Valley of Mexico that from this time on played a central role in Mexican history, the Teotihuacan people constructed the most massive of all structures in Mesoamerica, the Pyramids of the Sun and the Moon. At its zenith between AD 350 and 650, the capital had an estimated population of 200,000 and was a true city with extensive housing. It mysteriously fell into ruin in the 8th century.

A depiction of 'Dancers' in Monte Alban

In Oaxaca, to the southeast of the Valley of Mexico, there grew from about 600 BC an Olmec-influenced civilisation centered on Monte Alban, a mountain whose top had been levelled to create a ceremonial center. This became fully developed by the Zapotec people around AD 600, who were superseded by the conquering Mixtecs in AD 1000.

The Mayan civilisation arose in the highlands of southeastern Mexico and Guatemala, maturing in about AD 150, and progressed northward to Yucatan where it fell under Toltec influence from about AD 1000, reviving then declining to exhaustion in about 1450.

The Mayas were ancient Mexico's most profound thinkers, creators of the most advanced calendrical and astronomical systems, mathematicians who used zero, stone carvers of genius, builders of countless ceremonial cities, which fell into ruin for unknown reasons – possibly famine, war or insurrection.

One strong theory is for this decline, that each Mesoamerican civilisation fell under the weight of its population's demands on the surrounding countryside. Without the plough, the wheel or drought animals, both agriculture and transport were difficult, so that great pressure was put on easily accessible and workable land to produce food, which eventually became exhausted, weakening the civilisations, provoking internal conflict, and leaving them prone to attack by vengeful vassals or rivals.

Chac-Mool sculpture in the Temple of the Warriors, Chichen-Itza, Yucatan.

The Post-Classic Period

Certainly such turns of events could lead to militarism, which is indeed the dominant feature of the final phase of pre-Hispanic history, when warriors took over as the ruling class from the theocrats, who had perhaps been seen as failing in their job of ensuring that the gods brought peace and prosperity.

In central Mexico, the Toltecs ruled from about 950 to 1150, centered on Tula. Warlike, their influence is also strongly seen as far away as Yucatan in the final phase of Mayan culture.

It was not until after 1300 that the militaristic Aztecs arrived from the north in the Valley of Mexico and settled on islands in Lake Texcoco, now the site of Mexico City.

Tenochtitlan was their name for the place, which grew rapidly into a powerful city of possibly 300,000 citizens, with immense market places trading all the produce of Mexico. They also built numerous tall pyramid temples.

The Aztecs epitomise the warrior cultures which ruled Mesoamerica in the last centuries before the Spanish Conquest. Uncultured, but determined to succeed, they gradually conquered or subdued all the other peoples of central Mexico and held a large empire in thrall, demanding regular tribute and becoming fabulously rich in gold, silver and jade, jaguar skins and feathers of the rainbow-colored quetzal bird. To ensure continued good fortune, they made human sacrifices to their gods atop their pyramids, tearing out the hearts of captured enemies as ritual offerings. War was a way of life, but the Aztecs were also artists and philosophers. The emperor Moctezuma's reflective nature contributed to the downfall of the last great Mesoamerican civilisation.

The Spanish Conquest

In 1519, Hernan Cortes landed on the Gulf Coast and founded, with characteristic Spanish flourish, the settlement of La Villa Rica de la Vera Cruz, "The Rich City of the True Cross". Later shortened to Veracruz, the name epitomised Spanish imperialism in the Americas: the lust for gold and converts to Christianity, to which all else was subordinate. Despite their arrogance and avarice, however, Cortes's men were amazed and impressed by the great city they found in the Valley of Mexico.

The Aztecs were equally amazed to see strange men with blue eyes and beards, clothed in metal, riding upon large quadrupeds, and possessing noisy weapons which could kill from a distance. Though Cortes's men were few in number, less than 400, the Aztec ruler

Moctezuma decided they should be appeased and bribed to go away, partly on account of their magical-seeming equipment and also because their coming fitted a Mesoamerican legend about the god Quetzalcoatl, whose return to earth was predicted and who should be welcomed by them.

The gold merely whetted the Spaniards' appetite. They demanded more and, failing to get it, took Moctezuma hostage in his own palace. Heavily outnumbered, this required great bravado, but when Moctezuma died in their custody, they had to escape by night with great loss of life. They later returned with a large army of Mexican allies, the Tlaxcalans from the coast, and with a well-planned military strategy. Their defeat in 1521 of the almighty Aztecs was truly remarkable, for the Spaniards' technological and tactical superiority was far outweighed by the Aztecs' numerical and situational advantages, but there were good reasons for the defeat. The Aztecs were sapped by long-standing prophesies of doom and hampered by their practice of taking live captives for sacrifice. Tenochtitlan was weakened by small-pox and a three-month siege. The Spanish were extremely lustful for land and gold

EL Grito De Dolores

Revolutions don't usually have clear-cut beginnings, but the one that initiated the independence of Mexico has a time, a place and a name: *El Grito de Dolores* – The Cry of Dolores – a call to arms that issued from the mouth of Father Miguel Hidalgo y Costilla, the parish priest of Dolores in Guanajuato state, on the morning of 16 September, 1810. The date is now celebrated as Independence Day throughout Mexico with colorful patriotic parades and ceremonies, where the famous cry is repeated.

From the moment in 1808 that Napoleon invaded Spain and placed his brother on the throne, many in the Mexican *creole* middle class began seriously to contemplate throwing off the Spanish yoke. Hidalgo would meet in Queretaro with a magistrate named Dominguez and a captain called Allende, who together planned to rouse the crowds at a local festival to an uprising. But word leaked out.

Hidalgo decided to speak out at Sunday mass. He urged rebellion, the slaying of *gachupines*; he called for equality for all and land for the landless. With *El Grito de Dolores*, the revolution had begun. Father Hidalgo and Captain Allende led a rag-tag band of marchers armed with spears and sticks from town to town, gathering thousands of *mestizo* and In-

dian supporters. Though previously no saint, the priest had suddenly become a firebrand.

They took Guanajuato, a mining center, and then were confronted by a government army. Mayhem ensued. Hidalgo marched on to Guadalajara, sang a *te deum* in the cathedral, took the governor's palace, and set up an administration. Massacres of Spaniards ensued and emissaries spread out all over Mexico to foment insurrection. The movement was disorderly and bloodthirsty, and many *creoles* had qualms about it, even Hidalgo himself perhaps, because he withdrew when about to enter Mexico City. Confronted again by the Spanish army at Guadalajara, he was crushingly defeated in January 1811.

Hidalgo fled north, but was captured and shot in July. But his name lived on to inspire others; ten years later independence was achieved. Though repudiated by the church before his execution, Hidalgo is honored today as father of the nation. Every 15 evening of September, the President of the Republic, and governors and mayors all over Mexico lean from their palace balconies and shout to the assembled crowds "Long live Mexico! Long live the Virgin of Guadalupe! Death to the *gachupines*!" Spaniards take it in good heart these days.

and determined to kill so as to avoid capture and the horror of sacrifice, and to end it by converting the people to Christianity. Their Mexican allies were bent on avenging themselves against the brutal Aztec domination. These factors seemed to tip the balance.

New Spain

In mid 1521, the last emperor Cuauhtemoc was killed and the Spanish assumed power. One of their first

acts was to raze all the Aztec temples to the ground and to begin building a cathedral over the ruins of the principal pyramid. For precisely 300 years, Mexico was to be a Spanish colony.

Cortes and his men went on to conquer all of Mexico, leaving only minor pockets of resistance, and allocating themselves great estates. Systematic destruction of Mesoamerican culture and forced conversion to Catholicism were hallmarks of early Spanish rule, along with pillage of treasures and enslavement of the population.

Relics of the Mayan civilization – the double jaguar throne in the
Governor's Palace in Uxmal, Yucatan.

The Spanish king named the conquered land "New Spain", made Cortes Governor-General, but soon retired him to a vast estate in Oaxaca and introduced a viceroy from Spain to rule from Mexico City, the new capital, under the direction of the Council of the Indies. The country was divided into provinces and the church was allocated large dominions, eventually owning fully 30 percent of Mexico. Any resurgence of Indian power was prevented by brute force but mostly by the devastating spread of smallpox and by Catholicization of the ruling classes.

Even though royal decrees confirmed the rights of the Indians to their ancestral lands, estates called *encomiendas* were allocated to conquistadors and settlers with Indians as bonded labor, later to become amalgamated into vast haciendas.

By 1570 there were 70,000 Spanish; seeking but not finding El Dorado, they had become farmers and silver miners. Crops like wheat, barley and rice were introduced as were animals like mules, cattle, sheep, pigs and chickens. Rich lodes of silver were discovered and the silver cities of Zacatecas, Guanajuato and San Luis Potosi developed rapidly.

All the principal officials like governors, generals, judges and bishops were appointed from Spain; only middle and lower-level posts were occupied by Mexico-born Spanish, or *creoles*. The military conquest and political consolidation of Mexico were accompanied by a spiritual conquest which was considered the chief justification for the Spanish presence in the new world. The pope had granted Mexico to the Spanish monarchy for this purpose.

Catholic orders took charge of different regions and developed strong power bases allied to their vast land ownership. But the efforts of the religious orders to educate and assimilate the Indians were frustrated by hostile settlers who just wanted laborers on their farms, in their mines and on their building sites, so that the Indian folk cultures and languages persisted.

Two factors strongly influenced Mexico's destiny from the late 16th century: epidemics which wiped out most of the Indian population and profligate government in Spain.

At the conquest, central Mexico alone had an estimated 25 million inhabitants, three times that of Spain. By 1580, fully 90 percent of them were dead from white man's diseases and the ratio was reversed. The Indian civilisations had no hope of recovery and the colonisers were left short of labor. Slaves had to be imported from Africa.

In Spain, royal adventurism in European wars had bankrupted the country, despite the immense wealth in gold and silver that the Spanish galleons had carried across the Atlantic to the monarch. As a result, the crown began selling off land in the colonies. In Mexico, large estates became consolidated both through purchase and by landgrabbing from the Indians, who largely survived as serfs, or *peones*, on these haciendas run by powerful landowners. The church, though at times attempting to defend the Indians from exploitation, became a powerful landowner itself through tithes and bequests and one of the pillars of tri-partite power: church, army, and landed aristocracy.

The 17th and 18th centuries saw no grand events in Mexico, but firmly established a distinct Mexican society. Its economy was run largely via a monopoly of trade with Spain. Silver, sugar and tobacco were leading commodities. The Spanish-born *gachupines* continued to rule in all high positions, with the far more numerous *creoles* occupying lower positions of authority. Intermarriage of Spanish and Indians was common from the start, resulting in a large population of mixed race called *mestizos*.

Still the Indians were the largest group, and were the serfs and laborers, except in the more remote areas where they lived in a traditional manner. By the year 1800, their relative numbers were approximately: 30,000 *gachupines*, 1 million *criollos* or *creoles*, 1.5 million *mestizos*, 3.5 million *indigenas*.

Independence

This society, though far removed from Europe and North America, was already chafing at its injustices and not immune to the winds of change brought by the American and French Revolutions. The catalyst came when Napoleon in-

A wall-painting of the Tree of Paradise in the Tepantitla mural in which two rivers are shown to issue from the God's hands.

vaded Spain in 1808 – the *gachupines*, clinging to their power, accepted the legitimacy of French rule from Madrid, the *creoles* refused to.

Rebellion gathered pace among the local-born Spanish, who were increasingly determined to take control of the destiny, and wealth, of Mexico. In 1810 a liberal priest called Miguel Hidalgo led a movement calling for the abolition of serfdom, land reform and the end of Spanish trading monopolies, which precipitated an 11-year war of independence.

In 1821 independence was finally achieved, after the loss of 60,000 lives, but the character of the new state was not what the liberals had hoped for. *Gachupin* power was merely replaced by the rule of the *creole* elite; even though all citizens of the United States of Mexico were granted equal rights in the constitution, socio-economic relationships remained unchanged for the majority of the population.

The leading figure in the first decades of Mexican independence was General Santa Anna, a flamboyant figure who expelled the last Spanish troops and took office as president several times.

But in the Mexican-American War of 1846-48, which began over border disputes, especially over the ownership of Texas, Anna failed to prevent the United States from occupying Mexico City and then taking Mexico's vast northern territories of California, Arizona, New Mexico and Texas for a mere US$15

Moctezuma

Replica of Moctezuma's quetzal feather head-dress.

Moctezuma II became emperor of the Aztecs in 1502 when they were undisputed masters of Mexico. Their capital Tenochtitlan was greater than any in contemporary Europe, laid out on an island amid a lake, dissected by canals, approached by long causeways, studded with steep pyramids. In the temple to Huitzilopochtli, the god of war, the priests slew multitudes of captives, tearing out their hearts as sacrifices to placate the god and ensure the orderly working of the universe.

Moctezuma ascended the throne as a 34-year-old prince renowned for his valor, sagacity and piety. He consolidated Aztec power over the conquests of his predecessors, but he was repulsed by the nearby Tlaxcalans.

At his opulent palace, the emperor kept a botanical garden and a zoo and aviary filled with exotic animals and birds, jaguars and pu-

mas, toucans and macaws.

Moctezuma represented both the strengths and the weaknesses of the Aztec system. Brave in battle against his Indian adversaries, he could not cope with the unexpected and the inexplicable. He was superstitious, and strange happenings that he could not comprehend filled him with awe. When the Spanish ships first appeared on the Gulf Coast, his couriers brought him reports of towers that moved on the water, and of large beasts that seemed half man, half animal (horse and rider). In Tenochtitlan, there were weird portents of disaster: a comet "like a tongue of fire"; the mysterious burning of a tower of the great temple; a bird with a mirror in its forehead.

As the Spaniards approached Tenochtitlan, the Aztec ruler feared that Cortes was the legendary god-king Quetzalcoatl returning to assert lordship over his people. He also knew that the Spanish had defeated the Tlaxcalans in battle, something even the Aztecs had failed to do, and taken them as allies. Moctezuma was in a deep quandary. He at first ordered Cortes to stay

million. Losing half their land area in this way left a feeling of resentment among Mexicans towards their northern neighbor, which persists to this day.

After this, Santa Anna fell from power and liberals came to the fore, determined to abolish the excessive privileges of the church, army and *hacen-*

dados. In a popular movement, they instituted a constitutional democracy, promulgated freedom of education, freedom of speech and the press, and the separation of church and state. The vicious War of the Reforms ensued in 1858 between liberals and conservatives.

The liberals won under Benito

away from the city; after his warning was ignored, he welcomed the Spanish commander ceremonially. Bernal Diaz, a soldier-historian in Cortes's retinue recounted, "Moctezuma descended from his litter beneath a marvellously rich canopy of green feathers, worked with gold and silver, pearls and green stones... He was richly dressed and wore shoes like sandals with soles of gold covered with precious stones. The four chiefs who supported him were also richly dressed... Many other lords walked before the great Moctezuma, sweeping the ground where he would pass, and putting down mats, so that he would not have to walk on the ground. None of these lords thought of looking in his face; all of them kept their eyes down, with great reverence. When Cortes saw the great Moctezuma approaching, he jumped from his horse and they showed great respect toward each other."

Moctezuma hosted Cortes at a royal palace and attempted to use sorcery to defeat him. When Cortes later seized him and held him prisoner, Moctezuma submitted humbly. Why, with millions of subjects at his power? No explanation but superstition suffices. The emperor continued to rule, even when shackled, but when Spanish troops slew devotees at an Aztec religious rite, the people finally revolted and attacked the Spanish. Moctezuma, attempting to persuade them to lay down their arms, was wounded by a stone. He retired within, refused to speak, or to eat. He later died. The Spaniards fled, but returned to conquer. Moctezuma's name remains synonymous with hesitation, capitulation, and mystery.

Juarez, a lawyer of Zapotec Indian blood; as president he pushed through the reforms but inherited a ruined country heavily in debt to Britain, Spain and France.

All three countries together occupied Mexico to collect the debts, but the French decided to colonise the country, provoking another war and eventually installing Emperor Maximilian in the capital's Chapultepec Castle in 1864. This bizarre interlude lasted only three years, after which Juarez regained power and introduced land, economic and educational reforms. He was succeeded in the 1870s by Porfirio Diaz, whose domination brought industrial and economic modernisation and social and political stagnation in the long and paradoxical period of stability called the Porfiriato.

The Porfiriato

When Diaz took power in 1876, Mexico had 640 km (398 miles) of railways; when he left power in 1911, it had over 20,000 km (12,427 miles). He wanted "order and progress". Foreign capital poured in, paved roads stretched across the country, telephone and telegraph lines proliferated. He ruled as dictator, appointing his own legislators, and enforcing his policies with his army. Juarez's land reforms were suspended or even reversed, land was handed to his allies, the *hacendados*, and the plight of the *peones* worsened. Bandits were eliminated, protestors annihilated, peace was secured. He was ruthless, and successful, up to a point.

His agricultural and land policies were his downfall and weakened Mexico at the same time as his other policies strengthened it, and enriched the chosen few.

Most productive land came into the

Viva Zapata! Viva Villa!

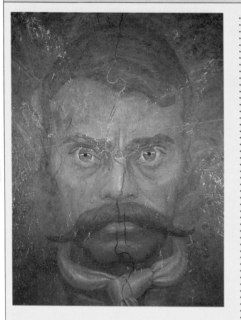

The legendary Emiliano Zapata.

Most people asked to name a Mexican would come up with Zapata or Pancho Villa. These two stars of the Mexican Revolution made such an impact worldwide with their flamboyant garb and dramatic exploits that they have become the most famous Mexicans in the world at large, thanks to photography, Hollywood, and our love of romantic heroes.

Who were they, and what did they really do? What is the story behind those richly atmospheric photographs of swarthy moustachioed men, with bandoliers slung across each shoulder, scowling fiercely beneath wide-brimmed sombreros?

They were quite distinct in character and background: one an idealist from the south, the other an ex-bandit from the north, but they were both men of the people and effective leaders of popular rebellions.

Emiliano Zapata was a peasant farmer in the state of Morelos, south of the capital. His family had suffered land expropriation by the *hacendados*, and he had personally experienced their violence. Following Madero's call to arms in 1910, Zapata roused a peasant army and helped bring him to power. When Madero failed to bring in the land reforms that were the peasants' chief aim, Zapata called for the immediate redistribution of property and set about doing it himself.

Under the banner "*Tierra Y Libertad!*" (Land and Liberty), he led his men, all dressed in traditional peasant sandals, sombreros and white cotton, to the *haciendas* of Morelos, where they took back properties lost under the Porfiriato and began tilling the land.

Zapata was always clear in his aims, close to his followers and always an inspiring leader. His sayings were potent spurs: when he urged, "It is better to die on your feet than live on your knees", it struck a deep chord in his men.

By contrast, Pancho Villa was an opportun-

hands of about 6,000 wealthy and powerful *hacendados*, who used it inefficiently, necessitating the import of corn, a staple food, whilst most peasants, rendered landless, became their laborers and barely survived. After three decades of increasing inequality and repression, even as Mexico modernised, something had to give.

The Revolution

"*Tierra Y Libertad!*" was the cry – "Land and Liberty!" – and Emiliano Zapata was the leader. Coming out of the southern state of Morelos, Zapata was an abused peasant who led other abused peasants in a crusade for their own land

ist, a rousing leader as much interested in his own profit and glory as in the people's progress. He represented the arid northern regions where huge cattle ranches predominated and he led an army of cowboys and former cattle rustlers like himself. Moody and given to random violence, Villa scared other leaders and citizens alike, but having himself escaped the *peones's* bondage, he understood the Revolution's fundamental issues and distributed land to the poor wherever his army occupied territory. Colorful and macho, he mesmerized a lot of women too.

Charismatic Leadership

By their charismatic and forceful leadership, these two men urged the basic issues of land reform and social change that led to the Revolution's most important achievements, but they were by no means the only revolutionary generals – many armed bands roamed the land – and they didn't have the political skills to take power. That fell to Generals Carranza and Obregon, the kind of men who had "always slept on soft pillows," complained Villa.

Zapata's and Villa's fame and fortune reached its height when their armies met to occupy the capital in late 1914, streaming through the streets, shooting in the air, singing and laughing. The caudillos sat and posed for photographers in the president's ornate chair in the National Palace, surrounded by bandoliered followers, but a month later they went home their separate ways.

Pancho Villa – the charismatic leader.

They had come together because they shared a cause, but their men didn't mix, they had no firm political agenda, and they later disagreed. Typical of the times, both were later assassinated by government agents: Zapata in 1919, Villa in 1923. But their legend lives on in Hollywood's makebelieve.

and the freedom to till it. From the north came liberal politician Francisco Madero allied with former bandit Pancho Villa, leader of a motley rebellion of peasants, farmers, miners and the middle class. Together they forced the ousting of Diaz in 1911. Madero became president, but was faint-hearted in his land reforms. Zapata refused to disarm, and returned with his men to Morelos to implement his own far-reaching reform plan. He grabbed land from the *hacendados*, distributed it amongst the peasants, and instituted democratic administration. Meanwhile, conservative forces led by General Huerta shot Madero and took power in 1913.

Huerta tried to impose his rule

Serpent wall in the temple at Tula, the Toltec capital. The middle freize depicts feathered serpents and skulls.

militarily, provoking several revolutionary movements in different parts of the country, notably those of Carranza and Obregon. A chaotic period of conflict eventually resulted in the coming to power of President Carranza in 1917, under a new reformist constitution which prescribed a single four-year presidential term and set up a federal state.

But the country was neither united nor pacified. Military chiefs and rebel leaders continued to control fiefdoms and to enrich themselves. By 1920 Mexico was near collapse – the conse-

tral order on it. With Obregon, the turbulent period of the Mexican Revolution came to an end. He pensioned off Villa with a huge *hacienda* (Zapata had been shot by Carranza's army in 1919). Obregon's presidency finally brought stability and enabled a national renaissance in the arts and the establishment of universal free education.

President Calles's term, which lasted from 1924-28, was notable for the curbing of the power of the Catholic church, long a political problem. The church opposed major provisions of the 1917 constitution like agrarian reform and secular education. Calles declared church lands state property and imposed severe restrictions on the clergy. An armed revolt of militant Catholics resulted in the Cristero Rebellion, but the church had to capitulate in 1929.

But it was not until 1934 with the accession of President Lazaro Cardenas, a socialist and nationalist, however, that real progress was made with the land reforms that had been the focus of the revolutionary movement. Cardenas redistributed almost 20 million hectares of *haciendas* into cooperatives, called *ejidos*. He also nationalised the oil industry and has come to be seen as the president who most embodied the ideals of the Revolution.

After him, Mexico, non-combatant in the Second World War, settled into a long period of consolidation and material progress with, in effect, a one-party political system under the Institutionalised Revolutionary Party.

quence of 10 years of disorder and conflict, the deaths of 10 percent of the population, perhaps even two million people, of weak central government and a crushing foreign debt.

In 1920 the revolutionary general Alvaro Obregon was elected president, he took charge of a drained, divided and devastated country and imposed cen-

Government & Economy

"The genius of revolutionary leadership lay in its capacity to harness the energy and grievances of the popular movement to antithetical ends – state building and capitalist development," wrote Alan Knight in his two-volume study *The Mexican Revolution*. After three decades of revolutionary and reactionary turmoil culminating in the firmly reformist government of Lazaro Cardenas (1934-40), the ensuing half century saw the consolidation of power under the monolithic PRI – Partido Revolucionario Institucional – and steady economic progress until the debt crisis of the 1980s.

The Palacio Nacional, official residence of the Mexican president.

Now in the 1990s Mexico is entering a new phase of its history with market-oriented economic reforms and membership of the North American Free Trade Association (NAFTA).

Since Cardenas, Mexico has experienced remarkable political stability by any standards but particularly in comparison

27

to all other Latin American countries. Functioning under the 1917 Constitution, presidents have been elected every six years, with the baton passed to a new one each time since their re-election is not permitted.

The Congress consists of a 64-seat Senate and a 500-seat Chamber of Deputies, both elected every three years. While numerous political parties participate in elections, one party – the PRI, or Institutional Revolutionary Party – dominates the legislature and has produced every president since the Revolution. In the year before each election, the incumbent PRI president gives the *dedazo*: he "points his finger" at the next PRI presidential candidate, who inevitably becomes the next president.

Mexico's governmental system is unique. Though changing in the 1990s, and due to change much more with the NAFTA agreement, it is still *sui generis*, resembling at one moment a communist one-party state, at another a liberal capitalist democracy. The PRI presents the face that suits the situation, left profile or right. Always nationalist in rhetoric, its foreign policy has been rigorously non-aligned, and pro-Latin America, in which it is a leader. [Mexico is second only to Brazil in population and GDP in Latin America and is the leading Spanish-speaking country in the Americas and the most populous one in the world.]

New Government Order

Inclusivity and patronage have been the ruling party's hallmarks for half a century. The party managed to co-opt, or at least placate, most political forces in the country, and has taken under its wing many significant sectors of the economy: the oil and steel industries, railways and airlines, electricity and telephones, banks and hotels. Jobs at all levels were given as political favors, and state subsidies covered operational losses: the country's economy became inseparable from its political management.

Examples are legion. The PRI handed out political appointments from municipal dogcatcher to president of the republic. Every *campesino* who wanted access to credit, water, or a place to sell vegetables had to negotiate with

The Cathedral and Constitution Square in Mexico City.

the local PRI official. All Mexico City taxi drivers had to carry PRI propaganda in their cabs. Most newspapers and radio and TV stations were under PRI control. Though under President Salinas, most state enterprises were sold off and the media liberalised, the pa-

tronage system largely remained.

The one-party system, has served the nation well during its transition to a modern state. It has assured a peaceful succession to power along with a fair level of civil liberties – a noteworthy achievement in the Latin American con-

The Pull of the North: *Maquiladoras,* Wetbacks and NAFTA

The border between the United States and Mexico provides the starkest contrast in living standards of any frontier on the planet: nowhere else is there such a huge divide between neighboring nations in the quality and the way of life. Consequently, for several decades now, Mexico's northern border, and beyond, has exerted a strong pull on job seekers and made a significant effect on the Mexican economy and society.since at least the 1920s, Mexican migrant farm laborers have travelled legally to the United States to work the harvest in the tomato and lettuce fields of California. In recent decades, illegal migrants have persistently found their way across the border to seek their fortune in any job available. Known as "wetbacks" because so many have had to swim the Rio Bravo (which flows from Mexico's Rio Grande) to get into the United States, they have become a significant proportion of the population in the cities of Texas and southern California. Current illegal and legal immigration combined is reckoned at between 200,000 and 300,000 annually, whilst at least 1.5 million cross the border for temporary jobs.

Needing to stem this flow of humanity, the US and Mexican governments' most imaginative tactic has been the creation of tax-free manufacturing plants within Mexico along the length of the northern border. In addition to reducing the migrant flood, these factories benefit Mexico by providing hundreds of thou-

sands with work and the United Staes by providing cheaper production costs for goods destined for the American market.

They are called *maquiladoras.* They are assembly plants which put together parts mostly manufactured in the USA and export the finished goods mostly back to the USA. Electronic and automotive products predominate. In 1990 there were about 2,200 *maquiladoras* employing 560,000 Mexicans generating US$3.6 billion in foreign exchange. They are located in cities all along the border from Matamoros on the Gulf Coast to Tijuana on the Pacific. Most of these cities face US cities directly over the frontier: Nuevo Laredo and Laredo, Ciudad Juarez and El Paso, Tijuana and San Diego, and so on. Some even have the same name on both sides: Nogales, Sonora and Nogales, Arizona, for example.

A *Maquiladora* City

Tijuana is a prime example of a *maquiladora* city. Located just over the border from San Diego, California, right on the Pacific Coast, it has about 600 assembly plants employing 65,000 workers. They put together anything from integrated circuits to Barbie Dolls, from televisions to Disney teething rings. Unemployment is less than 2 percent and workers come from all over Mexico. *Newsweek* magazine re-

text. Part of the reason for this is the minor role assigned to the armed forces since the 1930s which has kept the military from the kind of political interference or domination that has been so common and so violent elsewhere in 20th-century Latin America.

There have however been, and there continue to be, significant human rights abuses such as police torture and extra-judicial execution, and corruption has

been endemic in the system, particularly since the 1950s. The weakest part of the population has also become mired in poverty in recent decades: notably the pure-blood Indian population and the unemployed urban poor. Some estimates put half the population on or beneath the poverty line.

Until the setbacks of the 1980s, Mexico's economic growth in four decades had been tremendous. In 1910,

ported in 1991 on Dalia Costa who came up from Sinaloa with her husband and got jobs with Deltec, a San Diego-based maker of electric surge protectors for computers. "It is a good place to get a job," she said. Not only manual workers find it attractive; many jobs are created for managers and professionals too.

Previously known as a naughty night out or souvenir stop for southern Californians, Tijuana has boomed on the income from *maquiladoras*. The population has almost trebled since 1980 to over one million, housing has generally improved, a cultural center has been built.

But still Tijuana is dogged by pollution, with millions of gallons of raw sewage and untreated industrial wastes sloshing into the Tijuana River daily, and by the social and environmental problem of squatter shacks smothering hillsides and creeks. Then again, if workers usually get about double the official minimum wage, that still only comes to about US$1 per hour, far less than across the border. To improve matters, NAFTA is the great hope of the future. The free trade area will benefit the *maquiladoras* as much as Mexican manufacturing in general, it is reckoned, but it should also enforce pollution control and reduce the influx of squatters to the border cities and the flow of wetbacks across the border, by providing increased job opportunities all over the country in both manufacturing and agriculture. *"Viva NAFTA!"* could well soon be a popular Mexican cry.

Mexico was basically a rural nation with over 70 percent of its population living off the land. In 1980 only one third of the workforce was in agriculture, while the same percentage worked in industry. Mexico's agriculture and mining continue important to the economy, just as they were during colonial times, but now the oil industry and manufacturing are the two largest contributors to the gross national product.

Mexico's industrial transformation has resulted not only from oil, but also from the manufacture of processed food, motor vehicles (such as the famous Volkswagen Beetle, still produced today), chemicals, paper, and tyres. The change in the complexity of Mexico's economy can be seen from its list of major exports, which a few decades ago were silver, sugar, coffee, lead, copper and zinc but which now include oil, frozen shrimp, chemical products, cars and electrical machinery. From a country that had hardly entered the industrial age in 1910, Mexico has grown into a nation crisscrossed by highways, including some freeways, and barricaded with dams for irrigation and electrical power. Even remote rural areas are now served by buses and electricity, whereas mule and candle power were predominant only 20 years ago.

The people have benefitted from Mexico's political stability and economic progress, but persistent pockets of poverty remain. While Mexico's middle class has grown and the majority of the population enjoys an improved standard of living, millions of Indian peasants still have not been assimilated by the new Mexico. Remaining outside the mainstream of the economy, millions speak only their Indian language, and many own no shoes and live on the edge of survival. Mexico's recent economic problems have only worsened their situation

From Olmecs to Oilmen

The Gulf Coast state of Tabasco is the cradle of Mexico's culture, the land of the Olmecs who made the first great Mesoamerican civilisation. Twenty-five centuries ago the area was studded with immense sculpted stone heads and tall ceremonial pyramids. Now the skyline is punctuated by oil derricks, drilling rigs and refining towers: Tabasco is the center of Mexico's petroleum industry, the most dramatic and dynamic example of modern Mexico's industrial economy. You could say that Mexico's history is summed up here: from Olmecs to oilmen.

Oil has played a considerable part in the history of modern Mexico. Deposits were first discovered and extracted by British and US companies during the Porfiriato; oil production was one of the marks of the beginning of the modern industrial period, as was the foreign investment in it.

Qualms about foreign control of an increasingly important product surfaced in the Revolution when the Constitution of 1917 called a halt to oil exploration by foreign companies. In 1921, Mexico was the world's largest producer. The qualms came to a head in the late 1930s.

After oil workers had struck for higher wages and been baulked by the foreign oil companies, in defiance of the Supreme Court, President Lazaro Cardenas took the drilling bit between his teeth and nationalised the petroleum industry. This bold move was billed as Mexico taking charge of its own economic destiny and was heartily seen that way by most Mexicans, who proceeded to club together to pay for it, with even peasant farmers donating chickens to the cause. It cost $24 million for the Americans and $81 million for the British.

The result was Petroleros Mexicanos, or PEMEX, an enormous state monopoly which was to fuel Mexico's rapid industrial development from the 1940s onwards, and to lead it to boom and bust in the late 1970s and early 1980s. Adding to those already known, huge offshore oil deposits were discovered in the early 1970s in the Gulf of Campeche. The Tabasco region was drenched in oil and towns like Coatzocoalcos and Minantlan became soaked in money, rampant development and pollution. At a time of high oil prices, the Mexican treasury overflowed with funds and the country looked very good to foreign bankers and investors. The government set about ambitious development projects and was showered with foreign loans for them.

In the early 1980s, with a sharp drop in oil prices and after rampant siphoning of oil revenues, Mexico fell into a debt crisis, even as it was earning US$15 billion annually in oil sales. Oil was the fool's gold of the era: it was seen as the solution to all problems, but turned out to

and their plight continues to concern the nation. The Chiapas peasant revolt of early 1994 brought the situation to international attention.

In the cities especially, unemployment is a curse. The national rate is currently reckoned to be at least 18 percent, despite much lower official figures. Under-employment is reckoned at 50 percent though there is a significant black economy which is reckoned at 22 percent of the whole; Mexico City, for example, has an estimated 500,000 street vendors. Mexico City's main square, the Zocalo, which the presidential palace overlooks, is usually lined with tradesmen like plumbers and bricklayers, seeking a day's work. Jobless oil workers have camped out there in protest. On top of this, two million young people enter the job market yearly.

In decreasing order of importance, the Mexican economy's main divisions are mineral exploitation, manufacturing, agriculture and services. The agriculture proportion is representative of a

be the cause of new ones. Today Mexico is back on its feet financially in a new era of fiscal rigor and privatisation, and PEMEX has been reformed. The Salinas government reined in both the oilworkers' union and excessive operational costs to make PEMEX more like a private corporation – but one thing is not going to change: state ownership of PEMEX is holy writ.

PEMEX is in *Fortune's* Top 50 list of the world's industrial corporations; its revenue represents 6 percent of the GDP, 23 percent of exports, and the largest source of tax income for the government. Once a mighty fiefdom riddled with corruption and inefficiency, featherbedding its workers and their families and building its own huge infrastructure, PEMEX has lost a third of its previous workforce of well over 200,000 since Salinas tightened its belt as a showcase piece in his effort to modernise Mexico's economy. In 1921, Mexico was top oil producer but by 1971 it was a net importer. The 1972 finds radically changed that, but unless new finds are made, it could be an importer again due to the country's burgeoning fuel needs. In 1993, Mexico was the fourth largest producer with 3.1 million barrels daily of oil and gas, 65 pecent of the crude coming from offshore and 28 percent from Tabasco and adjoining lowland Chiapas. Official reserves are quoted at 65 billion barrels.

long-term decline, whilst manufacturing is the main growth sector.

Mineral and Natural Resources

Mexico's mineral resources have been renowned since the early colonial days and the mushrooming of the silver cities. The country is rich in precious metals and is the world's leading silver producer, but low prices have closed down many silver mines. The most important mineral by far is oil, of which Mexico is the world's fourth largest producer with 3.1 million barrels daily. Dozens of other minerals are extracted, from arsenic to antimony, graphite to gold, mercury to magnesium. The potential is enormous: only 5 percent of Mexico's territory has been thoroughly explored whilst 60 percent is reckoned to contain useful substances.

Many of the enduring images of Mexico are of its agricultural workers: the *campesino* in his white cotton garb and sandals, the tight-trousered *charro* (cowboy) on his horse, both in sombreros. But both are more common in folklore than in reality to today. Now only 20 percent of the labor force works in agriculture, most likely wearing jeans, and their product constitutes only 9 percent of the GDP. About 13 percent of the land surface is under cultivation, over half of it in the interior highlands where rainfall is more frequent.

Mexico comes right after Brazil and Colombia in coffee production and is the world's largest avocado producer. Fishing, shrimp farming and fruit growing are important. The most productive region is the irrigated northwest where the desert has bloomed with alfalfa, wheat, safflower, soybeans, cotton and tomatoes. With vast areas of untillable and sparsely inhabited land, the north is full of cattle ranches.

Wherever subsistence farming is practised, which means in every state to a greater or lesser degree, corn and beans

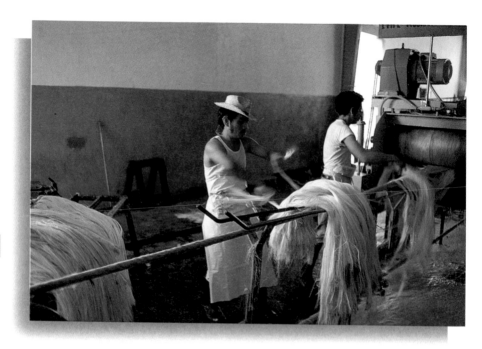

Sisal processing, fibers which make rope strong enough to
hoist great blocks of stone.

are the staples.

New 1992 laws have freed commu-
nal land farmers, of the *ejidos* created by
Cardenas in the 1930s, to become private property owners, which is supposed
to improve their lot by giving them
better access to bank loans.

Mexico has been a manufacturing
country for a century now, with serious
industrial growth dating from the 1940s.
This sector is set to grow quite rapidly
under the NAFTA Agreement which went
into operation in January 1994. Its GDP
proportion is 23 percent and almost
half the employees work in the capital;
the government is trying to rectify this
imbalance with relocation incentives.
Some factories have been shut down by
the government so as to reduce air pol-

lution in the Valley of Mexico, including a major oil refinery. Guadalajara
and Monterrey are next in importance
as manufacturing centers. Major products are steel, petrochemicals, pharma-
ceuticals, electricals and motor vehicles. Along the northern border, assembly plants called *maquiladoras* [see box]
employ over half a million workers. In
the service industry, tourism is a large
foreign exchange earner and employer,
with over US$4 billion in annual rev-
enues. The vast majority of tourists come
from over the border.

The last two decades have sent
Mexico on a roller-coaster ride. The
economy's steady upward progress ac-
celerated in the late 1970s on the back of
huge new oil finds and high oil prices.

Agriculture ranks third in importance in Mexico's economy.

The country went on a binge of heavy borrowing and ambitious investment, in the belief that oil prices would remain high. Then came the crunch: the world recession of 1982 and a sharp drop in the oil price. Mexico came under the burden of heavy foreign debt which it was in a weak position to service.

The economy flagged, inflation soared, and the Mexico City earthquake of 1985 only made things worse, killing at least 30,000 people and costing billions of dollars in damage and disruption. Debt renegotiation became the theme of the times. Mexico lost a decade in the 1980s, when the slump saw Mexicans' purchasing power cut by half.

Mexico's fate over the last two presidencies has been held by *tecnicos*, for-eign-educated economists: Miguel de la Madrid (1982-88) and Carlos Salinas de Gotari (1988-94). A principled and popular opponent with the magical name of Cuauhtemoc Cardenas put up a strong challenge – magical because it represented two great national heroes, the last Aztec ruler who valiantly defied Cortes until his death, and the great reformist president of the 1930s who was his father.

President Cuauhtemoc Cardenas

With this pedigree and the quiet manner of a professor, Cardenas stumped the country in support of peasants' and

Making tequila, a drink long associated with Mexico.

workers' causes at a time when the PRI was in trouble. The PRI claimed to be the party of the revolution, committed to nationalism and economic progress, but with the deteriorating economy in hock to foreign creditors, its revolutionary legitimacy was fast evaporating.

Taking office in December 1988, the Harvard-educated economist Salinas, then just 40 years old, surrounded himself with an equally youthful and highly-educated team of technocrats and economists. They consolidated a sense of economic order, ceded some political power to opposition parties in some states, notably the more rebellious ones like Chihuahua on the US border, and got the PRI through a tough time.

Salinas began to untangle the web of protectionism which had kept Mexico out of the global market. Mexico joined the GATT (General Agreement on Tarriffs and Trade) and opened its borders to imports, which flooded in; a goodly number of its consumer electronics, processed food, toy and garment manufacturers went to the wall as a result, but consumers were pleased with the improved choice and Mexican exporters benefitted. The president set about privatising state enterprises in industry and banking, transport and telecommunications, which filled the treasury's coffers with funds for much-needed social programmes. Full foreign ownership of business was permitted and laws were changed to allow for-

The Perpetual PRI

The Institutional Revolutionary Party: the very name embodies the perpetual paradox of modern Mexican politics. A revolution by its very nature is a dynamic process; an institution is by definition something fixed and ordered. So how do you have an "institutional revolution"? What sort of a party can run it?

Many Mexicans might say: the kind of party into which everyone can fit, the same people keep getting re-elected, anyone can say socialistic things, and no one does them. That's a cynical view, but Mexicans are pretty cynical about their ruling party, even in the 1990s when serious change is afoot.

Recipe for Success

The PRI has succeeded because it has been all things to all men, and women too, once they got the vote in 1955. It keeps business happy and the unions, it accommmodates peasants and bankers, it appeases the left and the right. It used to do this by nationalisation of major enterprises like petroleum, steel, banking, railways, airlines and telephones, by manipulating the unions and keeping the workers sweet, by protecting domestic industry with high import tariffs, and by handing out land to the peasants. Its secret has been inclusivity and patronage: getting as many social, economic and political groups under its umbrella as possible, and then handing out jobs, perks and subsidies to keep them happy.

But the balancing act has changed of late.

Since 1988, under President Salinas, many state enterprises have been sold off, resulting in a shake-out which has alienated some workers and unions, but it was a necessary move in the grand strategy of joining the global market, and has brought the PRI increased support from the business community.

Evidence of the PRI's ability to respond to new constituencies was previously seen in its support of equal rights for women, for which a law was passed in 1974. The PRI's monopoly on government has also been greatly facilitated by its domination of the mass media.

It's been a recipe for social stability and steady growth over the last fifty years, marred by inefficiency and corruption which have at the same time held the country back.

With the economic crisis of the 1980s, public dissatisfaction grew by leaps and bounds. At the 1988 presidential elections when opposition parties made their strongest showing ever, the PRI, running the ballot as well as running in it, as usual, scraped itself in with 50.4 percent of the vote.

The opposition loudly cried "Fraud!" but President Salinas took office and rapidly set about major economic reforms to show his mettle and to demonstrate that the PRI had imaginative life in it yet.

In the 1980s, an opposition party office hung this slogan across its frontage, well-placed on Mexico City's central Alameda Park: "Mexico, creere en ti, cuando desaparezca el PRI" – "Mexico, I'll believe in you, when the PRI is through." As the 1990s progress, it may get its wish.

eigners to buy land. The process became known as the *apertura*, the opening.

NAFTA

The *apertura* reached its apotheosis with the 1993 signing of the NAFTA Agreement, which took effect on 1 January, 1994, creating a trading block of 370 million people in Mexico, the United States and Canada. It will be 15 years before all trade barriers come down between the three countries because some industries will have interim protection of varying length, like banking (for Mexico's benefit) and citrus fruit (for the United State's benefit). NAFTA will al-

Mexico's economy is boosted by its shrimp farming industry.

low a free flow of investment capital across borders and establish an US$8 billion North American Development Bank. Its standardisation provisions should bring progress on environmental, sanitation and safety matters, which Mexico, like all developing countries, is much in need of.

Whilst the Salinas government banked its reputation on NAFTA, and got it, Mexicans are ambivalent about it. Industrial workers see hope in it for higher wages; currently 20 percent of the workforce earns only the minimum wage of US$5 daily. It is estimated that Mexico will quickly gain 600,000 jobs through new industrial investment. But many peasant farmers, such as those that took part in the early 1994 Chiapas revolt, fear a further widening of the gap between rich and poor, as dynamic US agribusiness undersells them with its cheap maize and other produce.

Salinas's free market reforms have brought a general increase in the standard of living. But a 1993 UN report calculated 16 percent of Mexicans to be living in extreme poverty and another 27 percent as struggling to make ends meet. With an annual growth rate of 2.3 percent, Mexico's population will reach 90 million in 1994. It's a young country: currently 80 percent of Mexicans are under 40 years of age. A lot of hopes are riding on NAFTA from the National Palace down to the shacks of the urban and rural poor as Mexico's youthful and burgeoning population approaches the 21st century.

Y ou could call Mexico the world in one country. From deep canyons to soaring snow-covered peaks, from dry desert to lush rainforest, from tequila-clear seas, glistening coastlines and spectacular islands, to fertile basins and high plateaux, from swampy lowlands and desolate wilderness to overcrowded cities...Mexico has it all. The country is shaped like a curved horn, if you block out the peninsula of Baja California sticking out on the left.

Mexico is huge, covering an area of 1,972, 538 sq km (761,601 sq miles) or one-quarter of the size of the United States. It is Latin America's third largest country, after Brazil and Argentina. Its land mass extends across 1,930 km (1,200 miles) at its widest part in the north and narrows down to 217 km (135 miles) at the Isthmus of Tehuanatepec in the south. Lengthwise, it stretches 2,977 km (1,850 miles) from north-

Cultivation along the delta in the Puerto Escondido area.

Geography & Climate

41

Rugged desert scenery in Matehuala, en route to Zacatecas.

west to southeast. It boasts an extensive coastline of 2,795 km (1,737 miles) on the Gulf of Mexico and the Caribbean Sea on the east; on the west it enjoys 7,401 km (4,600 miles) of coast on the Pacific Ocean and Gulf of California.

Mexico has three neighbors: the largest is the United States in the north with which it shares a common border that stretches 3,343 km (2,078 miles) across. A 875-km (544-mile) land and river border in the south divides Mexico from Guatemala while in the southeast, Belize is separated from the Yucatan by

activity. Mexico sits on the western edge of the vast North American plate which interacts with the Pacific, Cocos and Caribbean plates. The earth moves when these plates shift in relation to one another thus molding the physiography of the country, resulting in some extremely complex land forms.

Indeed, it is these tectonic forces that have built up a fair bit of the central and southern areas of Mexico and are responsible for the volcanic peaks of Popocatepetl (5,451 m/17,887 ft) and Pico de Orizaba (5,700 m/18,701 ft) also called Citlaltepetl, which are very young in geologic terms.

The map of Mexico shows two long mountainous chains almost paralleling the coasts stretching from the US border near Arizona on the east (Sierra Madre Occidental) and from near Texas on the west (Sierra Madre Oriental) all the way downwards, stopping short just north of Mexico City, a distance of some 1,287 km (800 miles). Below the two arms in the south is the Sierra Madre del Sur rising from the coast in the state of Guerrero to end at the Isthmus of Tehuantepec.

In between the two main mountain chains lies the vast Mexican Plateau with intermontane basins containing pockets of settlement and cultivated areas. The two principal arms of the Sierra Madre give Mexico much of its topographical character. The volcanic Sierra Madre Occidental which joins the Sierra Nevada range in the United States, rises up to 2,743 m (9,000 ft). Westward-

a 252 km (157-mile) boundary.

"Ring of Fire"

Mexico may be geographically very diverse but it is also very volatile. It forms part of the Asia-Pacific "Ring of Fire" and is prone to seismic and volcanic

Park and preserve in Cozumel, Yucatan.

flowing streams have cut deeply into the mountains to carve out a series of canyons or barrancas, the most famous of which is the Barranca del Cobre, or Copper Canyon, Mexico's Grand Canyon. Just as highly dissected are the limestone-and-shale mountains of the Sierra Madre Oriental with peaks towering above 3,658 m (12,000 ft). The southern end of the Mexican Plateau is bounded by the Neo-Volcanic Cordillera which extends east to west and gives rise to the majestic volcanic peaks of Ixtaccihuatl, Popocatepetl, Orizaba, and

Majestic volcanic peak in Colima.

Nevado de Toluca.

The Mexican Plateau can roughly be divided into two parts: Mesa del Norte stretching from the US border to around San Luis Potosi where the Mesa Central starts, terminating just below Mexico City. The more rugged Mesa del Norte is dry and its desert soil is not conducive to cultivation, hence it supports only about 20 percent of the total Mexican population despite occupying 40 percent of Mexico. In contrast, the flatter Mesa Central receives copious amounts of rainfall. What's more, rich volcanic soils in this region and good drainage contribute to make this fertile heartland of Mexico the country's breadbasket.

The 2,134-2,743 meter high (7,000-9,000 ft) high Mesa Central is actually made up of several intermontane basins interrupted by volcanic mountains. The biggest basins – Guadalajara, Mexico and Puebla – are some 259 sq km (100 sq miles) in size; the rest are much smaller. Many of the basins were once major lakes that had been drained by the Spanish to make way for settlement. Today, only Lake Patzcuaro and Lake Cuitzeo remain.

Though the Mesa Central constitutes only 14 percent of the country, its agricultural wealth has attracted half of the population to live there.

The south is another montage of mountains and plateaux. The corrugated Sierra Madre Del Sur runs out to the Pacific coast giving rise to attractive coastal areas dubbed as the Mexican

Humid green gorges and canyons framed by dramatic rock formations make up the Barranca del Cobre.

Riviera dotted with resorts such as Acapulco, Ixtapa, Zihuatenejo, Puerto Escondido and Huatulco. Beyond the coast stretches an infertile basin unsuitable for cultivation. The Madre del Sur rises to about 1,524 m (5,000 ft) to the northeast, sliced by ridges and valleys of which the picturesque Oaxaca Valley is the biggest.

The Oaxaca Valley is poor and heavily populated, mostly with Indians whose colorful traditional costumes have nevertheless made this area a tourist draw. The tableland ends at the Isthmus of Tehuantepec, is a neck of land that is no more than 274 m (900 ft) high and is flanked by narrow coastal plains.

In the southeast, the mountain ranges of Central America push into Mexico to form the Chiapas Highlands, a series of faulted mountains encircling a high rift valley beyond which more faulted mountains extend to the Tabasco Plain which is the southern end of the Gulf Coastal Plain. Northeast of the Tabasco Plain, sticking out into the Gulf of Mexico like a thumb, is the relatively flat Yucatan Peninsula. Ample rainfall in this area has made it an important cattle-raising and agricultural center.

Coastal Lowlands

Mexico's coastal lowlands are extensive, flanking both sides of the Mexican Plateau. On the east, the Gulf Coastal Plain runs 1,448 km along the Gulf of

Arid grasslands in Iguala, south of Mexico City.

Mexico from the Texas border to the Yucatan Peninsula. A mix of lagoons and swamps, the plains start off as a 160 km (100-mile) broad ribbon in the north and taper into a narrow strip near Tampico to extend in a jagged fashion into the Isthmus of Tehuantepec.

On the west coast, the Pacific Coast lowlands are narrower and more irregular. Also 1,448 km (900 miles) in length, they stretch from Mexicali in the north to Tuxpan in the south with a good portion of the lowlands facing the Gulf of California. Characterized by coastal terrace after terrace, mesas and tiny basins with riverine deltas in between, irrigation is practised and crops have been successfully grown in this normally arid region.

World's Longest Peninsular

Baja California is unique. A finger of land no more than 160 km (99 miles) wide, the 1,287-km (800-mile) peninsula is the world's longest. It is arid and desolate supporting small populations in scattered areas, mainly at the top and bottom of the peninsula. Yet this inhospitable landscape has managed to nurture some of Mexico's most beautiful plant life and it is home to a wide variety of animals (see *Flora and Fauna*).

Baja California is covered in the middle with a granite faulted mountain block that is more than 2,7743 m (9,000 ft) high. It slopes gently westwards into the sea while its formidable eastern es-

Waterfalls in the jungle south of Palenque.

carpment is a barrier to communications from the Gulf of California.

Rivers and Lakes

Mexico lacks major rivers and natural lakes. The most important ones are found in the Mexican Plateau. West of Mexico City, the Lerma River drains the Toluca Basin and flows westwards to form Lake Chapala, the country's largest. Out of this lake flows the Rio Grande de Santiago which cuts across the Sierra

Madre del Sur. It has been tapped as a source of hydroelectric power. Three main rivers in the south – the Grijalva and the Usumacinta which drain the Chiapas Highlands and the Papaloapan which pours into the Gulf of Mexico – carry some 40 percent of Mexico's river waters. The Mesa del Norte has only small rivers to speak of. They tend to be short and steep since the Sierra Madre Occidental and Oriental from which they originate lie close to the coast.

The most important river is the Rio Bravo del Norte in the east which flows out of Texas as the Rio Grande and forms part of the US-Mexican border. Its tributary, Rio Conchos, drains a major portion of the Mesa del Norte. On the Pacific side, Rio Yaqui, Rio Fuerte and Rio Culiacan have been dammed and their waters are used to irrigate the arid coastlands.

Climate

Mexico's climate is as diverse as its topography. But despite its wide latitudinal range, the climate is determined more by altitude. Nearly half of the country lies south of the Tropic of Cancer where the coastal plains are hot and humid. Yet, if you move inland to places enjoying higher elevations like Guanajuato and Guadalajara, you will notice a distinct drop in temperature. The air is also drier and mountain peaks are often covered with snow.

Indeed, there are five vertical cli-

Madre Occidental in the northwest to empty into the Pacific.

The Moctezuma and Panuco rivers drain the eastern section of the Mesa Central, slicing out gorges as they cut through the Sierra Madre Oriental to flow into the Gulf of Mexico, the Rio Balsas, draining the Balsas Depression. The Rio Balsas springs in the Sierra

Keeping track with nature.

matic zones in Mexico south of the Tropic of Cancer. The hot and humid tropics, characterized by the Yucatan Peninsula, extend from sea level to 914 m (3,000 ft) high. This is the *tierra caliente* (hot land) with average temperatures of 25°C (77°F). The *tierra templada* or temperate zone has a climate which is mild, about 19°C (66°F), but the mercury dips to much lower at night. *Tierra fria* (cold land) as its name implies is much colder, extending up to 3,352 m (11,000 ft) with day temperatures in the mid-50s. Creel and the little towns on the rim of the Barranca del Cobre are a case in point.

After the *tierra fria,* just above are the alpine pastures or *paramos.* The highest level of all is the *tierra helada* (frozen land) at an altitude of over 3,960 m (13,000 ft) where mountain peaks (for example Popocatepetl and Orizaba) are permanently snow-capped.

North of the Tropic of Cancer, Mexico experiences extremes in temperature typical of desert areas, especially in the northernmost interior of the Mesa del Norte. In Baja California and the deserts of Chihuahua and Sonora, the summer temperature can go up to 43°C (110°F) and plunge to below freezing in winter. Rain too is scarce in northern Mexico.

The Baja, Chihuahua and Sonora areas receive no more than 254 mm (10 inches) of rain a year. The rest of the country north of the Tropic of Cancer fare only a little better with an annual rainfall of 508 m (20 inches) while the

Thatched riverside home.

highland areas of the two Sierra Madre chains and the Gulf Coastal Plain are better off as they receive more.

The rainfall situation improves south of the Tropic of Cancer with central and part of southern Mexico enjoying some 1,016 mm (40 inches) of rain a year. However, it is the extreme south of Mexico that rain falls all the year round resulting in a lush rainforest vegetation. This is in the Gulf Coastal Plain and the surrounding areas, stretching from Tampico to Villahermosa, the Chiapas Highlands and the southern portion of the Yucatan Peninsula. The heaviest rains fall in the wet season from June to September with tropical hurricanes occurring off the Gulf and Pacific coasts from August to October.

Mexico has a wealth of colorful bird species thanks to its abundance of hot, humid tropical forests. It is a mind boggling fact that Mexico has 1,018 recorded species of birds compared to about 500 for the whole of Europe, a third more birds than the United States and Canada put together, earning it the rank of 13th in the world for bird variety.

Flora & Fauna

Indeed, the story goes that the Spanish Conquistadores were stun-ned when they first saw the bright and beautiful birds presented to them as gifts.

Mexico has an astonishing variety of flora.

Many of the bright and beautiful birds can still be glimpsed by the visitor today, although 10 percent of the species have been placed on the endangered list due to the destruction of ecosystems, excessive hunting, trafficking and pollution. But the Mexican government is taking steps to combat this and recently formed the National Commission for the

53

Mexico is a tropical paradise for birds, among them the keel billed toucan...

Study and Utilization of Bio Diversity to gather information to provide for the protection of endangered species.

Though only the more exotic birds such as the scarlet macaw and the keel billed toucan are found in the lush rain forests, there are birds everywhere in Mexico, even in its dry deserts and snowy mountain peaks.

Seventy-eight species are endemic to Mexico and found only in specific areas. Among them are the long-tailed wood partridge that makes its home in the cloud pine and oak forests on the

inhabiting the coastal swamps, lagoons and estuaries, such as the roseate spoonbill and northern jacanda on the Gulf of Mexico and the Pacific Coast. These too are the temporary homes of some migratory duck species every year for six months. Egrets and herons are plentiful along the coast and on the lakes.

Spectacular Bird Species

In the swamplands of the southeast lives the jabiru, a rapidly dwindling species of stork that is Mexico's highest flying bird. The more remote landscape here attracts the ornate hawk eagle and the king vulture. Among the more spectacular birds in Mexico is the rainbow-

neo-volcanic axis in central Mexico, and the eastern thick billed parrot found in the forests of Coahulla, Nuevo Leon and Tamaulipas. The rocky outcrop of San Pedro Martir in the Gulf of California or the Sea of Cortes is the habitat of thousands of pelicans, blue footed boobies, gulls and tropical birds.

Then there are the lowland birds

... and the heron.

Birding in Mexico – by Morten Strange

Mexico straddles two major zoo-geographical regions, the Neoarctic which includes North America and the Neotropical which extends all across the South American continent. That means that in the north of Mexico the birdlife has northern affinities, in the south of the country it is mainly tropical and the birds are shared with many of the Central American countries. There are a wide range of habitats across this big nation from barren deserts in the north and tall mountains in the interior to low-land evergreen rainforests in the south; the birdlife is equally varied. Including migrants and rare stragglers more than 1,000 different species occur.

Yellow-breasted chat.

American Dipper

Some Endangered Birds

Within the last few years great efforts have been made to preserve some of Mexicos natural heritage – just the way its rich cultural heritage has been protected for centuries. At the time of the Aztecs all of Mexico was heavily forested and rich in wildlife, now only shrinking pockets, especially in the south are left.

In its survey of threatened birds published in 1988 the International Council for Bird Preservation described a number of unique Mexican birds now very rare and threatened with total extinction. The thick-billed parrot occurs in the northern states of Chihuahua and Sinalos in pine-oak forests in the Sierra Madre Occidental. During a recent survey only 55 nests were found, the forest where this parrot lives is no protected against logging and although capture of the bird is illegal according to Mexican law, enforcement is difficult and many still end up in the pet trade. Another parrot, the maroon-fronted parrot, lives in a similar habitat within the same region which is continuously being degraded by logging, clearing and slash-and-burn farming, only an estimated 2,000 of this species are left in the world today.

Other rare and threatened Mexican birds include the bearded wood partridge, the altamira yellow-throat and the red-crowned amazon, all occuring within a small range in the northeastern part of the country, the socorro mockingbird which was thought to be extinct until its dramatic rediscovery in 1988 can also be seen.

According to a recent survey only eight of Mexico's 51 national parks really serve their purpose in protecting the habitat and its wildlife. Like other developing countries Mexico is at the moment engaged in finding a balance between economic progress for the rural population and conservation and protection of the natural foundation of the land.

Places to Go

Around Mexico City itself some common park birds like rufous-backed thrush, bald-headed crosbeak and orchard oriole, can be seen inside Chapultepec Park. In the dry outskirts of the city look out for desert birds like vermilion flycatcher, brown towhee and canyon wren. The Desierto de los Leones to the southwest has a varied habitat including some forest cover holding arboreal birds like chickadees, arens, flycatchers and many warblers. Close to the southeast of the city, on the road between two extinct volcanoes, Iztaccihuantl and Popacatepetl, there is spectacular mountain scenery and forests and birdlife including hummingbirds, thrushes, towhees, swifts and many others.

Orchard oriole.

Belted Kingfisher

Insurgente Miguel Hidalgo and Costilla National Park is also well worth a visit both for historical and natural reasons. It is a volcanic area with spring water and meadows and forested hillsides, good for birding in the mornings. Tufted flycatcher, slate-throated redstart, pine siskin and golden-crowned kinglet are some of the species to look out for.

For waterbirds the Laguna de Catemago at the Gulf of Mexico east of the capital is probably the best destination. This is a rich area of sea coast, freshwater swamps and dense forest inland close by. The freshwater segments have divers, cormorants, gulls, and kingfishers, the open country has many cuckoos and weavers building their pouch nests in dense clutches low in the trees.

North of Mexico City the habitat is typical scrubland, with extensive stretches of barren deserts, ideal for shooting western movies! The desert habitat is largely shared with the southern United States and some birds considered rare in Texas, New Mexico and Arizona can be seen well here like elf owl, violet-crowned hummingbird, golden-fronted woodpecker, tropical kingbird and many others.

Shorebirds and terns are plentiful, sea birds like boobies and pelicans move along the coast. The forest to the north of the city has parrots, yellow crosbeak, magpie-jay and many other good Mexican resident birds. The hilly back

country here is well forested, also further south extending behind the town of Tepic, explore the back roads and find good highland birds like mountain trogon, white-striped woodcreeper and the rare tufted jay. There are also military macaws and other parrots to look out for in the early mornings and late afternoons.

West of Tepic at the coast, San Blas is a famous birder's destination, mangrove trips can be arranged and you get good views of many Central American water-birds in the heron, rail and kingfisher families. The forest of Singaita holds many aboreal birds including specialities like squirrel cuckoo, russel-crowned motmot, red-crowned ant-tanager, collared forest-falcon and the orange-fronted parakeet.

The southeastern coastline facing the Caribbean is generally a bit wetter than the Pacific coast with denser forest-cover and patches of lowland tropical rainforest, but the area around Merida is an exception. It is quite dry, getting gradually wetter as you move further south and this whole area holds many special Mexican and Caribbean birds.

The coast is good for flamingos, spoonbills, frigatebirds and shorebirds, the scrub behind the beach has white-lored gnatcatcher, Mexican shertail, telchac puerto and black-throated bobwhite (in the pheasant family).

There is good forest inland nearby Uxmal and Chichen-Itza with hummingbirds, jays, wrens and buntings. On the east coast of the Yucatan Peninsula, Cozumel Island is one of Mexico's largest and has many birds not found anywhere else in the country. If you drive on the main road south towards Chetumal and eventually into Belize, you come through good habitats holding fine southern Mexico species that you will never find up north, like white hawk, stripe-tailed hummingbird, back-crested coquette, lovely cotinga, refous piha and many others.

In the far south of the country the state of Chiapas bordering Guatemala has some of the best lowland rainforest in Mexico. Here you are well into the Neotropical zoogeographical region and the richest bird area on earth.

An iguana basking in the sun.

colored quetzal, Guatemala's national bird. So beautiful is the quetzal's plumage that pre-Hispanic Mexicans used the feathers to make headdresses. The ocellated turkey from the Yucatan Peninsula and the parrots found in Mexico are birds with dazzling plumage.

Yet another species that Mexico has in common with Guatemala and which is found in the south of the country, in the cloud forests of Chiapas and Oaxaca is the rare horned guan, so called because of the red horn on its head.

Animals

The diversity of ecosystems and the wide range of climatic zones have given

The Puerto Escondido mangrove swamps host a variety of birds.

Hog-fish hovering in a reef off Cozumel.

Mexico a variety of wildlife, from the tropical tapir to the antelope. In reptiles alone, Mexico has 717 species – the largest number of species in the world, of which a third are endemic. Because of its long coastline, Mexico has exceptionally varied marine life. Indiscriminate hunting in the past almost led to the extinction of the gray whale, elephant seal and Guadalupe fur seal, but they are now found in abundant numbers along the coast of Baja California. Every year, thousands of gray whales migrate to the Baja's west coast to breed.

The Cedros, San Benitos and Guadalupe Islands off Baja's Pacific coast are home to hundreds of elephant seals (also known as sea elephant) while some 500 fur seals thrive near Guadalupe Island. Cedros is also the habitat for a small species of deer.

Baja California is also home to some of Mexico's most exotic animal species. On San Pedro Martir, in the nutrient rich waters of the Gulf of California where numerous sea lions frolic, exotic lizards and rattlesnakes with no rattles in their tails roam among the cacti. The rattlesnakes can also be found on Catalina Island.

The poisonous scorpion lizard found along the Pacific Coast from Sonora to Chiapas is endemic to Mexico. It lives in dry, rocky areas, dry tropical forests and desert bush country. This huge green lizard which can grow up to 1.8 m (6 ft) long can be found in the evergreen

The scarlet flower of the agave plant which provides fruit for the famed tequila.

forests from southern Tamaulipas and Sinaloa along the Pacific Coast and along the coast of the Gulf of Mexico.

The boa is Mexico's largest snake and is commonly found in the tropical areas of the Republic. These tropical jungles are also home to big cats such as the puma, jaguar and cougar.

Three species of desert tortoises are found in Mexico. They feed on cactus flowers and shoots and can live up to 100 years. Then there is the volcanic rabbit which lives among the tall grass of pine forests growing above 9,900 feet. The coffee-colored rabbit with short, round ears is found principally on the slopes of Popocatepetl and Iztaccihuatl.

Mexico has several other exotic animal species now on the endangered list.

Among them is the handsome Mexican wolf, inhabiting the mountains of Chihuahua and Durango, the nocturnal porcupine feeding in the pine forests of Chihuahua, Sonora, Sinaloa and Coahuila and the beaver which roams the waters of the Rio Bravo and Colorado in the north. The golden possum with its silky thick fur used to be abundant in the humid forests of Veracruz, Tabasco, Chiapas and Oaxaca but the destruction of forests and their conversion to pasture land has led to a reduction in their population. Also to be found in declining numbers in the humid forests from Sonora to Chiapas on the Pacific Coast and from Tamaulipas to the Yucatan Peninsula are the ocelot, a beautifully spotted cat, and inhabitant of the forests in the south of Mexico, while the ghost bat which used to haunt the Pacific coast from Nayarit to Chiapas is now rarely seen.

Flora

Mexico abounds with vegetation even in the wilderness areas. Baja California, for instance, has the red flores de San Miguel (flowers of St Michael), the yellow morning glory and the vine creeper calledjicama,with its red trumpet-shaped flowers. Where there's water, you will find the area bursting with fig trees, dates, pomegranates, grapes and sugarcane. In the dry northern and central regions of Mexico, you will find an astonishing variety of cacti, agave plants, cassava, mesquite and brush plants that thrive in arid conditions.

The ever present Bougainvillea.

The cloud forests in northern Mexico are home to 40 species of colorful orchids, some so rare that they lack common names. Some thrive in soil while others feed off the rain, air and dust from their perches atop trees. In the south where the climate is hot and humid, there are lush rainforests. On the tropical eastern and western coasts savannah landscapes can be found. Pine and oak forests dominate the slopes of the more mountainous regions with temperate climates. Many tropical and temperate type flowers flourish in Mexico. They include the dahlia (Mexico's national flower), hibiscus, bougainvillea, prickly poppy, gardenias, camellias, marigolds, the flame vine and the poinsettia, the floral symbol of Christmas.

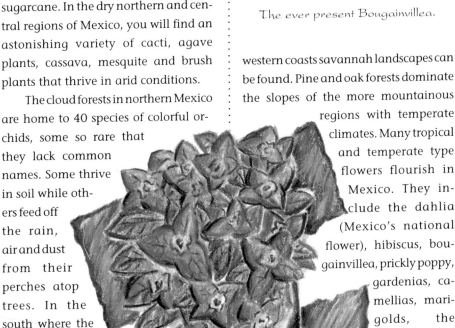

Mexico is truly an ethnic melting pot. It stands out as the most racially and culturally integrated of all Spain's former colonies in Latin America. The stock is a mixture of mainly Spanish and Indian to which other European, as well as a sprinkling of African elements have been added.

Mexico has 81.25 million people earning it the rank of the 11th most populous nation in the world and the third most populous on the American continent. It is a young country with half of its people under 19 years of age.

Mexico is thought to have been first settled during the Ice Age, more than 40,000 years ago, by nomadic tribes from Asia. They had roamed over to the American continent in search of food, crossing the land bridge which links Alaska with Central Asia. All these movements stopped when the Ice Age ended and the bridge melted into what is now the Bering Strait

People

63

A sensuous beauty from Oaxaca.

The ubiquitous charro...

criollos or *creoles* and in time to come, became the new ruling class.

Indeed, it was the *creoles* who later distanced themselves from Spain and started the movement for an independent Mexico. Many of the early Spaniards, however, also married Indian women. The mixed children of these marriages were the first of the *mestizos* who make up two thirds of Mexicans today. But not all the Indians were integrated as rural isolation enabled several communities to survive intact.

Moreover, because of ill treatment and the savage killing of many tribes by the Spanish, many Indians were distrustful of the colonists and tried as best as they could to cut themselves off and preserve their own identity. The exist-

separating America from Asia. The Asian features of many of today's Mexicans, especially the pure Indians, does seem to lend weight to this theory.

Spanish Conquistadores

Then the Spanish Conquistadores arrived seeking new lands and wealth, often engaging in warfare to achieve their goals. Since women and children had no place in such a violent atmosphere, most of the men came alone. When they decided to settle and make the New World their home, some of them later brought in their own womenfolk. Their children, who were born and raised in Mexico, were known as

... and his counterpart, the charrlada.

The Spiritualistic Huichols

Deep in the mountainous pockets of the rugged Sierra Madre in Jalisco, live the Huichol Indians, perhaps the most traditional of all Mexico's indigenous groups.

The inaccessibility of their villages have enabled the Huichols to hold out against the domination of the Spanish Conquistadores and the influence of Catholic missionaries.

The Huichols are known for their beaded and yarn art. Using colorful glass beads and acrylic yarn, they weave designs in the form of animals and birds. Each symbol and color expresses a meaning. Yellow and orange for instance represent the sun, a sacred place the Huichols journey to after death. The eagle is a god, one of the 57 deities the Huichols venerate. The cornstalk is also a god as it is considered by the Huichols (and other Indians) to be the source of all life.

The most important deity of all is undoubtedly the peyote, a plant of the cactus family. The peyote is taken by the Huichols for its hallucinogenic effects in the belief that it will enable them to communicate better with the gods. How the Huichols got to worship the peyote is unclear as the plant itself is not found in the Jalisco region. Tribal members are chosen each year to make the long trek to the desert of San Luis Potosi where it grows, to harvest the plant. Members selected to do the pilgrimage are deemed holy as they are considered to have made a visit to the land of the gods.

ence of these groups who still wear the same costumes as their ancestors and live much as they did, have enriched the cultural tapestry that makes up Mexico.

Indians

The pure Indians are said to constitute one quarter of Mexicans but according to estimates in 1990, only 7.9 percent of the population, or 6.4 million, actually speak an indigenous language. Although 139 Indian languages were wiped out as a result of Spanish rule, fifty Indian languages have survived and are still spoken today, some by a mere few hundred people, others by more substantial numbers.

Nahuatl is a the language spoken by the greatest number of Indians – 1.5 million – who are spread over a dozen states, mostly in Guerrero, Puebla, Veracruz and San Luis Potosi. Other Indian languages still spoken by considerable numbers in Mexico include the Tzotzil and Tzeltal in Chiapas, the Maya in the Yucatan Peninsula, the Tarastec, Totonac, Otomi and Mazahua on the Mesa Central and the Zapotec,

Starting them young.

Mixtec and Mazatec in Oaxaca. Some four million Mexicans are of pure European ancestry, the result of migration in the 19th and 20th century, while those with African heritage can trace it to the trickle of former slaves who came to Mexico's Gulf coast from the Caribbean islands. Mexicans are predominantly Catholic with 95 percent claiming adherence to the faith. However, many of the Indian Catholics also happily worship their old gods; the rest practise paganism.

The Mexican Character

In order to impress other males, the Mexican male adopts an exaggerated

The spirit of Mexico is captured in its dances.

The Church of Our Lady of Guadalupe

It is a moving sight: Men and women crawling on their knees, some stumbling, all the way from the plaza, up and down steps, their hands fingering rosaries.... When they finally reach the altar, their pace quickens a little and their eyes light up with joy and adoration.

The scene is repeated every day at La Basilica de Nuestra Senora de Guadalupe (the Church of Our Lady of Guadalupe), the most venerated shrine in Mexico, dedicated to the Virgin Mary. Wave upon relentless wave of pilgrims arrive, bearing images of the Virgin, banners proclaiming their adoration and whence they came, and floral floats carrying the Virgin's image. The crush of pilgrims starts on the long road, Caldeza de Guadalupe, that leads to the church with some pilgrims dropping on their knees, to begin their crawl.

It is on 12 December (the Day of the Race or *Dia de la Raza* in Mexico (Columbus Day in the United States) that celebrations peak. For it was this date in 1531 that marked the last of the three consecutive days on which an Indian by the name of Juan Diego saw the vision of the Virgin Mary. Although the Indian had told his priest about it, he was not believed until the third day, when the Virgin made an imprint of her image on his cloak.

On seeing the image, the priest ordered a church to be built on the spot where she was seen and Juan Diego's cloak was preserved. She was declared the patron saint of Mexico and her shrine has since been visited by pilgrims from far and wide.

The volume of pilgrims became so overwhelming that a bigger church with a capacity of 20,000 was built in 1976 next to the original basilica, now a museum of religious artifacts. Juan Diego's cloak, enclosed in glass and framed high on a wall in a corner of the new Basilica may be viewed briefly from a moving walkway below. The week before and after 12 October sees one dizzying procession of pilgrims after another with continuous performances by Indian dancers in traditional costumes in the plaza outside the church. The Basilica lies just outside Mexico City, in the suburb of La Villa de Guadalupe (metro stop: La Villa).

masculinity called "machismo". This is manifested in a orm of aggressive driving, weapon carrying and heavy drinking. Thus the Mexican male is often labelled "macho". With his swaggering walk and cowboy hat and boots, he certainly is a picture of overstated masculinity. In the past, he has often been caricatured as hard drinking, out carousing with friends in men-only *cantinas* and rarely lifting a finger at home. Octavio Paz, the poet, concedes in his *Labyrinth of Solitude* that the Mexican male's conduct is a mask to conceal his solitude.

Lulu, a thirty-something Mexican pediatrician says: "I remember an incident when I was a teenager and my older brother and I were in the kitchen washing dishes. My father suddenly stormed in and dragged my brother out, saying he shouldn't be doing women's work!"

Attitudes are slowly changing and the modern Mexican man, especially if he has lived abroad, is beginning to share household tasks. Still, there are some aspects of the Mexican machismo that will take time to disappear. Lulu explains: "Mexican men are a jealous lot. They like to keep their women to themselves. They discourage the use of makeup on their girlfriends or wives for instance because they don't want them

Dressing up is part of the fun at fiestas.

to look attractive for other men. Also, when they marry, they feel it's okay for them to have mistresses while their wives must remain monogamous! They would prefer too if their wives didn't work as there would be fewer opportunities then to meet other men.

As Lulu confides, "it's the mother who is at fault by doting on her sons and spoiling them. Hence, boys grow up with the notion that only women should do all the cooking and cleaning. What's more, the sons end up glorifying their mother and try to seek a wife like her

Oaxaca dancer in traditional dress.

Mexican man adores children. On weekends, he delights in playing the role of the family man and spending time with his kids. Indeed, the sense of family is very strong among Mexicans. Whenever there is a celebration or event, all family members attend in full force. This includes not just immediate members but also the relatives and very close friends as the family circle is an extended one. At the core of the unit is the mother who cooks, looks after the household, takes care of the children and passes on to them religious and cultural values. So strong is the family unit that many young men and women continue to live at home even after they have started work, moving out only when they marry.

when they marry. If the wife falls short, they take a mistress. "

But, there's hope. As more women become educated and they learn to bring up sons and daughters on a more equal basis, machismo among Mexican men is likely to decline in future.

Despite his macho attitude, the

Because of their unique history, in which a major world religion was imposed on ancient peoples of a totally separate religious tradition, Mexicans today, continue to follow a kaleidoscope of faiths under the nominal umbrella of Christianity.

The great majority call themselves Catholic, but usually their Catholicism is mixed with varying degrees of observance of the pre-Columbian rituals; if not, as amongst the pure European stock, then it will certainly include worship of local saints, above all the Virgin of Guadalupe.

The Catholic church has been a pillar of the state for centuries.

Religion

Human Sacrifice

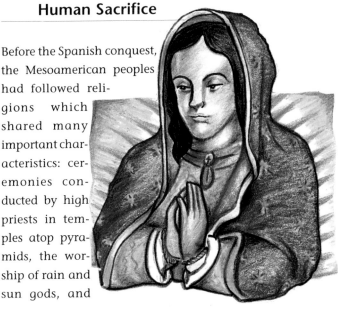

Before the Spanish conquest, the Mesoamerican peoples had followed religions which shared many important characteristics: ceremonies conducted by high priests in temples atop pyramids, the worship of rain and sun gods, and

Religious iconographic souvenirs on sale near a church.

propitiation of the gods, through human sacrifice.

The Mesoamericans believed in an elemental universe that was constantly under threat of destruction, and their religious practices centered upon preventing this through worship, ritual and sacrifice. The great civilisations had state religions guided by high priests at mighty temple complexes; at the same time, folk religions of the rural and tribal peoples like the Huichols and Tarahumaras emphasised worship of the spirits in nature.

A devout moment in a church in Zapopan.

Spanish Missionaries

In the first two centuries of colonisation, Spanish missionaries made strenuous efforts to convert the indigenous population to Christianity, but the usual re- sult of their proselytizing was a veneer of Catholicism pasted upon the pre- Hispanic religions, which continued to guide the people's lives. Old gods would survive under Christian saints' names and pre-Hispanic festivals and rituals would be observed still, celebrated on a

Altar for the Dead.

saint's day which was conveniently close to the traditional date. Over time a synthesis developed, with characteristics differing by region and people. Despite a gradual erosion of traditional practices as the people became more exposed to the modern world this pattern persists today.

Day of the Dead

This native diversity, creates a religious panorama today which reaches from a service in Mexico City's cathedral, resembling a high-level Catholic rite anywhere in the world, all the way through to the observances in a remote church in a full-blood Indian region where tradi-

tionally-clothed worshippers practise magic and witchcraft. The synthesis is most prominently and dramatically seen in the great national festival of the Day of the Dead, one of the most highly distinctive facets of Mexican-ness.

Indian traditions see a world in which all natural phenomena have spiritual significance, be they climatic like the wind and rain, or celestial like the sun, moon and stars, or animal like jaguars, deer and snakes, or vegetable like trees and flowers. Gods which derive from these natural features vary from place to place. They form pagan pantheons which Indians worship alongside the Christian trinity and the saints.

Altered states of mind are a surviving feature of Indian religions. Hallucinogenic mushrooms are used by some Indian peoples. Peyote, a hallucinogen derived from a cactus, is taken ritually by the Huichols of Jalisco; the Tarahumara of the Copper Canyon become intoxicated with alcohol at certain festivals. Fertility rites permeate some supposedly Christian festivals, especially in spring. The Totonac Voladores of Veracruz exemplify this; in Oaxaca, ancient maize god rituals live on in the summer Guelaguetza dance festival.

In some remote areas, clearly pagan rituals survive. Among the Trique of Oaxaca, oxen are sacrificed and an ox broth is spread over the church floor for the Festival of the Dead. The Huichols of Jalisco worship the fertility goddess Nakawe above Christ, of whom they have two versions. In Chiapas, some

Priests receiving the image of Our Lady of Zapopan.

highland Indian churches have no pews, altars are made on the church floors, and worshippers sacrifice chickens there. In many regions, such as amongst the Yaquis of the northwest, Indian witch doctors called *brujos* use rituals to cure the sick, who are believed to have lost their soul through bad deeds or by being hexed by an enemy. This undercurrent of ancient beliefs runs through a land in which over 90 percent of the population professes the Catholic faith, and in which the Catholic church was for centuries one of the pillars of the state.

The church came to Mexico with Cortes himself, in the persons of friars. Its representatives flocked into the territory and established bishoprics, missions and monasteries.

Unifying Influence

In the colonial period, the church was second only to the crown in importance, and it exerted a useful unifying influence on the formative nation. It was also almost the only provider of education. Its power was bound to cause problems as Mexicans sought independence and social justice; it was wealthy, landed and conservative.

Successive governments restricted its privileges, notably by nationalising its land. The 1917 constitution forbade the church to comment on government actions and banned property ownership. In 1926, President Calles clamped down severely on the church, provoking

Interior of chapel in a colonial hacienda.

a three-year armed rebellion by the Cristero guerrillas.

Provisions of this time, like the banning of the clergy from wearing their vestments in public and the cutting of diplomatic relations with the Vatican, have only just been overturned by Presi-dent Salinas, marking a growing normalisation of state-church relations in the 1990s. At the same time, Protestantism is growing fast under the influence of aggressive evangelists from north of the border and now has the support of at least 5 percent of the population.

Portrait of Nuestra Sonora, a much revered saint in Mexico.

Catholicism is nevertheless still one of the most obvious marks of Mexico as a nation, and Mexico's diverse peoples are unified in adoration of the brown-skinned Virgin of Guadalupe. Faith is deep-rooted and nothing brings this home to a visitor like the common sight of a pilgrim at a revered church, approaching the altar on his/her knees, starting not just from the aisle but from the stony churchyard outside, or even from far down the access road, arriving bloody and in pain. NAFTA may change a lot of things, but it won't change that.

"The art of the fiesta has been debased almost everywhere else, but not in Mexico. There are few places in the world where it is possible to take part in a spectacle like our great religious fiestas with their violent primary colors, their bizarre costumes and dances, their fireworks and ceremonies, and their inexhaustible welter of surprises: the fruit, candy, toys and other objects sold on these days in the plazas and open air markets....Fiestas are our only luxury".

Octavio Paz in the celebrated *The Labyrinth of Solitude.*

In true Latin American spirit, Mexican fiestas are celebrated with lots of color, fervor and fun, featuring traditional costumes, music and folklore dances. Hardly a week goes by without one being celebrated somewhere in the country. Several are celebrated nationwide; some are special to a village or town. Big or small, the display of exuberance is undeniably catching.

Celebrant in Aztec finery.

Festivals & Celebrations

79

Mexico has one of the world's richest folk dance traditions.

Many of the festivals are religious in origin, held in honor of Catholic saints, but there are also some that commemorate ancient Indian rituals as evidenced by the use of elaborate costumes, feathers and masks.

Posadas

Ranking as the most important – and unique – event on Mexico's calendar of festivals are the *posadas*. The *Posada* is a fiesta that every Mexican child eagerly looks forward to, for it signals the advent of Christmas. There are nine *posadas* performed from 16 December through 24 December, one for each night. These are parades in which children and adults alike dress up to re-enact the journey of Joseph and Mary to Bethlehem asking for a room at a *posada* (inn). On the ninth and final *posada*, on Christmas Eve, the scene and re-enactment are the same as the past eight nights – with one difference, Joseph and Mary come upon an inn, which though full, has a stable where they are allowed to stay and here Jesus is born.

The *posada* is celebrated in private homes where friends and relatives of the host family gather. Occupying centerstage are the "pilgrims" which are clay figures of Joseph, Mary and the Guardian Angel. Behind them, guests line up in a procession singing the traditional litany "*Ora pro Nobis*" and asking for "a room at the inn".

Ballet Folklorico dancing in the streets in Mexico City.

A small group made up of the host family, waiting behind the main door to their house, answers in a chorus, first denying them entrance then finally admitting them. The pilgrim procession reacts joyously. The hostess expresses her happiness in being chosen to give the Holy Family a night's lodging. Then the baby doll of Jesus is placed in the arms of a child in the role of Mary who places him in a cradle in a manger scene. The enactment of the religious part over, the host family distributes gifts such as porcelain, papier-mache

Origin of *Posadas*

The *Posadas* are one of Mexico's more enduring traditional customs. To put it in a nutshell, they are the Mexican dramatization of Nativity. No one's certain of their exact origin although it's been conjectured that they probably dated from the period just after the Conquest when conversion of the Indians to the new religion had also begun. Historians believe they were likely to have come from Andalusia and were brought by colonists to New Spain, to give a familiar touch to Christmas. Celebrations were held in homes, convents and monasteries. To the surprise of the Spaniards, the *posadas* took root very quickly in Mexico where they were embraced with much enthusiasm.

Perhaps it was because the nine nights of pre-Christmas celebrations fell close to the Day of the Virgin of Guadalupe (12 December), a religious day that is deeply rooted in the ancient Anahuac civilization, and this struck a chord with the Indians. Whatever the reason, the *posadas* have since been celebrated with a fervor that even surpasses that for Corpus Christi and Holy Week. The *posadas* were first introduced in Mexico in the village of San Augustin de Acolman, near the sacred site of Teotihuacan which the Aztecs who had been conquered by the Spanish, called the "Place where the gods were made". It was coincidental that the Aztecs also honored the birth of their god Huitxilopochtli during the time around Christmas by gathering in homes to feast and eat tzoat, corn paste in the shape of their idols. This was apparently capitalized by the Au-gustinian priests who emphasized the similarity of the two fiestas to get the pagans to accept the new religion. Thus the novena of the *posada* representing the nine-day journey of Joseph and Mary (and representing also the nine months of pregnancy) is celebrated in Mexican homes today using Christian forms, rather than idols venerating the sun-god Huitxilopochtli.

Spanish customs and Indian rituals blended to give the colonial *posada* a truly Mexican flavor. There is the creche that occupies pride of place, a pitcher of *tepocote* punch, a traditional feast and exchange of gifts using figurines (a remnant from a pre-Columbian ritual) and the breaking of the *pinata* which represents the triumph of good over evil. The decorated pa-per-covered clay jug filled with gifts and candies is the symbolic representation of temptation or the spirit of evil that attracts humanity. The goodies inside the *pinata* are the unknown pleasures causing the temptation. The blind-folded person wielding the stick to break the suspended jug represents faith which should be blind and which ultimately must triumph and destroy the spirit of evil.

In the past, the *posada* was celebrated in a communal fashion – out in the streets, in the zocalos and was even dramatized in the theaters and dance halls. Castanets from Spain, tambou-rines, guitars and bagpipes combined with na-tive drums and flutes to produce a distinct Christmas music that accompanied the festivi-ties. Today, however, the *posadas* tend to be celebrated indoors, among family and friends.

and palm-leaf containers filled with cin-namon and fruit candies to symbolize the food offered to the Holy Family.

Then comes the moment all the children have been waiting for – the breaking of the *pinata* (see box). The blindfolded guests take turns to burst open the suspended candy-filled *pinata* with a stick and everyone rushes to gather its contents the moment they spill out.

Christmas Eve celebrations then begin in earnest as guests are served a *tejocote* fruit punch made with myrtle and raisins, or *rompope* liqueur. Supper follows, comprising asparagus soup, tur-key with chestnut dressing and a tradi-tional Christmas salad. After the feast, the entire party moves on to a nearby church to attend *"Misa de Gallo"* (Christ-

Mexican folk ballet in full swing.

mas Eve midnight mass).

In Oaxaca and Queretaro, the occasion is particularly memorable. Here the faithful in these two cities celebrate the festivities in a communal fashion, just like in the old days.

In Oaxaca, it's a grand affair involving much pageantry. After the last *posada* on Christmas Eve, the *calendas* or pilgrims' processions leave each church with lighted torches to drop by at the house of the "godmother" of the Child Jesus to pick him up for the grand procession preceded by splendid floats that wend their way to the Zocalo. After the march through the streets, the procession return to their respective churches to attend mass. At the stroke of midnight, the Child Jesus is placed in a crib and hymns which herald his birth are sung.

On 18 December, there are double celebrations as the *posada* coincides with the festival of Nuestra Senora de la Soledad (Our Lady of Solitude) marked by a spectacular fireworks display, an impressive procession, and the performances of Oaxaca's folk dances.

Christmas may come and go but the children still do not get to unwrap their presents until 12 days later, on 6 January with the arrival of *Los Reyes Magos* (The Three Kings of the Orient), who present gifts to the Child Jesus, another occasion for celebration. The New Year, of course, is ushered in with as much a carnival atmosphere as anywhere else in the world.

In the tradition of the conquerors.

Festival of Our Lady of Guadalupe

Matching the *posadas* in importance nationwide is the festival of Our Lady of Guadalupe on 12 December. The Ba-

silica de Guadalupe in Mexico City is of course, the main center of celebrations, but fiestas are also held in other cities at churches named in honor of the Virgin. Thousands of pilgrims from all corners of Mexico file into the Basilica from as early as dawn carrying floral images of the Virgin, some crawling in on their knees, to celebrate mass.

Outside in a plaza, performers in the morning sing *Las Mananitas*, the saint's day serenade played on Mexican birthdays. Then Indian dancers dressed resplendently in pre-Hispanic costumes perform traditional native dances such as *Conquista* (Conquest), *Moros y Cristianos* (Moors and Christians) and *Arrieros* (Mule-teers) in gusto, throughout the day.

Tecate in Baja California Norte celebrates the festival with a stunning parade in which *charros* in splendid cowboy costumes participate showing off their dazzling rope skills.

For the colorfully dressed Tzotzil and Tzeltal Indians living in San Cristobal de Las Casas and its environs, the Festival of Our Lady of Guadalupe is a very special one. It's held over two days, starting on 10 December, with a parade of costumed riders on horseback leading a procession of carts covered with cyprus branches, flowers and moss across the town to the Hill of Guadalupe where the church dedicated to the Virgin stands. The portico of the church and the streets leading to it are magnificently decorated. On 11 December, marimba and string music, fireworks displays and processions kick off, continuing through 12 December.

Matching the crowds in enthusiasm and numbers, flocking to worship at the Church of Our Lady of Guadelupe on 12 December, is the one million-strong congregation filing into Guadalajara on 12 October for the Procession of Our Lady of Zapopan. The religious parade starts as early as 5 am as dancers accompany the image of the Virgin Mary at the head of an adoring procession en route from the city center to the church (an annex of the Franciscan Monastery in Zapopan) dedicated to her.

Carnival Time

Carnival time in February and March explodes in riotous merrymaking in the streets in many towns and cities in Mexico. It takes place in the week before Ash Wednesday and is the Mexican version of the Mardi Gras.

It takes on a distinctly maritime note in the coastal towns of La Paz and Manzanillo. Masked and costumed merrymakers take to the streets. There are parades, flower contests and dancing in the salons. Boats in La Paz join in with elaborately decorated masts and at night, the port is ablaze with a fireworks display. In Manzanillo, fishing and watersports contests cap the day-long fiesta. Revelry during the "Carnaval" in

Festival of the Dead

Offerings of chocolate skulls.

Macabre, some would say about Mexico's grand celebrations for the souls of the dead on their annual *Dia de los Muertos* (Day of the Dead) that takes place every 1 November. Perhaps, but it shows just how comfortable the Mexicans are with the concept of death which they accept as a natural part of life and with resignation, even affection.

Incredibly, the Mexican Festival of the Dead celebrations have a parallel among the traditional Chinese who devote an entire month dubbed the Festival of the Ghosts (usually mid – August or September depending on the lunar calendar) to give offerings at an altar and to entertain with street opera the souls of the dead as they leave the underworld to visit the living. In Mexico, the Festival of the Dead coincides with the Catholic All Souls' Day and is a unique marriage of Christian customs and the pagan traditions of the indigenous Indians. It is a festival that is colored with joy, humor, imagination and a dash of the bizarre.

A few weeks before the festival, stores and street stalls throughout the country sell sugar and chocolate skulls, skeletal figures, cut-outs and pop-up skeletal toys, used as offerings and decorations on the altar to the dead. There are art exhibitions highlighting skeletons in various poses, concerts featuring appropriate music, dances and even discos staging Festival of the Dead themes.

On the Dia de los Muertos, the souls of the dead are believed to return to earth to indulge in earthly pleasures and to visit their living relatives who welcome them with flowers and honor them with offerings of food and drink that they had enjoyed when alive.

Even in the most urban, sophisticated Mexican *mestizo* home where the religious significance of the festival is perhaps a little muted, there is a still an *ofrenda* (offering table) of some kind. But it is in the rural areas, among particularly the Indians, that the occasion is infused with deep religious meaning and is a cause for celebrations on a grand scale.

It is a time when the entire family gathers to remember the dead. Members living away from home make an effort to return to join in with the celebrations. Nowhere in Mexico is the festival more movingly celebrated than in Patzcuaro

the high-spirited resorts of Acapulco and Mazatlan on the Yucatan Peninsula and in the sunny islands of Cozumel and Isla Mujeres offshore, reaches almost fever pitch. It takes place on the Sunday before Ash Wednesday with extrava-

gant floats, dancing in the streets and flower battles.

In Mazatlan, the fun continues through Tuesday with masquerades and even pleasure boats joining in with night-long floating parties on board. In

among the Tarascan or Purepeche Indians, especially those living on the island of Janitzio in Lake Patzcuaro and in the villages dotted along its shores.

A festive air reigns in Janitzio and other parts of Patzcuaro on the eve of 1 November as the Purepechans go shopping for sugar skulls, candy, bread, fruit, candles and flowers as they prepare to welcome back for a day their departed relatives in a ceremony known as "*Animecha Ketjtzitacua*" in the Purepeche dialect.

All day long, families in Janitzio tend to the tombs of their beloved who lie buried in the cemetery behind the church dedicated to the patron saint of San Jeronimo. They lovingly decorate the tombs with flowers, especially marigolds which have been associated with mourning since Aztec times, and set up altars or *ofrendas*. The *ofrendas* are elaborately decked with *tepejilote* (palm) leaves, flowers, sun and star decorations fashioned out of the *palma de coyol* (a kind of palm), and offerings which differ according to the deceased age. For little children who had died before they could get to enjoy them, candy, chocolates and toys are among the offerings; for those who had died in adulthood, the favorite delicacies and drinks they which enjoyed while they were alive, are placed on the altar. At dusk, family members huddle around the tombstones to keep vigil and offer prayers. The glow of flickering candles adds a touch of mystery and magic to the solemn occasion. At midnight, the church bells toll invoking the spirits of the dead who rise from beyond their graves to join the living and to receive their offerings. As the bells toll all night long, the Purepechans chant in accompaniment, asking for peace for the departed and happiness for the living.

Merida, the partying lasts five days.

Carnival celebrations in two Indian villages in San Cristobal de las Casas in Chiapas include rites that hark back to pre-Hispanic times. The beautiful hand-woven colorful costumes and be-rib-

boned and tasseled hats that the Indians in both villages wear daily add to the festive atmosphere.

In San Andres Chamula, villagers gather at the main square to watch the unfolding of a rather bizarre spectacle. Indian actors with faces blackened and dressed in black European-style clothing chase a group of children into the village church where they pretend to behead the youngsters. The Indians then ride on horseback to an arch where a black rooster has been hung and proceed to pluck out its feathers. One of them then bites off the rooster's head while the rest mimics him.

For the Indians of San Juan Chamula, the festival is conducted on a more fiery note. Pre-Carnival celebrations begin a few days before Tuesday. The Chamula Indians take to the streets costumed in Napoleonic-style dress coats and wearing monkey hats, playing and dancing to the carnival music of the *bolonchon*.

The highlight takes place on Tuesday when the Indians perform a dramatic purification rite that involves leaping over a barricade of fire between the San Juan church and a cross placed before the entrance.

Holy Week

Semana Santa, or Holy Week, is a time of repentance and joy. Mexicans throughout the country also take their holidays during this week. If you intend to join

Almost every festival culminates in a celebration of dance.

them in their celebrations, secure a reservation at your intended destination well in advance or arrive a week early to look for accommodations.

Holy Week starts with Palm Sunday and continues through Easter Sunday. In villages, towns and cities, processions commemorating the Stations of the Cross are held on Good Friday, ending in worship at the local church. Penitents, some holding a huge cross, walk behind gaily decorated floats carrying images of the Virgin and Jesus Christ.

Each region has its own variation of the procession and two places may be singled out for their unique presentations. The most moving spectacle of all is held at Ixtapalapa in Mexico City, where hundreds of villagers re-enact the

drama of the Passion which ends in the Crucifixion taking place on the historic Cerro de la Estrella (Hill of the Star).

In Patzcuaro, it's no less dramatic. In the mountains and towns around Lake Patzcuaro, Indians bring their crosses, specially made from the paste of corn stalks, to take part in a magnificent procession held in Patzcuaro on Good Friday. The giant crosses, some 1.8 m (6 ft) tall, are truly an impressive sight.

Corpus Christi in Papantla is a four-day celebration of native dances by the Totonac Indians. The most spectacular, the forerunner of today's bungee jump, is the Flying Pole Dance or Voladores. Thrice daily, the Totonacs climb up a 30-m (100-ft) high pole for the ritual. Tying themselves to long ropes attached

An eyeful at a local festival.

to the top of the pole, they leap off into space, making 13 revolutions before touching the ground.

Residents of San Miguel de Allende and San Felipe, 85 km (53 miles) away, gather in September to venerate the Nino Miguelito or Little Boy Michael – the patron saint of San Miguel – with marigolds. St Michael's Day in San Felipe marks two days of pomp and pageantry beginning on 28 September. The event attracts masses of devotees from surrounding towns in this northern part of Mexico, carrying images of the saint, banners and leading mules with "Treasures of the Kings" (wooden boxes of candied fruit) on their backs. In an impressive procession led by Aztec and Otomi dancers, the faithful make their way to the barracks near the sanctuary of St Michael. The following day, the barracks serve as the castle for the grand re-enactment of the battle of the Moors and the Christians. The cavalry and infantry in San Felipe join in and suchiles or marigolds are used as cannon fodder.

After the "castle" is taken, the vanquished are made to carry the image of Little Boy Michael to the sanctuary to the cheers of the crowd as they walk on the carpet of flowers.

Thousands of miles south of Mexico, the small Indian village of Huistan 45 km (28 miles) from San Cristobal de las Casas, also celebrates the Festival of St Michael who was adopted as their patron saint and from whose baroque image the Indians had apparently copied their traditional costume.

Romantics should head for Aguascalientes, in Mexico's north, for the *Feria de San Marcos* (Fair of St Mark) on 25 April. That's when they can hear soothing serenades in the town's famous St Mark's Garden or watch the stirring native *Matachines* dances. For those who prefer more excitement, there are bullfights and cockfights to watch. And in August, religion and wine mix as Aguascalientes holds its annual grape fair in the first two weeks of August, culminating the revelry with the Festival of the Assumption of the Virgin Mary on 15 August. *Matachines* dancers perform daily near the Cathedral and the warm summer nights are illuminated by a grand parade of floats circulating through the city.

Sugar Skulls and Sugar Animals

Colorful sugar skulls, figurines and animals appear in market and street stalls a couple of weeks before the Festival of the Dead celebrations on 1 November. They are bought as offerings for graves and to put on *ofrendas* in people's homes. Children also receive them as gifts with their names carved in icing across the skulls. The animals come in a wide range; sheep, lambs, cows, cats, giraffes, chickens and pigs, while the skulls have a number of expressions – cheerful, soulful or ferocious. The figurines are usually in the form of winged angels.

The origin of these sugar images is unclear. Some believe they were connected to the amaranth dough figures used in Aztec religious ceremonies while others believe they came from Europe. Whatever their origin, the images are popular. Although the sugar images can be eaten, some people prefer to keep theirs on display even till the following year. The sugar images are made from a mixture of icing sugar, egg white and lemon juice. Sometimes, a powder from the chaut root is used to bind the ingredients. Molds are used to create the shapes and after they have hardened and are turned out, details such as eyes and other trimmings are added by hand, or are piped on. Chocolate is also often used to make the images. They are made from cacao, hard boiled egg yolks, powdered cloves and cinnamon.

Festival of the Dead paraphernalia.

Independence Day

On 15 September, religion takes a back seat in Mexico as the entire nation celebrates Independence Day. Each town and city sets its own tone and pace with festivities starting even a few days earlier. In Tijuana, for instance, the celebratory mood begins on 11 September and the town turns into a big country fair with horse and auto races, folklore dances, regional costume contests and *mariachi* entertainment.

However, at 11 pm in Tijuana and elsewhere, townsfolk will gather in the main square to join in and shout "Viva Mexico!" and enjoy the concerts and dances that follow, usually until the early hours of the morning.

In Dolores Hidalgo, where the "Grito" by Miguel Hidalgo was first given, it's a very special occasion, indeed. So too in Mexico City where Independence Day is feted in grand style. Celebrations center on the Zocalo where

Independence Day celebration at the Zocalo.

the National Palace stands.

Days before the event, buildings in the Zocalo have been decorated and they are beautifully illuminated at night. At 9 pm, the tempo builds up. Fireworks light up the sky and it is standing room only in the Zocalo.

At 11 pm, the President of the Republic leads the waiting crowd to repeat the "Grito of Dolores" ending with "Viva Mexico!" *Mariachi* bands strike up, more fireworks shoot into the sky and folk dancers kick off. Celebrations continue the day with a stirring military parade and display of strength featuring the armed forces and various military schools in Mexico. The march-past takes place from the Zocalo to the Independence Monument.

20 November also marks a very important day on the national calendar for Mexico City – the anniversary of the Revolution of 1910.

The highlight is a colorful parade in which practically every social group is represented. There are bands, sporting groups, skaters, motorcyclists, football teams, labor groups and even schoolchildren performing their special routines to the delight of locals as well as tourists. The parade is topped off with a magnificent performance by Mexico's famous *charros*.

Mexico City joins Puebla on 5 May (Cinco de Mayo) to commemorate the Battle of Puebla. The historic battle in Puebla for the forts of Loreto and Guadalupe took place in 1842 and it

Indian dancers in a parade of colorful and exotic headdresses and costumes.

ended in a shattering defeat for the French enemy forces.

The exciting battle in Puebla is simulated on the mounds of Loreto and Guadalupe and in Mexico City at El Penon, a hill behind the international airport. Participants dressed as either French or Mexican soldiers and carrying thundering muskets include the Zacapoaxtla Indians whose fearlessness and fighting prowess during the battle more than 150 years ago helped the Mexican Army secure victory.

Flower Festival

Flower power reigns in Cuernavaca from 2 May to 6 May when the town hosts its annual Flower Festival that exhibits glorious blooms which includes the dahlia, Mexico's national flower, in the Borda Garden. The focus on flowers in Cuernavaca continues at the Festival of the Birth of Our Virgin Mary on 15 September. Held at the Sanctuary of Our Lady of Miracles in Tlaltenango, participants carry flowers, set off fireworks, and also perform native dances in celebration.

For a truly folkloric fiesta, go to Oaxaca for the Guelaguetza Folk Festival on the third and last Monday of July. It's an ancient Zapotec ritual staged on the Cerro del Fortin (Hill of the Small Fort). It pays tribute to an important figure – who it was originally has been lost in the mists of time – but gifts are

Re-enactment of the Crucifixion in Easter celebrations.

still brought and dances performed in the person's honor. The color and exuberance of Oaxaca's folk dances executed with flourish by the Mixtecs, Zapotecs, Mazatecs and Mijes, are truly fascinating and breathtaking.

Those who enjoy eating radishes will appreciate the unusual Festival of Radishes hosted by Oaxaca on 23 December. But the radishes here are solely for admiration as horticulturists show off skills in carving the radishes into various shapes and using them as part of floral arrangements.

A flourish is added to the festival by the throwing of plates into the air after the traditional *bunuelos* (doughnut-shaped bread) which were served on them, have been consumed.

Breaking the pinata.

Art & Culture

Mexico has one of the longest and richest cultural histories in the world. Its first high civilization developed around 3,000 years ago and successive native cultures of high achievement flourished up until the Spanish conquest of 1521.

Thenceforth Mexican culture split into two currents: the native Indian tradition, which contracted to its folk roots, and the imported Hispanic tradition, which superficially dominated. Whilst an indigenous mixed culture thrived at the folk level by the 18th century, and religious art and architecture had distinct local touches during the colonial period, it was not until the 20th century that Mexico truly found its own artistic culture, especially in painting where the muralists forged a new national consciousness.

Today, Mexico presents to the world a vibrant and distinctive national culture, the colorful off-

The grandeur of ancient civilizations lives on in sculptures.

Churrigueresque-style facade — a vibrant mix of Spanish-Mexican temperament.

spring of two strong parents: Europe and Mesoamerica.

The Ancients

Starting with the Olmecs and ending with the Aztecs, our knowledge of the ancients reveals a striking continuity. These civilizations built cities with ceremonial centers dominated by pyramid temples. They were adept at astronomy and developed complex calendrical systems. They worshipped various gods and made blood sacrifices to them. They prized jade and gold. Their art was largely religious but also ornamental. They were notable creators in architecture, stone carving, sculpture, pottery,

painting, jewelry and featherwork.

Pyramids, ball courts, sculpture, stone carving, mural painting: these were the constants of ancient Mexican architecture. The paint faded centuries, even millennia, ago; much carving has been obliterated, much sculpture destroyed. Ball courts and even pyramids have been demolished, by the Spanish, or by succeeding civilizations, or even by the same civilization, for reasons we can only guess at. But enough of all this remains for us to have a reasonably useful view of these civilizations.

The dominant artifacts of Mesoamerica were its pyramids. These symbolically reached for the heavens and were topped by temples dedicated to a god – of rain, fertility, war, and so on. All

Details on the facade of a Zapopan building.

were stepped but there was considerable variation in steepness and mass.

The Totonacs built squat, thick-layered pyramids with niches. Some precipitous Mayan pyramids look very much like miniature Matterhorns. The Aztecs also built them very steep and with twin temples on top. All were painted with religious motifs and in sacred colors.

The grandest pyramid complex known, is still largely intact: Teotihuacan, with its massive, gently graduated mounds. This is also an excellent example of ancient urban planning, with its central axis called the Avenue of the Dead. The largest known pyramid complex is the pyramid at Cholula, partly destroyed by the Spaniards, who then built a church on top of it. In this they were actually imitating the ancients: pyramids were often built over the top of each other successively by different rulers, or by conquerors.

Stone carving was the natural complement to monumental building. The Olmecs are famed for their massive basalt heads. Their significance is unknown but they are thought to be formal representations of rulers.

The Mayas were supreme stone carvers, whether in relief or in statuary. Mayan monumental art is mathematical, with each column, figure, face, animal, frieze, stairway, and temples expressing a date or time relationship.

The Olmecs were expert sculptors and jade carvers. They made marvellous jade figurines with mask-like faces.

The Ballet Folklorico

The Ballet Folklorico present artistic adaptations of Mexican folk dance traditions.

Mexico has one of the world's richest folk dance traditions. This is the art which most fully represents the meeting of the Indian and Hispanic cultures which make up Mexico. A great range of folk dances can be seen at festivals and celebrations all over the country, but you'd need to travel an awful lot to see them all. How do you get round this?

In the early 1950s Amalia Hernandez hit on the idea of creating a permanent ballet company which would perform the best folk dances of the regions of Mexico and display the vibrant festive costumes of the diverse localities. The Ballet Folklorico de Mexico was born in 1952 and her concept was an instant success. It has gone on to garner worldwide acclaim and to become firmly established as one of the pillars of Mexican cultural life.

Dance as a celebration and dance as a spectacle are two different things: one is a participatory activity marking a festive event, the other is a performance directed at a paying audience. The Ballet Folklorico is in the business of spectacles and therefore the dances and music it presents are not authentic folk examples but artistic adaptations designed to entertain, necessarily so. And in this the Ballet is amongst the most brilliant of entertainments in the world.

The Ballet Folklorico is theater, not anthropology: dazzling, exhilarating, kaleidoscopic. It presents dances from across the spectrum of Mexican history: dances that clearly date from pre-Hispanic times, like the *Dance of the Deer*, in which a solitary man wearing an antlered deer's head leaps and springs around the stage while being hunted; or *Los Dioses*, a dance based on Aztec rituals featuring brilliant quetzal-plumed costumes. It includes dances based on the ballads of the Revolution, with full-skirted *soldaderas*

They made jade masks portraying mythological beliefs. They also fashioned basalt and clay figurines that were naturalistic, such as of a wrestler or a wailing infant.

The Mayas excelled in this kind of art. They left wonderful figurines: two common motifs found at Jaina, show a woman sheltering a grown man beneath her and an ugly old man making

advances to a handsome female. The Mayas were notable painters too: they adorned temples with strongly colored wall paintings of richly attired figures, probably both human and divine, and pottery with quaint designs. Seated lords were a very common subject of carving and painting.

Turquoise mosaic masks are a distinctive feature of Mesoamerican art,

and Zapata-like figures, both with bandoliers slung recklessly over their shoulders.

But its main meat is the extraordinary range of regional dances that have come out of Spanish traditions rooted in Mexican soil, or of Indian traditions adapted to changing needs, transformed by spectacular choreography and costumes and bravura performances. There is the fish dance from Michoacan featuring a huge fishnet, and the Puebla dance of men in vertical circular headdresses of ribbons which look like catherine wheels; the tropical whites of a fiesta in steamy Veracruz, and the exuberant courtship ritual of the *Jarabe a la Tapatio*, with its echoes of flamenco.

The women's costumes are absolutely stunning: the red, white and gold of the china *poblana*, the flowered dresses evoking Chiapas, the swirling skirts of the Alazanas dance. The music is expert and varied: *marimba* music from the south, a *mariachi* band from Guadalajara, accordions and flutes, violins and drums. And there are dramatic demonstrations of country skills like lassoing.

The Ballet Folklorico has had a permanent home in the ornate setting of Mexico City's Palacio de Bellas Artes since 1959, supported by the government. Since then, Amalia Hernandez has created choreography for 30 ballets made up of 56 different dances. Highly disciplined and professional, the Ballet regularly tours abroad and has won over 100 awards. Currently Norma Lopez Hernandez, the founder's daughter, is its artistic director.

for which Teotihuacan is famous. The Zapotecs excelled in featherwork and gold jewelry. The Mixtecs who succeeded them at Monte Alban were expert in pottery decoration. The Toltecs, who flourished in Central Mexico between the Teotihuacan and Aztec periods, were notable for their massive statues of warriors which served as pillars to a large temple. They also left a unique mother-

History in perspective at the Anthropology Museum.

of-pearl mosaic ornament of a warrior's head peering out from the gaping mouth of a coyote.

The Aztec Calendar

The most celebrated piece of Meso-american art was produced by the Aztecs: the Sun Stone or Aztec Calendar. This massive disc almost four meters across, is densely carved with calendrical information and represents the sum of Aztec astronomical knowledge.

The center portrays the Sun God and the surrounding concentric rings of symbols concern chronology and the five successive universes of Aztec mythic history. The magnificent stone stood

Diego Rivera

A mural depicting the pleasures of family life.

Diego Rivera (1886-1954) is the most important cultural figure in Mexico's 20th century history. He allied first-class artistic technique with revolutionary politics and proud nationalism to stand at the forefront of the movement forging a Mexican national culture.

His medium was mural painting and his work still adorns many public buildings and spaces in the capital and elsewhere. His heritage to the nation is most clearly exemplified by the magnificent series of murals evoking Mexican history which line the courtyard of the National Palace in Mexico City's Zocalo.

Rivera, born in 1886, spent 14 years studying art in Europe, especially Paris, where he knew Picasso amongst others and painted in a Cubist style. Two events were crucially formative near the end of his exile: he met the young painter David Alfaro Siqueiros fresh from fighting in the Revolution, and he went on a tour of Italy to see its Renaissance fresco tradition. Siqueiros fired him with revolutionary ideals, and frescos inspired him to paint on is a grand scale and in public.

Returning home in 1921, he went to discover the Maya lands and revisited the ancient monuments of central Mexico; his country was revealed to his mature eyes for the first time, just when the Revolution had turned to concerted creative endeavor.

All these things combined to impel Rivera on a life-long project of representing and advancing Mexican nationhood and the Mexican people through public art. The early 1920s were a time of great creativity and energy in the political and cultural fields, ably fuelled by the pioneering radical Minister of Education, Jose Vasconcelos, who in particular saw the potential of the mural in Mexican nation-building. Rivera joined the nascent mural movement sponsored by Vasconcelos to decorate the National Preparatory School, where he worked for the first time with Siqueiros and Orozco, also destined to be great muralists.

In 1923, Vasconcelos gave him a solo commission to paint the courtyard walls of the colonial palace housing the Ministry of Education. In dozens of roughly three-by-two meter

halfway up the Great Temple of Tenochtitlan.

A distinctive feature of Mesoamerican art was featherwork. The region was replete with brilliantly colored birds whose feathers were worked into tunics and headdresses for the nobility. The quetzal was the most highly prized bird and the greatest artifact left to us is Moctezuma's huge fan-like headdress fashioned from its long, bright green tail feathers.

The Aztecs prized their featherworkers, potters, jewellers and painters,

spaces between doors along the cloister-like corridors, Rivera set about depicting scenes of national life and recent history, idealising the disadvantaged – the peasants, workers and indians, and satirising their exploiters – the rich, the church, and the industrialists.

With this opus, Rivera became the leading figure in the surge of national consciousness and cultural renewal which followed the turmoil of the Revolution of 1910-20. A member of the communist party from 1922, his murals were instrumental in creating a new sense of nationhood and in impelling the national reform movement of the 1920s and 30s.

Drawing on all of Mexico's diverse history and honoring its common people, he created a proud, vibrant and all-inclusive vision of a complex and unique nation, inspiring Mexicans with a new sense of their own worth and heritage. Along with Siqueiros and Orozco, he took Mexico onto the world stage of modern art. But it was Rivera's brilliant evocations that most impressed the world at large, and it was Rivera who stood firmly at the center of Mexican cultural life until his death in 1954.

All of Rivera's work is politically charged and nationalistic, varying from simple idealisations and satires of Mexican people to epic recreations of Mexico's history and quasi-religious images of primal energy and a utopian future. When given the commission to paint the National Palace, seat of the president, in the capital's historic heart, he created large panels teeming with characters and incident, representing ancient civilisations like the Totonacs and the Mayas, or the turbulent struggles for Independence and the Revolution.

In works such as this, Rivera's achievement

Evocative art along the Ministry of Education corridors.

was to set before all Mexicans, but especially the illiterate, the fullness of their own history, to instill a pride in its cultural diversity, and to inspire future progress.

Despite distortions, such as portraying the Aztecs as noble and the conquistadors as savages, the poor always dignified and the rich always disgusting, overall he left a brilliant legacy to the nation and a potent inspiration for the post-colonial world.

composing poetry in their praise; they danced and made music with gourd rattles, drums and flutes.

Mesoamerican cultures were rich in ceremony, ritual, music and dance. These living elements persisted longest after the conquest.

The Colonial Period

The only artistic continuity between the Mesoamerican and Spanish colonial periods was in the dominating importance of religion. The most notable ar-

Frida Kahlo

The painter Frida Kahlo is a central figure in Mexico's modern cultural history and is today the most highly valued female artist in Latin America. Born in 1907, she so identified with the Revolution that she would later always give the year as 1910. Encouraged by her husband Diego Rivera, she developed a unique personal style which is sometimes called surrealist but is really *sui generis*, taking a Mexican popular art tradition and moulding it into her own mode of expression.

Much given to self-portrait, her work is colorful in treatment, dreamlike in aspect, personal in subject, and visceral in effect. Working when Mexico was creating its modern nationhood, she probed questions of identity – personal, cultural and political – at a time of great flux and paralleled the nation's search for itself. Through her work and her life, she significantly assisted that national self-discovery and is unquestionably the most outstanding Mexican woman of this century. Strong-minded and devoted to folk dress, she favored the costumes of Tehuantepec, a region famed for its bold women.

The crucial event of her life was a terrible accident which occurred at the age of 18. A bus she was riding in was hit by a tram and a handrail was sent plunging through her abdomen and back, rendering her unable to bear children and liable to severe back pain all her life. Passionate for life but often confined to bed or a wheelchair, painting became her outlet. It began as she lay at home recovering and borrowed her father's box of paints. With a mirror fixed above her bed, she started on the self-portraits which dominate her oeuvre, later saying, "I paint myself because I am so often alone and because I am the subject I know best."

Kahlo's painting was consciously rooted in the *retablo*, or votive painting of Mexican popular religious tradition: simple images of miraculous events with inscriptions beneath. Her subject was most often herself: dressed in a variety of beautiful ethnic costumes, wearing extraordinary jewelry, with tropical fruit or flowers, or with a pet monkey or parrot.

She deliberately stressed her facial peculiarities: her thick black eyebrows that almost met and her faint moustache. Strongly autobiographical, her work is expressive of much more than herself: of the Mexican condition and of the human condition.

She often employs Mexican cultural motifs: in one pencil sketch, her eyebrows become a bird, echoing the snake-surrounded eyes of the Aztec rain deity Tlaloc. In *My Grandparents, My Parents and I*, she depicts herself as a child and shows her *mestizo* origins; the family tree floats in front of an arid, mountainous, cactus-dotted backdrop. In *Self-Portrait with Cropped Hair*, she sits in a man's suit and shirt, scissors in hand, her long tresses lying on the floor all around. At the top are two lines from a popular song: "Listen, if I loved you, it was for your hair; now you're bald, I don't love you any more." Her husband was frequently unfaithful, causing her pain; she herself took lovers of both sexes.

One of them was Leon Trotsky, a close friend of Rivera and herself when he went into exile in Mexico City. Frida Kahlo, like her husband, was fiercely committed to left-wing causes and to the ideals of the Mexican Revolution; she often took part in political parades and campaigns. But if you go today to her family house, the "Blue House", now the Frida Kahlo Museum in Coyoacan, Mexico City, you will encounter none of this; you will find yourself in a place of extraordinary beauty and charm, filled with the fine Mexican folk arts that she adored.

tistic achievements continued to be in religious architecture and stone carving. The Spanish had brought a strong tradition of church-building with them and found a people who were excellent workers in stone. The result over the three centuries of Spanish rule was as many as 12,000 Catholic churches built in a variety of styles which followed European trends but which took shape

Traditional Mayan home.

with unique local touches and embellishments, often extravagant.

The religious orders built widely from the 16th century. With vast courtyards, chapels, cloisters, gardens and aqueducts, their institutions were the first centers of the new culture and they were often magnificent. The Franciscan structures tended to be austere, the Augustinian rich and spacious, the Dominican defensive and massive. They were remarkable for the eclecticism with which they combined Romanesque, Gothic and Renaissance elements. For the better instruction of the Indians, they were decorated with fresco painting. In secular architecture, fine Renaissance style palaces for the new nobility arose; extant examples are Cortes's at

Cuernavaca and Montejo's at Merida.

Mexican art first came into its own with the Baroque period. The combination of the exuberant Spanish-Latin temperament with the Indian love of color and decoration gave rise to an ultra-baroque explosion.

The most extreme example of this tendency was the Churrigueresque – the baroque gone wild. Surfaces were a riot of ornament: elaborately-carved stone facades and lavishly-moulded stucco interiors, dripping with gilding and vivid multi-colored painting. In a reaction to this colonial opulence, Mexico took to neo-classicism as an expression of enlightenment and progress in the late 18th and the 19th century.

Though Mexico produced notable

Sculpture outside the Rufino Tamayo Museum, Mexico City.

Baroque religious artists and Romantic landscapists, especially Velasco with his series of paintings of the Valley of Mexico, the nation's first artist of real repute and indigenous inspiration was the engraver Jose Guadalupe Posada [1852-1913]. Famous for his skeleton and skull cartoons, drawing on Mexican motifs with strong lines and black humor, Posada was a vigorous nationalist inspiration to the next generation: the muralists.

The Muralists

Modern Mexican art is inseparable from the muralists. With its 1922 manifesto, the Mexican mural movement went into battle for "a fighting educative art for all". Murals adorning dozens of public buildings in Mexico City and the provinces, helped create a national consciousness, urged on social reform, and inspired youth and painters worldwide. Diego Rivera [see box] became the acknowledged leader but he was not the only accomplished muralist; David Alfaro Siqueiros and Jose Clemente Orozco were at work at the same time during the movement's height, from between 1920-50, producing boldly dynamic works that contrasted with Rivera's tighty-packed tableaux.

The movement's direct inspirations were the frescos of the Italian Renaissance, the Russian revolution in its first bloom and the turmoil of the Mexican

Revolution then in progress. Its leading promoter was Jose Vasconcelos, Minister of Education, philosopher and revolutionary himself. Both quantity and quality were stunning. Dozens of artists joined the movement and the best produced world-class work.

The revolution was spurred on by ubiquitous artistic images of nationalist and progressive passion – in ministerial and municipal buildings, in churches and palaces, in colleges and hospitals, in patios, in stairwells, on facades, wherever there was a suitable blank space, big or huge.

The first major commission was at Vasconcelos's own Ministry of Education, which he gave over in 1923 to the immense newly-matured talent of Diego Rivera. Rivera set to work "to produce the pure basic images of my land. I wanted my painting to reflect the social life of Mexico as I saw it, and through my vision of the truth to show the masses the outline of the future." He went on to paint the National Palace and numerous public buildings.

Siqueiros and Orozco stand out for the boldness of their images and directness of impact. Siqueiros was a life-long communist and the muralist most committed to fitting art to its setting. Producer of the first muralist manifesto, Siqueiros stuck to his guns all his life,

which culminated in his seventies with two masterpieces, *The Mexican Revolution* in Chapultepec Castle and *The March of Humanity* in the Siqueiros Polyforum, Mexico City.

Orozco was ultimately pessimistic about revolutionary Mexico, but his expressive powers never diminished. His most gripping work was done in Mexico's second city Guadalajara in the late 1930s. There he expressed the physical and mystical conflicts of humanity in broodingly magnificent murals, embodying his ideals in the fresco *Man of Fire* in the dome of the Hospicio Cabanas, in which a swirling burning man is purified through fire.

Mexican muralism in all its extraordinary variety is not just a national treasure but one of mankind's most noble achievements, a vibrantly lasting demonstration that art which is most deeply and most skillfully national, can reach out to the whole world.

Modern Art

Mexico has been in the forefront of Latin American art in this century, not only through the muralists but also through painters like Frida Kahlo [see box] and Rufino Tamayo. Tamayo was both an easel painter and muralist, but not of the didactic or dynamic kind like

Octavio Paz

Octavio Paz is Mexico's foremost literary figure, a poet and essayist of the highest caliber. Nobel Prize winner for Literature in 1990, Paz is most widely known as the author of the seminal work on Mexican-ness, *The Labyrinth of Solitude*.

Born in Mexico City in 1914, he began writing at an early age under the influence of classic Spanish poets. In 1945, he joined the Mexican diplomatic service. His first important collection of poems came out in 1949, *Libertad bajo palabra*, and *El laberinto de la soledad* appeared in 1950. His quirkily questing mind has since regularly produced collections of poems and essays inspired by a variety of philosophical traditions.

From 1962 he was Ambassador to India, becoming absorbed in oriental art and thought, but resigning in 1968 in protest against the Mexico City student massacre. His 1969 poetry collection *Ladera este* came out of his Asian experience; all phases of his poetry are sparkling in their imagery and restless in form. By this time he was recognised as Latin America's most scintillating poet.

He taught at Cambridge in 1970 and returned to Mexico in 1971 to found the cultural magazine *Plural* which was very influential in Latin America. When it suffered from government interference in 1976, he started another monthly called *Vuelta*.

Such is the importance of his best-known work, that many commentators say you cannot understand Mexico unless you've read it. In *The Labyrinth of Solitude*, Octavio Paz portrays and dissects the Mexican character as evidenced by Mexico's history and culture. With a poet's passion and a philosopher's acuity, he focuses on fundamental themes like death and individuality. A highlight of the book is his examination of the fiesta; this excerpt shows to advan-

tage his deep affinity for his nation and his exceptional descriptive and analytic powers.

"In all of these ceremonies, the Mexican opens out. They all give him the chance to reveal himself and to converse with God, country, friends or relations. During these days of silent Mexican whistles, shouts, sings, shoots off fireworks, discharges his pistol into the air. He discharges his soul. And his shout like the rockets we love so much, ascends to the heavens, explodes into green, red, blue and white lights, and falls dizzily to earth with a trail of golden sparks. This is the night when friends who have not exchanged more than the prescribed for months get together, trade confidences, weep over the same troubles, discover that they are brothers, and sometimes, to prove it, kill each other. The night is full of songs and loud cries. The lover wakes up his sweetheart with an orchestra. There are jokes and conversations from balcony to balcony, sidewalk to sidewalk. Nobody talks quietly. Hats fly in the air. Laughter and curses ring like silver pesos. Guitars are brought out.

Now and then, it is true the happiness ends badly, in quarrels, insults, pistol shots, stabbings. But these too are part of the fiesta, for the Mexican does not seek amusement: he seeks to escape from himself, to leap over the wall of solitude that confines him during the rest of the year. All are possessed by violence and frenzy. Their souls explode like the colours and voices and emotions.

Do they forget themselves and show their true faces? Nobody knows. The important thing is to go out, open a way, get drunk on noise, people, colours. Mexico is celebrating a fiesta. And this fiesta shot through with lightning and delirium is the brilliant reverse to our silence and apathy, our reticence and gloom."

"The Big Three". His work is poetic and warmly colored, impressionistic and semi-abstract, the product of a lyrical imagination. A master of form, he could make a child assume the dimensions of its mother's heart. The Museo Tamayo in Mexico City shows many of his works. Nearby in the Museum of Anthropology is a notable Tamayo mural, *Combat of Night and Day*.

Imposing La Valenciana church facade.

In the 1980s a new generation of painters came out from under the long shadow of the great muralists to make their own mark with works reflecting contemporary Mexico. Elena Climent is a leading example with her boldly colored paintings of shrines, walls, cupboards and shopfronts showing the things of everyday life.

Literature

Writing in Mexico began with the ancient civilizations who recorded events in glyphs or symbolic pictures, either on monuments in stone or in codices, on deerskin or bark parchment. Glyphs are complex symbols first used by the Olmecs and developed by the Mayas into a sophisticated communicative system. The Mayan glyphs notate astronomy, history and myths; they were produced by scribes and sculptors whose patron "saint" was the howler monkey.

The codices, of which there are several Maya and Aztec examples extant, were documents which folded up like a screen. Calendrical and astronomical data, historical events, religious myths and administrative matters were recorded on them by means of painted objects and symbols. The Mayas, through transcription in the early colonial period, have left us extensive chronicles and mythic histories in the books called *Chilam Balam* and *Popol Vuh*. There was also an imaginative oral tradition:

we know that the Aztecs composed epic "nationalistic" songs and individual poetry which could be surprisingly philosophical in mood, and it is reasonable to assume that earlier peoples had similar traditions.

Some Spaniards of the conquest period wrote fascinating accounts of the Indian societies and cultures. The soldier Bernal Diaz recorded his experiences with Cortes's expedition in *The Conquest of New Spain*. The Franciscan missionary Fray Bernardino de Sahagun recorded the *General History of the Things of New Spain*, a treasure trove of information about the Aztecs and central Mexican cultures. Bishop Diego de Landa, who burned the Mayan codices, partially redeemed himself with *Yucatan Before and After the Conquest*, his account of Mayan culture.

Literature in colonial Mexico was highly derivative of European styles and themes, with the notable exception of a remarkable 17th century woman called Sor Juana Ines de la Cruz, a liberal nun who wrote love poetry and comic dramas. For most of the period, only works approved by the Spanish authorities could be published. In 1816, the first Mexican and Latin American novel, *The Itching Parrot* by Joaquin Fernandez de Lizardi, was printed. Nineteenth-century Mexico produced a great deal of poetry, novels and drama drawn from European models, especially French; it took the 1910 Revolution to inspire a distinctively Mexican literature.

"The Novel of the Mexican Revolu-

tion" was thus born. A notable example is Mariano Azuela's *Los de abajo* (The Underdogs), about the lowly soldiers of the revolutionary turmoil, of which he was one. Martin Luis Guzman produced dramatic novels arising from his reporting experiences with Pancho Villa and others, but he's best known for *La Sombra del Caudillo* (The Shadow of the Dictator), an indictment of the 1920s' political heirs of the Revolution.

Famous Authors

Juan Rulfo's [1918-86] high reputation rests on two works of the 1950s: a short story collection called *El Llano en llamas* (The Burning Plain) and a novella called *Pedro Paramo*. Regional and rural in setting, depicting the revolutionary period, these works concern father-son relationships, and themes such as death and guilt, paradise and hell. Enigmatic and poetic, Rulfo's work represents the Mexican psyche as no other novelist's does and prefigures the magic realism which later took Latin American literature by storm.

Two writers have been pre-eminent in recent decades: Octavio Paz and Carlos Fuentes. Poet and essayist Octavio Paz achieved supreme acclaim with the 1990 Nobel Prize for Literature [see box]. Carlos Fuentes is Mexico's foremost novelist and most widely translated author. From a brilliantly inventive well-spring of ideas which bridge the divisions of our world – industrialised and develop-

Mexico's rich culture is prevalent in its architectual and design traditions.

ing, white-skinned and brown-skinned, post-modern and traditional – he creates complex and sparkling imaginative worlds.

Born in 1928, the product of a cosmopolitan upbringing as a diplomat's son, Fuentes draws on a wide range of cultural and historical references, a fascination with the fantastic and fabulous, and a preoccupation with the Revolution's failings. Among his works are *La Muerte de Artemio Cruz*, the deathbed memories of a revolutionary officer turned capitalist opportunist; and *Terra Nostra*, a vast rumination on Latin America combining Renaissance thought, Aztec mythology, present reality and future projection.

A newcomer who has made a con-

siderable mark is Laura Esquivel. She had an international success with *Como Agua Para Chocolate* (Like Water For Chocolate), in which recipes lead to much more than food.

Cinema

The heyday of the Mexican cinema, like Hollywood, was in the 1930s and 40s. Big stars of the Golden Age were the comedian Cantinflas, actor Jorge Negrete, actresses Maria Felix and Dolores del Rio, whilst Lupe Velez, the "Mexican Spitfire", also starred in Hollywood. The great director of the period was Emilio Fernandez, whose most acclaimed works are *Maria Candelaria* (win-

Mexican music, song and dance evoke images of a strong, spirited people.

ner at the 1943 Cannes Film Festival) and *La Perla* [1945].

In the 1950s and 60s, the industry became relentlessly commercial and downmarket, producing popular films with stars like Pedro Infante. In recent decades, popular melodramas known as *pulquerias* have predominated.

An internationally acclaimed film of the 1980s was *Frida*, directed by Paul Leduc, an impressionistic portrait of the painter Frida Kahlo, her life and her world. The 1990s have brought something of a renaissance in film-making: a new wave of films about Mexican life and mores has arisen, such as the sex comedy *La Tarea* (Homework).

Another production was *El Mariachi*, made for just $7,000, a highly original

and entertaining mix of genres – western, musical, comedy, gangster – and an exemplary triumph of talent over resources. The most famous example so far is *Como Agua Para Chocolate*, after the best-selling novel.

Mexico has attracted the talents of some major foreign directors who made films redolent of its unique flavour. Eisenstein made the classic *Que Viva Mexico!* in the 1930s. Bunuel spent a long exile in the 1940s and 1950s making classics like *Los Olvidados* about Mexico City's poor and *Nazarin* about a latter day Christ figure, as well as numerous commercial movies. Though Hollywood productions, John Huston made three notable movies in Mexico, which includes *The Night of the Iguana*.

Music and Dance

Music, song and dance occupy a special place in the heart of the expressive Mexicans. Throughout the country, on the streets, plazas, metro trains and sometimes buses, you will hear the soulful strains of music played by buskers trying to earn a living.

Mexican music stems from two main origins: Indian and European. The earliest Indian music before the arrival of the Spanish was mainly wind and percussion related with flutes and drums dominating. The imaginative Indians fashioned instruments out of natural materials: reeds were turned into flutes, rattles and shakers were made from gourds while shells were used as horns.

Religious and somber in its tone and beat, traditional Indian music is the kind heard today accompanying Indian dances during fiestas. The Spanish Conquest brought in Spanish instruments and rhythms which were incorporated with native styles. After independence, other European instruments such as the accordion and the saxophone made their appearance, altering the blend even more. The result is a melodious music which has broad appeal, particularly among the *mestizos*.

Mexican Music

Central to typical Mexican music is the basic rhythm or *son* layered over by backing instrumentals. Each region has created its own characteristic *son*, although the accompanying music is composed from the same instruments such as large and small guitars, the violin and the harp.

The best known rhythm, without a doubt, is the *son mariachi*. Around the Gulf Coast, where African and Caribbean influences played a part, the mellifluous *marimba* is more often heard.

Most Mexican dances are traditional, embodying ancient rituals, or because there's a story to tell, costumes and masks are also often used. Among the better known dances are those of the Concheros (in Indian costumes), Voladores (Flying Pole) and the dances of the Tarascans such as the Dance of the Elderly (Danza de los Viejitos). If you like ballads or tales of romance, you will enjoy Mexican song. There are basically three types: The *corrido*, an adaption of the Spanish ballad; the *cancion* (song), whose theme is a tragic or impossible romance, and the *ranchero*, the Mexican version of country and western. A derivative of the *ranchero* is the *mariachi*, Mexico's best-known sound.

Tijuana
Mexicali
Ensenada
Puerto
Penasco
San Quintin
Nogales
Ciudad
Juárez
U
Baja
California
Ojinaga
Hermosillo
Chihuahua
Isla
Cedres
Guaymas
Cuauhtémoc
Santa
Rosalia
Cuidad
Obregon
Delicias
M
Loreto
Gulf of
California
Baja
California
Sur
Los
Mochis
Torreon
Culiacán
Continental Divide
La Paz
Durango
Fresnillo
San Lucas
Zacatecas
Sierra Madre Occidental
Tuxpan
San Blas
Aquascal
Islas
Marias
Tepic
Guadalajara
Pacific
Ocean
Puerto
Vallarta
Barra de
Navidad
Colima
Ur
Manzanillo
Lazaro
Cardenas

N

0   Kilometers   240

STATES

Nuevo
Laredo

onterrey

Matamoros

*Gulf of
Mexico*

Cuidad
Victoria

Cuidad
Mante

uis
si

Tampico

ato

Sierra Madre Oriental

Hidalgo

Poza Rice

taro

Pachuca

Mexico City

Xalapa

oluca

Tlaxcale

Veracruz

*Bay of
Campeche*

navaca

Puebla

Orizaba

Morelos

Distrito
Federal

Coatzacoalcos

Villahermosa

ilpancingo

Acapulco

San Cristóbal
de Las Casas

Tuxtla Gutierrez

Oaxaca

Puerto
Escondido

Salina
Cruz

Comitan

*Gulf of
Tehuantepec*

Tapachula

GUATEMALA

Progreso

Valladolíd

Cancún

Merida

*Isla de
Cozumel*

Chetumal

BELIZE

HONDURAS

EL
SALVADOR

Mexico City

115

Mexico City is like no other metropolis in the Americas. Many others have its skyscrapers and boulevards, a vibrant cultural and commercial life, surrounding mountains and sprawling suburbs. They may also have colonial quarters and shanty towns, they may have pollution problems and high altitude locations too. But none have all of this together, in spades, lying atop an ancient civilisation whose remains sprout forth all around.

The many faces of Mexico City.

Comparisons within the Americas are inadequate. Mexico City is more like Rome than anywhere else. It has that depth of history, that sense of surprise around every corner, and yes, that urban anarchy. Walking around the colonial quarter is like wandering through Renaissance and Baroque Rome. Standing in the Zocalo with its remains of the Aztec Templo Mayor, is akin to being in the Roman Forum. Negotiating the

Illuminated splendor of the Zocalo's Cathedral.

Paseo de la Reforma is comparable to dealing with a modern Roman boulevard. But Mexico City is also much more than this because it is the capital of a multi-ethnic third world nation, replete with the contrasts of rich and poor, its streets alive with the color of Indian vendors and beggars as well as the chic boutiques and fashions of the wealthy, a place where you can as readily munch a tortilla on the sidewalk as drink a fine wine in a fancy restaurant.

And with all this, Mexico City has also long been reckoned the world's

But a large population and a long history also enable the city to offer a range of services and attractions incomparable within Latin America. From shops and markets to churches and museums, from quaint old alleys to broad modern boulevards, from bawdy nightclubs to grand opera, from ancient ruins to modern art galleries, from taco stands to three star restaurants, Mexico City has it all and has much of the best in the Americas.

Add to this a heady location in a mountain-ringed basin at an altitude of 2,255 m (7,400 feet), with views of snow-capped volcanoes on a clear day, and you have one of the world's great cities by almost any measure.

There are broadly four layers to Mexico City's history: the Aztec origins in and around Lake Texcoco, the Spanish colonial city which gradually filled in the lake, the 19th-century independence expansion which virtually eliminated it, and the modern one that has burgeoned in recent decades. All of these overlap and mix with each other to create one of the world's most fascinating and multi-faceted metropolises.

Aztec City

The Aztec settlement of Tenochtitlan was founded in 1325 in Lake Texcoco, whose shores were already inhabited by other peoples. By 1500 the Aztecs were supreme and Tenochtitlan was dominant over two other large cities called

largest city; with a population now around 20 million, and there's no sign of it stopping as the national total burgeons towards 100 million by the year 2000. This ballooning of humanity and activity puts great pressure on public services like the metro and on housing and road traffic, but manifests itself most severely in its air pollution.

The Aztec Calendar

The face of the Sun God lies at the center of the basalt slab.

The finest piece of Aztec art left to us and the pride of the Museum of Anthropology in Mexico City is the Sun Stone or Aztec Calendar. The largest Aztec sculpture ever found, the circular slab measures almost 4 m (about 13 ft) across and weighs 24 tons. It was discovered in 1790 at the site of Tenochtitlan's great ceremonial precinct. At the basalt stone's center is the face of the sun god, its tongue hanging out of its mouth, the fearful countenance of Tonatiuh who was the lord of the earth.

Around this are concentric rings of symbols which represent the history of the universe according to Aztec belief. This belief was absolutely fundamental to their psyche as a people and the reason for their warlike way of life and bloodthirsty religious practices. They believed that the world had gone through four creations.

The first was the world of the Jaguar Sun ruled by giants who ate acorns; it ended when jaguars devoured the giants and was succeeded by the world of the Wind Sun. This ended in hurricanes, to be replaced by the Fire Sun, presided over by Tlaloc the Rain God, which ended in turn in a great fiery rain. The Water Sun came next, which was eventually engulfed by a flood, after which the fifth world came into being, supposedly at ancient Teotihuacan.

Known as the World of Motion, it was all to end on the Aztec calendar day "4 Motion", when the world would be destroyed by earthquakes. Tonatiuh was its god. On the Sun Stone, Toniatuh's face is flanked by claws clutch-

ing human hearts, and this motif points gorily to the linchpin of the system.

The Aztecs believed that the fifth sun was the last and that the universe would end when it was destroyed by the order of the gods. To prevent this, the gods had to be well fed, and their diet was human hearts. Out of a deep sense of insecurity, the Aztecs took the age old Mesoamerican practice of human sacrifice to extreme lengths. In order to ensure the continuation of the universe, they offered to their gods an endless stream of victims upon the sacrificial altars. The high priests cut open their chests, tore out the still beating hearts and raised them aloft in offering.

On the Sun Stone, surrounding Tonatiuh's ghastly face and claws, are four square panels representing the four previous worlds – of jaguar, wind, sun and water. The whole configuration of the central part of the stone around the face forms the fateful sign of 4 Motion, the day of the end of the world, and the face depicts the sun's death. The design of the stone shows clearly the sense of foreboding that permeates Aztec religion. The fifth sun, which gave light and life to their world, was a concession by the gods, which they would take away unless fed enough human blood. Through the gods' travail the world had been created; through man's sacrifice it would be perpetuated.

The Sun Stone also portrays other leading gods of the Aztec pantheon: Smoking Mirror, the Plumed Serpent and the Rain God. The stone was originally colorfully painted. Though it is also often called the Calendar Stone, strictly calendrical information is limited to the third concentric ring which depicts the twenty day-signs of the solar calendar, which had eighteen months and five nameless "unlucky" days. The "centuries" lasted 52 years.

Street performers taking a break.

Tlatelolco and Texcoco.

Tenochtitlan housed some 500,000 people and the Valley of Mexico had about one million inhabitants by the time Cortes arrived. Such an impressive urban concentration was far bigger and much more populous than any in Europe at the time; even Constantinople was smaller, and the Spanish royal capital of Toledo had a mere 18,000 souls. The Aztec capital was at least ten times bigger than any city the Spaniards personally knew, covering about 15 sq. km (6 sq miles). They were astonished.

Nevertheless, within two years of their arrival in 1519, they had razed the splendid city to the ground, burned what they couldn't plunder, and decimated the population through disease, starva-

tion or the sword. Tenochtitlan was left a smouldering ruin.

One year later Cortes decided that the best place to build the capital of New Spain was upon the same site. Its center was placed upon the Aztec ceremonial center: the great open square called the Zocalo lay over the Aztec public plaza, the viceroy's palace replaced Moctezuma's, and the cathedral rose at the site of the Great Temple of the Aztecs. The symbolism was deliberate: Spain had crushed Mesoamerica. What we see today of Aztec architecture – the remains of pyramids at a few sites – was unearthed in later centuries during rebuilding work.

The Spanish proceeded to build a colonial city whose main outline and

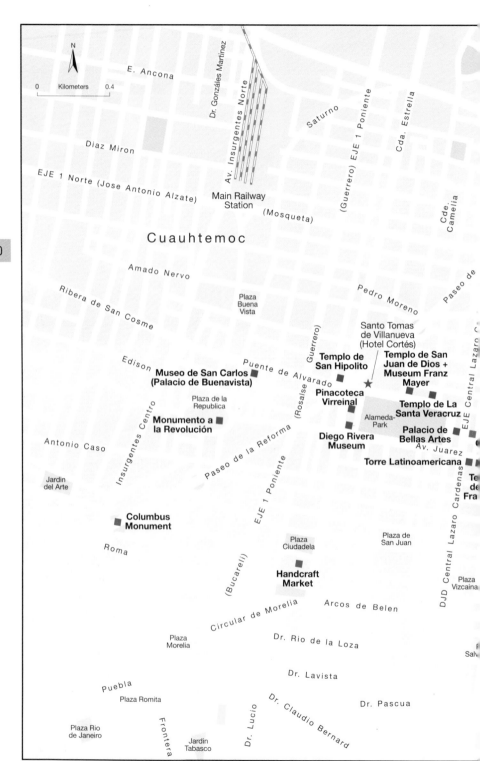

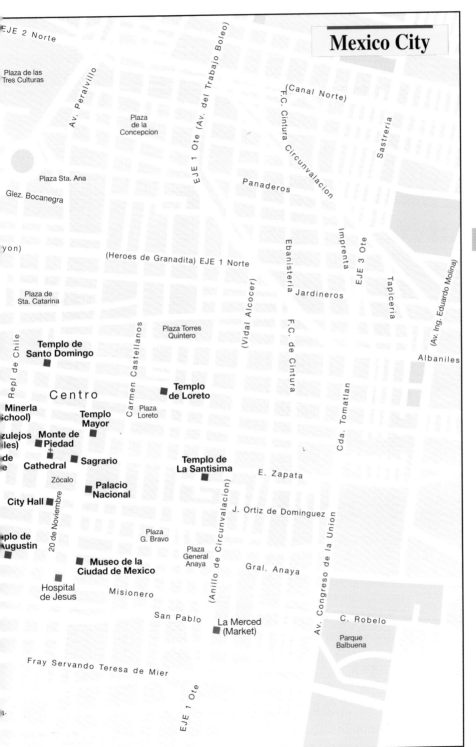

Mexico City

EJE 2 Norte

Plaza de las
Tres Culturas

Av. Peralvillo

Plaza
de la
Concepcion

EJE 1 Ote (Av. del Trabajo Boleo)

(Canal Norte)

F.C. Cintura Circunvalacion

Sastreria

Plaza Sta. Ana

Glez. Bocanegra

Panaderos

yon)

(Heroes de Granadita) EJE 1 Norte

Ebanisteria

Imprenta

EJE 3 Ote

Tapiceria

(Av. Ing. Eduardo Molina)

Plaza de
Sta. Catarina

(Vidal Alcocer)

Jardineros

F.C. de Cintura

Albaniles

Repl de Chile

Carmen Castellanos

Plaza Torres
Quintero

**Templo de
Santo Domingo**

Cda. Tomatlan

Centro

**Templo
de Loreto**

Minerla
chool)

**Templo
Mayor**

Plaza
Loreto

zulejos
les)

**Monte de
Piedad**

**Templo de
La Santisima**

E. Zapata

de
e

Cathedral

Sagrario

Zócalo

**Palacio
Nacional**

City Hall

20 de Noviembre

J. Ortiz de Dominguez

Av. Congreso de la Union

plo de
ugustin

Plaza
G. Bravo

Plaza
General
Anaya

Plaza
(Anillo de Circunvalacion)

Gral. Anaya

**Museo de la
Ciudad de Mexico**

Hospital
de Jesus

Misionero

C. Robelo

San Pablo

**La Merced
(Market)**

Parque
Balbuena

Fray Servando Teresa de Mier

EJE 1 Ote

.

The Palace on the main square.

substance still exists at the heart of to-day's Mexico City. Officials, soldiers, clerics and merchants built themselves palaces, churches, monasteries, courts, warehouses and barracks. Residential streets and marketplaces accommodated the citizens. A grid-iron of streets had spread out from the Zocalo over an area of several square kilometers by the time of independence in 1821.

Thenceforth the city spread outward, particularly with the construction of the great boulevard called the **Paseo de la Reforma**. Built by Emperor

of gravity shifted to this area, the most important for both business and pleasure. With Mexico's rapid industrialisation from the 1940s onwards, almost half of it in the Federal District, the city's expansion gathered pace until it became the world's largest, with over 20 million people in 1994. Most citizens are poorly housed in outer neighborhoods though there are some very wealthy suburbs in the south. Meanwhile the city center retains considerable dignity although under great pressure from people, traffic and pollution.

Though the city was traumatised by the 1985 earthquake which killed an estimated 30,000, toppled hundreds of buildings and caused severe economic losses, it has since bounced back with the better times of the 1990s. Mexico City has many lives and many faces: here's the way to find them.

Around the Zocalo

There's no better place to start than the **Zocalo**, the focal point of Mexican history, of the nation and of the capital. Officially called Constitution Square, it is an immense paved space around which stand the august structures of the Cathedral, the National Palace and the City Hall, built on top of the Great Plaza of the Aztecs. The Zocalo is a vast open stage for great events, festivals, parades and demonstrations, when it is full to bursting, or conversely, when empty, a magnificent vantage point.

Maximilian in imitation of the Champs Elysees in Paris, it connected the old city with Chapultepec and rapidly became the capital's most prestigious street, lined with *belle epoque* mansions during the Porfiriato and today with important corporate offices, embassies and department stores.

In the 20th century the city's center

Palacio de Bellas Artes, the Palace of Fine Arts, is Mexico's most important theater and opera house.

From its center flutters a huge national flag, which is raised every morning and furled at each dusk. To the north rises the massive, venerable, higgledy-piggledy pile that is Mexico City's Cathedral. Constructed over three centuries in various styles and subject to subsidence, its stone mellowed with age and its towers tilting at odd angles, it looks solid and precarious all at once. Reckoned the largest religious complex in the Americas, it was begun in 1573 and last added to in the 19th century, giving it elements of the Gothic, Renaissance, Baroque and Neo-classical.

Known as the **Metropolitan Cathedral**, it contains many side chapels and altars, the two most celebrated being the Altar de Perdon and the Altar de los Reyes, both elaborately carved in the 18th-century Churrigueresque style, as is the stone facade of the Sagrario, built onto the east side. There are several notable frescos and paintings within this ornate place of worship, which is Mexico's principal church.

To the Zocalo's east stands the long uniform facade of the **National Palace**, office of the President of the Republic and seat of the federal government. This was begun early in colonial times as the Viceroy's Palace, destroyed during a 17th century rebellion and quickly rebuilt, and has been enlarged and modified ever since, most recently in the 1920s when a third storey was added.

From its front hangs the Bell of Dolores which Hidalgo rang in 1810 to start the independence movement and which the President rings every eve of Independence Day to a Zocalo jammed with celebrants. Some parts are open to the public, in continuation of a long tradition.

Its original inner courtyard was the ring for Mexico's first bullfight and the same space served as a marketplace until the 18th century. Emperor Maximilian furnished it splendidly and Porfirio Diaz modernised it with telephones and lifts. Glorious finishing touches were added by Diego Rivera's murals in the country-yard stairway and upper cloisters. These can be viewed daily from 9am till 5pm.

Rivera and his assistants rendered a magnificent panorama of Mexican history which portrays with idealistic reverence and vibrant colorfulness the civilisations of ancient Mexico, and dramatically depicts the turbulence of the independence and revolutionary struggles. Working intermittently from 1929 to 1945, they covered almost 111 sq m (1,200 sq ft) of wall space and left one of the 20th-century's greatest legacies.

Beside the National Palace to the east of the Cathedral, ruins of the **Great Temple of the Aztecs** were revealed in 1978. Here can be seen how the ancient Mexicans constructed new pyramids over the top of older ones in layers. Great stone snake heads which lay at the temple entrance have been unearthed; the **Museo Templo Mayor** exhibits 3,000 excavated items.

Two blocks north in **San Ildefonso**

Finely-executed details on the Cathedral's facade.

Street is the National Preparatory School where the muralists began their movement in the early 1920s. Close by is the Ministry of Education where Diego Rivera painted his first major mural commission in 1923.

A little to the west is the **Plaza Santo Domingo**, a gem of a square ringed by buildings redolent of the city's history: a Dominican church, the old Customs House, the former tribunal of the Inquisition and arcades in which professional scribes work at battered typewriters, assisting the illiterate with their business or love affairs.

Walking back to the Zocalo along Calle Monte Piedad brings you to an aged curiosity, the city pawnshop (Monte de Piedad), still going strong, facing the

Diego Rivera's vision of history in the National Palace.

Cathedral. On this spot stood the Palace of Axayactl in which Cortes and his men were housed upon their arrival. Back at the Zocalo, two beautiful hotels are worth a look-in, the Majestic to its west which has a great view over the square from its rooftop restaurant, and the Gran Hotel Ciudad de Mexico round the corner in Calle 16 de Setiembre which has a splendid Art Nouveau atrium.

The streets which lead west from here are the main business ones of the old city where colonial monuments jostle with 19th-century mansions and early 20th-century commercial premises. **Calle Madero** is a case in point with the Palacio de Iturbide, a baroque palace turned into a bank; the Iglesia de San Francisco, a 16th-century church favored

by the viceroys and once a resting place for Cortes's body; the Casa de los Azulejos, a duke's mansion with beautiful blue-tiled facades, now housing a splendid Sanborn's restaurant in its roofed patio. By night these streets glow in the warm light of gas globes.

Around the Alameda

Calle Madero leads out to the **Alameda Park**, the popular formal gardens which bridge the old and new parts of Mexico City. This is a fine place to join the Mexicans at leisure – whether businesspeople taking a break from the surrounding offices or country folk new to town. A rich variety of vendors, busk-

Chapultepec Castle – Maximilian in Mexico

Chapultepec is full of history. The Aztec settlers held their first "new fire" ceremony here in 1266 marking the beginning of a new 52-year cycle. They gave it its name, "Grasshopper Hill", and declared it a holy place. From its springs Moctezuma I built an aqueduct to supply Tenochtitlan with fresh water and in its woods Moctezuma II went hunting. The emperor built himself a palace there with swimming pools and fishponds. Cortes the conquistador fought a battle with the Aztecs there in 1521, took the hill and cut the aqueduct as part of his successful siege of Tenochtitlan.

The Spanish viceroys followed the Aztec emperors' suit and made a palatial retreat out of Chapultepec. Late in their rule a castle was erected atop the hill. After independence the first president began a botanical park, then in 1841 the castle became a military academy and the scene of an event that all Mexican schoolchildren learn about. In the Mexican-American War of 1846-48, the US invaders reached the capital and attacked the last hold-out on the hill. Nine hundred soldiers and 47 cadets defended the castle to the end, and the six cadets who fell wrapped in the national flag are commemorated as the *Ninos Heroes* (Boy Heroes) by a monument below the hill.

In 1864 Maximilian von Hapsburg was placed in power over Mexico by the French as part of their forced reclamation of debt. The Emperor set about rebuilding and remodelling the castle within and without as his imperial residence. It is from this period that the castle as we know it today dates. Now a museum, some of the imperial rooms remain as they were lived in by the Emperor and the Empress Carlota, a Belgian princess. They are furnished in the contemporary style of the French Second Empire. The Empress's bedchamber, for example, has elegant blue and gold armchairs and tables, bed and drapes.

The Empress quickly made a name for herself as a wonderful hostess and Chapultepec Castle became the peak of the capital's social life. She and Maximilian would wear Mexican attire, walk out amongst the people and eat Mexican food as signs of their commitment to their new territory. They spoke Spanish and toured the provinces. They supported the arts and sciences. The Emperor wrote a 600-page book on court etiquette for his new subjects. But all this was hardly enough to successfully rule a strange and turbulent country.

Maximilian's main qualification for his task was his bloodline. Apart from that, the 32-year-old Austrian archduke was ill-suited to further the imperial ambitions of Napoleon III, yet not disliked by the Mexicans due to his quickly developed love for the country. He turned out to be a progressive who wished to advance the cause of the people, much to the dismay of his conservative backers in Mexico.

From 1865, however, his situation became undermined as the United States began to support the ousting of the French occupiers by Juarez, and Napoleon III and the Pope began to back out. The Empress Carlota went on a traumatic trip to Europe to try to persuade the people in power there, of the importance of her husband's mission, but her failure sent her mad, and she was never to return to Mexico. Proud Maximilian stayed to fight Juarez's forces, lost and was put before the firing squad in 1867. The whole bizarre and tragic episode had lasted just three years.

With Porfirio Diaz, the castle became the presidential residence and stayed so until 1949, after which it was transformed into the National Museum of History. The 2,100 acres of wooded parkland and ornamental lakes are now a public park understandably well-liked by the *capitalinos*. And the Presidents still have their residence in the park at the executive mansion of Los Pinos.

ers and beggars ply their trade around here. In Aztec times, this area had been a marketplace.

The Alameda's principal monument

is the **Palacio de Bellas Artes**, the city's opera house. Begun in Belle Epoque style, its construction was halted by the Revolution, so that the interior ended

Cultured greenery in Alameda Park.

Chapultepec Park is one of Mexico City's major attractions.

up in Art Deco style, very finely too. The upper galleries of its lobby serve to display some stunning works of the great muralists: Rivera, Siqueiros, Orozco and Tamayo. The 2,000-seat auditorium has a brillant Tiffany glass curtain depicting the volcanoes Popocatepetl and Ixtaccihuatl which overlook the city from the east.

Nearby stands the **Torre Latino-americana**, until recently the city's tallest building, whose 42nd floor observation deck gives you an unbeatable central panorama. Choose a clear day for this one!

Diego Rivera painted a fascinating late work called *Dream of a Sunday Afternoon in the Alameda,* now displayed in the **Museo Mural Diego Rivera** at the west side of the park after removal from the earthquake-damaged Hotel del Prado which stood on the south side.

The 1985 earthquake ruined many of the Alameda's surrounding hotels and office blocks, radically altering its profile. Also on the west side is the **Pinoteca Virreinal**, a gallery of fine colonial religious art. The park's north side has the fine old Hotel Cortes, a warm reddish-walled structure of Augustinian monastic origin.

Reforma and Chapultepec

To the west of Alameda begins the capital's modern business district with its gleaming steel-and-glass office towers. The main artery is the **Paseo de la Reforma**, a broad tree-lined boulevard which runs all the way down to Chapultepec Park. Central statues commemorate national heroes like Cuauhtemoc, the last Aztec ruler, and figures like Columbus (but not Cortes!)

Along the Reforma lie embassies and airline offices, multi-national corporation offices and department stores. Off to the south is the **Zona Rosa**, long the city's leading shopping and nightlife area containing fashionable boutiques, restaurants and cabarets, though the **Polanco** district on the north side has taken over the lead in recent years.

Chapultepec Park is one of the city's major attractions on several counts; as a refreshing green lung, a place of historic interest and a site of major museums.

Originally the hunting ground of the Aztec rulers, it has hosted palaces of Aztec emperors, Spanish viceroys and Mexican presidents. The extensive 670-hectare park's centerpiece is a large boating lake.

Atop its hill stands **Chapultepec Castle** as left by Emperor Maximilian. Its crenellated roof has a garden with wonderful views of the park and city. Within its walls is the **National Museum of History** displaying some imperial and presidential chambers as used by the former rulers as residences, historic coaches of Maximilian and Juarez, historical paintings, and a powerful panoramic mural on early 20th-century Mexico by Siqueiros, called *Del Porfirismo a la Revolucion.*

National Museum of Anthropology

Located in the park's northern section, the **National Museum of Anthropology** is the world famous showcase of Mexico's ancient history and civilisations, and of extant indigenous cultures. Spacious and modern, rectangular in form and arranged around a large central courtyard, the lower galleries display artifacts and information about distinct historical periods, peoples or regions – the Preclassic era, the Toltecs or the Gulf Coast, for example.

The upper galleries are concerned with ethnographic exhibits on the way various Mexico people live today. This museum is a must-see and worth at least one whole day's visit.

Highlights include the Aztec Calendar [see box], a replica of Moctezuma's quetzal feather headdress and a huge Olmec head sculpture.

Nearby is the **Rufino Tamayo Museum of Contemporary International Art** which displays many of the modern master's works along with his own modern art collection in a gallery which is a work of art itself. Also within Chapultepec Park is the **Museum of Modern Art** with works of Mexico's best artists, especially Rivera and Kahlo. In a tradition started by the Aztecs and continued by Cortes, there is a small zoo here too.

The National Museum of Anthropology showcases Mexico's ancient civilizations.

North to Guadalupe

A ride back northwards all along the Paseo de la Reforma takes you through an interesting cross-section of the city and brings you to two important sights. First is the **Plaza de las Tres Culturas** at Tlatelolco. Formerly the greatest Aztec marketplace, it became the site of a colonial church, and in this century was ringed with modern office and residential blocks.

These three cultures are together presented to the eye in a remarkable historical perspective: the pyramid of Tlatelolco, the church of Santiago, and the Foreign Ministry. This was also the site of the 1968 student massacre in which several hundred young protesters were shot dead by the security forces at an anti-government demonstration during the Mexico City Olympics. After the 1985 earthquake, hundreds of homeless people camped out here.

In the northern suburbs stands the shrine which for the average Mexican is the supreme monument of the nation, the **Basilica of Guadalupe** [see box under *Religion*]. A trip further out to **Tenayuca** takes you to the most intact Aztec temple ever found, its base surrounded with stone serpents.

Southern Suburbs

The city's southern suburbs contain a

Tenochtitlan

When Cortes's men came over a mountain pass and looked down on the Valley Of Mexico in 1519, they saw an amazing sight which they could hardly believe.

"When we saw so many cities built both on the water and on dry land, and their straight level causeways, we could not restrain our admiration. It was like the enchantments in the book of Amadis, because of high towers, temples and other buildings, all of masonry, which rose from the water. Some of our soldiers asked if what we had seen was not a dream," wrote historian Bernal Diaz.

A wonderful city lay before their eyes, set on an island in a great lake, criss-crossed by canals, graced with floating gardens, studded with whitewashed temples – the Aztec capital, Tenochtitlan, at that time the focal point of Ancient Mexico. But when they discovered the bloody human sacrifices that took place atop its tall pyramids, the Spaniards' admiration changed to horror.

Apparently the fruit of a long civilisation by its size, beauty and complexity, Tenochtitlan was in fact an upstart metropolis founded on a small reedy island less than two centuries before. A wandering tribe from the north, the Aztecs had a legend which said they should settle in the place where an eagle landed on a cactus. So the legend goes, they duly saw this phenomenon at Lake Texcoco in the Valley of Mexico in AD 1325, and set to building.

Such was the aggressive ambition of the Aztecs that within a century and a half they had dominated all the peoples of central Mexico, brought them into tribute and built themselves a great imperial capital. The original island had multiplied a thousandfold connected by bridges and causeways, all dead straight, to create a chequerboard Venice. Long causeways joined the island city to the lakeshore, which was

Ruins of the Great Temple.

rimmed with satellite cities.

The citizens of Tenochtitlan supported themselves through trade, manufacturing, farming and fishing. They had a highly specialised method of agriculture: they constructed reed rafts on which they placed earth and sowed seeds, creating floating fields called *chinampas*. These would eventually adhere to the lakebed and become solid land. So the city expanded and fed itself with basics.

The Aztec markets were truly remarkable. The major market of Tlatelolco was said to serve 70,000 customers daily with every saleable item

cluster of interesting sights and museums, many connected with Diego Rivera and his circle. These include the houses of Rivera and Frida Kahlo, and of their friend Leon Trotsky. These three houses

are now museums. They stand in the pleasant suburbs of **Coyoacan** and **San Angel** which were villages within living memory and have a long colonial history. Coyoacan's pedigree goes back to

of Mesoamerica. Bernal Diaz recounted that there were dealers in gold, silver, precious stones, feathers, cloaks, embroidery, slaves, cotton goods and fabrics made of twisted thread, chocolate, sisal cloth and ropes and sandals, skins of jaguars and lions, otters, jackals, and deer, badgers, mountain cats, kidney beans, sage, turkeys, rabbits, and so on, with an amazing range of fruit and vegetables. All was well ordered and located by category of merchandise; while inspectors toured the market and magistrates sat in judgement of disputes in a central hall.

The city was well run, with public services and sanitation that had no equal in Europe. The streets were swept and sprinkled by night and guarded by watchmen, and reed huts were placed at regular intervals as toilets. Fresh water supplies were assured by aqueduct from the mainland. A dyke separated the main body of the brackish lake from the waters around the city, which were fed by sweet water springs that assisted agriculture.

The focal point of the city was the Great Temple, a very high pyramid topped by two shrines dedicated to the gods Tlaloc and Huitzilopochtli, which dominated a complex of pyramids within a walled precinct. Three causeways linked the city to the mainland from the north, west and south and led to broad avenues which met here. Palaces of the nobles surrounded the precinct and served as seats of government. Farther out the citizens lived in adobe houses and travelled about largely in canoes along the canals.

Within two years of Cortes's arrival, all this was gone. The Spaniards razed and burned the city to the ground, and began to build their own city on top. Yet, so great had it been, not till the late 19th century did Mexico City reach the size and population of old Tenochtitlan.

Cortes and his cohorts who first settled here after the conquest and whose office is extant, the Casa de Cortes, in the leafy Plaza de Hidalgo. In San Angel stands the Carmelite Convent and Church,

dating from 1617, with charming cloisters, fountains and gardens, and a museum of religious art and oddities.

The painter Frida Kahlo was born, grew up, lived most of her married life, and died in the Kahlo family residence in Coyoacan known as the **Blue House**. This became a museum after her death and is a place of great beauty full of indigenous art as well as her own and Diego Rivera's paintings and the religious folk paintings called *retablos* on which her own style was based. The rooms still have the warmth of a lived-in house and exude a feeling of love, both personal and for Mexico's culture.

Rivera's studio in nearby San Angel is now the **Museo Estudio Diego Rivera**; he worked here from 1928 onwards and died here in 1957. Shown here are some of his personal effects and mementos and changing exhibitions on his life and work.

Anahuacalli is another Rivera museum in nearby San Pablo Tepetlapan which he built himself in the shape of a Mayan tomb to display his extraordinary collection of pre-Columbian art.

Trotsky fled Stalin's wrath to exile in Mexico in 1937. He was welcomed to the houses of Communist Party members Rivera and Kahlo, and had a brief affair with the latter. He then moved to another house in the area which rapidly became a fortress with steel doors, crenellated roofs and a watchtower. Though Trotsky survived a machine gun attack led by the muralist Siqueiros, then a Stalinist, he succumbed in 1940

The Smog Bowl

Mexico City has the misfortune of containing a goodly proportion of the country's industry and motor vehicles and of also lying in a high altitude basin encircled by mountains. Misfortune because this acts as a sun-heated pan in which huge quantities of noxious emissions brew up what is reckoned to be the world's worst urban air.

Consequently, respiratory and related diseases are rampant amongst the population. This is naturally not something Mexicans are proud of or happy about – though it has afforded plenty of black jokes like "See Mexico City and die!" – and in recent years serious measures have begun to be taken to tackle the problem.

The capital contains some 20 million people, 16,000 factories producing half the country's non-oil manufacturing output, 19,000 other businesses and 3.5 million vehicles – all crammed into a valley 2,255 m (7,400 ft) above sea level and hemmed in by mountains.

12,000 tons of pollutants are spewed into the air daily. Slabs of cold air above the city trap warmer polluted air at street level for hours, especially in winter. Vehicles are the worst cul-prits, issuing 80 percent of pollutants. For lack of oxygen, engines burn fuel inefficiently, releasing unburnt hydrocarbons which the sun turns into poisonous ozone. Some days the environment is so bad that factories are ordered to stop functioning and citizens are advised not to exercise.

The government is battling the problem with a multi-billion dollar programme which includes fuel quality improvement, incentives to switch to natural gas and diesel fuel, and the relocation of industry.

Some severely pollutive industries have been shut down and even the city's mammoth oil refinery was closed as the single worst polluter. Car owners have to leave their beloved buggies at home one day a week. "Green Patrols" hunt smoke-belching vehicles.

All this has diminished the problem, but environmentalists urge more action. For those who are still gasping, there are oxygen booths at downtown points where they can get some good lungfuls for a few pesos. But visitors won't necessarily suffer; it's quite possible to make a lengthy visit and not experience the problem, even in winter.

to the attack of a trusted aide with an ice-pick. The house remains as it was on that day, with Trotsky's trademark round glasses lying smashed on his desk, with books open for study. His ashes are kept in the garden.

The **University City** is a showcase of Mexican modern architecture and of monumental muralism. Most notable is the massive library whose four sides are completely covered with a mosaic mural by Juan O' Gorman depicting the history of Mexico culture and science. The administration building has an immerse mural by Siqueiros showing students benefitting the nation with their learning. The origins of the **Universidad Nacional Autonoma de Mexico** go back to 1551 and it currently has a student enrollment of 300,000, making it both the oldest and biggest University in the Americas.

On the southern outskirts, **Xochimilo** is a favorite recreation spot of *capitalinos* and features in many city tours. It's a relic of Aztec days, canals that run between garden plots similar to the old *chinampas* of Tenochtitlan.

Locals hire colorful flat-bottomed boats with canopies on top and tables between facing benches and go on waterborne picnics, especially on Sundays. Floating mariachi bands ply for trade, offering musical accompaniment. Famous for its flowers too, Xochimilco means "in the flower fields".

Markets

The Aztecs had a market at **Tlatelolco** that was quite possibly the world's largest in the early 16th century. You can see how it might have looked in Diego Rivera's marvellous mural in the National Palace. Modern Mexicans are no slouches at marketing either and today's Mexico City has some pretty big markets too.

Tlatelolco's spiritual successor was **La Merced**, an immense fresh produce and general goods market which was recently downsized when many functions were moved to the outskirts. Located about one kilometer southeast of the Zocalo, the market is still very active with an especially interesting offshoot called **Mercado de Sonora** peddling medicinal herbs, and also live animals and festive toys and crafts.

Another monster market is **La Lagunilla**. It is housed in huge buildings a few blocks north of the colonial center, and sells clothing, food and household goods. The wide range of *huaraches* (sandals) are well worth a look and the Sunday flea market in the streets around even more so. Here you'll find antiques, old books and appliances and all sorts of bric-a-brac.

For curios and crafts, the outdoor **Ciudadela Curio Market** is located a few blocks south of Alameda Park. Here you can find fine weaving, with Oaxacan women actually doing some on the spot with backstrap looms, bark paintings from Guerrero, guitars from Michoacan, and so on. Kitsch-lovers are well catered for too, plastic ducks dressed *mariachi* outfits to hang in the car, are favorite buys.

Along Avenida Juarez on the south side of Alameda Park are superior arts and crafts emporiums like FONART and the Museo Nacional de Artes e Industrias Populares.

In the Zona Rosa, **Curiosidades Mexicanas** is an indoor market that sells food, crafts, curios and souvenirs, such as woven *huipiles* and *serapes*, Toluca sweaters, charro sombreros and all sorts of knick-knacks. **Buenavista Crafts Market**, next to the main railway terminus, is a vast one-stop store crammed with "90,000 items" according to its sales pitch.

Even if you are limiting your stay to Mexico City alone, you can still discover the wonders of the country on sidetrips out of the capital. Indeed, many of the places that can be easily visited within a day from Mexico City form the historical heart of the country. There is Teotihuacan, for instance, Mexico's biggest ancient city and Cholula, site of the largest ancient pyramid in the Americas. The attractions are also varied. They include the popular resort of Cuernavaca, the lush national park of the Desert of the Lions, colonial Puebla and its fabulous churches and the colorful Indian market at Toluca.

Climbing up the Pyramid of Tepozteco.

Environs of Mexico

Aztec Myth

"When all was night, When there was no day, When there was no light. They gathered, The gods convened There in Teotihuacan".
Imagine such a sacred meeting

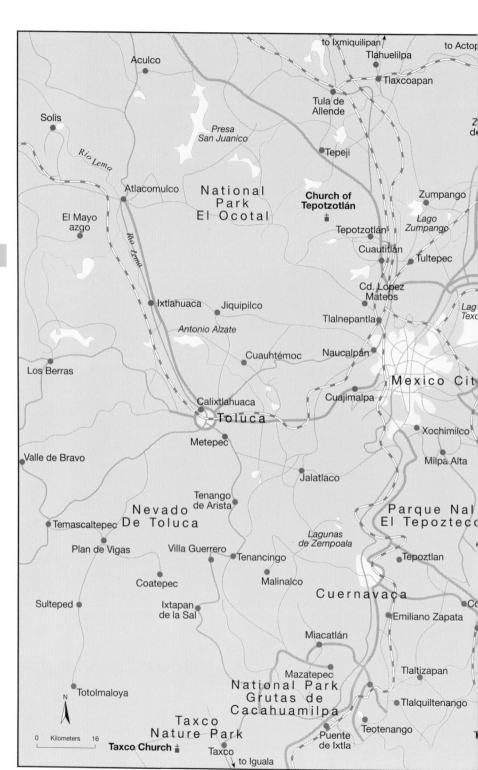

to Ixmiquilipan

to Actop

Tlahuelilpa

Aculco

Tlaxcoapan

Tula de
Allende

Z
d

Solis

Presa
San Juanico

Tepeji

Río Lema

Atlacomulco

National
Park
El Ocotal

Church of
Tepotzotlán
⛪

Zumpango

Lago
Zumpango

El Mayo
azgo

Tepotzotlán

Cuautitlán

Río Lema

Tultepec

Ixtlahuaca

Jiquipilco

Cd. López
Mateos

Antonio Alzate

Tlalnepantla

Lag
Texc

Cuauhtémoc

Naucalpán

Los Berras

Mexico Cit

Calixtlahuaca

Cuajimalpa

Toluca

Xochimilco

Metepec

Valle de Bravo

Milpa Alta

Jalatlaco

Tenango
de Arista

Nevado
De Toluca

Parque Nal
El Tepozteco

Temascaltepec

Lagunas
de Zempoala

Plan de Vigas

Villa Guerrero

Tenancingo

Tepoztlan

Coatepec

Malinalco

Cuernavaca

Sulteped

Ixtapan
de la Sal

Co

Emiliano Zapata

Miacatlán

Mazatepec

Tlaltizapan

Totolmaloya

National Park
Grutas de
Cacahuamilpa

Tlalquiltenango

N

Taxco
Nature Park

Teotenango

0   Kilometers   16

Taxco Church ⛪

Taxco

Puente
de Ixtla

to Iguala

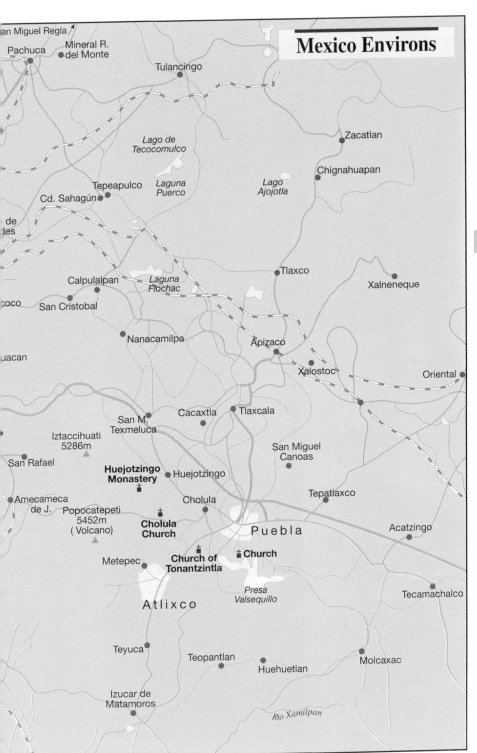

Mexico Environs

an Miguel Regla

Pachuca

Mineral R.
del Monte

Tulancingo

Zacatlan

Lago de
Tecocomulco

Chignahuapan

Tepeapulco

Laguna
Puerco

Lago
Ajojotla

Cd. Sahagún

de
les

Tlaxco

Calpulalpan

Laguna
Flochac

Xalneneque

:oco

San Cristobal

Nanacamilpa

Apizaco

uacan

Xalostoc

Oriental

Cacaxtla

Tlaxcala

San M.
Texmeluca

Iztaccihuati
5286m

San Miguel
Canoas

San Rafael

Huejotzingo
Monastery

Huejotzingo

Amecameca
de J.

Popocatepeti
5452m
(Volcano)

Cholula

Tepatlaxco

Cholula
Church

Puebla

Acatzingo

Metepec

Church of
Tonantzintla

Church

Presa
Valsequillo

Tecamachalco

Atlixco

Teyuca

Teopantlan

Huehuetlan

Molcaxac

Izucar de
Matamoros

Rio Xamilpan

Pyramid of the Sun at Teotihuacan.

taking place as you gaze upon the splendidly laid-out complex of pyramids, temples and courts that make up **Teotihuacan**, a major archeological site 45 km (28 miles) east of Mexico City.

The name, Teotihuacan, meaning "Place where the gods were made" was given by the Aztecs who held the site in considerable awe and respect. And well they might, for Teotihuacan was, at the height of its glory in AD 600, the sixth-largest city in the world. It belonged to a great ancient civilization at the time of the Early Classic sub-period from AD 300 to AD 600 but historians have been unable to determine exactly who the people were and how they disappeared in AD 700 when their power declined.

Historians have however, been able to identify some of the remarkably well-preserved structures in the 18-sq-km (7-sq-mile) city complex that the Teotihuacan culture built: more than 75 temples, over 2,000 apartment complexes and 600 workshops for the making of ceramics and other crafts and several hundred wall murals on its palaces and temples.

Teotihuacan was an important religious, political and trading center in Mesomerica. As the first true metropolis in central Mexico, Teotihuacan housed 250,000 people at the peak of its power. It was believed to have started as a string of villages in around the 2nd century BC growing into a city that was built upon modern lines around the time of Christ and existing for nearly

View of Popocatepetl at sunrise.

1,000 years.

When the Aztecs established Tenochtitlan, upon which Mexico City was later founded, Teotihuacan was in ruins. However, Teotihuacan was used as a ceremonial center by the Aztecs who sensed its significance. Indeed, they named it as the place of gods for they believed that the lords who were buried there had become gods.

Avenue of the Dead

Teotihuacan was simply laid out according to the four cardinal points. The main street – the 4-km (2.5 miles) Calle de los Muertos or **Avenue of the Dead** – extends in a north-south direction and cuts through the city. On the east side of the avenue and standing in the middle of the city was the magnificent **Pyramid of the Sun** looking towards the point on the horizon where the sun sets at the summer solstice. On the north end was placed the **Pyramid of the Moon** while the Cuidadela housing the important **Temple and Palace of Quetzalcoatl** was positioned on the southern end but on the east side, almost parallel to the Pyramid of the Sun.

The Avenue of the Dead was the name given by the Aztecs who thought that the structures flanking both sides of the thoroughfare were tombs, but they are now believed to be the ruins of palaces in which the priests lived.

The architectural harmony

Pyramids of Sun and Moon

Of all, the Pyramid of the Sun the ruins of Teotihuacan. It ranks as the third largest pyramid in the world, after the pyramid in Cholula and Cheops in Egypt.

The Pyramid of the Sun rises in five levels to over 65 m (215 ft) from a square base that measures 226 m (743 ft) on all sides, about the same size as that of the Pyramid of Cheops which however rises up to 144 m (475 ft). But while Cheops, like other Egyptian pyramids was built as a tomb for pharaohs, the Mexican pyramids constructed 3000 years later, served more as ceremonial centers. They had truncated tops crowned by temples; only a few pyramids in Mexico contained tombs. The Pyramid of the Sun was no exception. When it was built in 100 AD it had a temple on top and the Aztecs reckoned it was dedicated to the sun-god Quetzalcoatl. An underground chamber filled with religious artifacts excavated in 1971 seem to corroborate the Aztec belief that rituals were conducted here.

It boggles the mind to think that three and a half million tons of material were used for the pyramid which took 15,000 people to build. Made with adobe brick covered with volcanic stone and plaster, the pyramid was painted red which must have made it a glowing sight at sunset. A stairway on the west face brings you to the terraces and the top. It's best though to explore the pyramid in the morning as climbing up the steep stairs can be exhausting in the debilitating afternoon heat.

From the top, when you survey the grand architecture of Teotihuacan around you and examine the elaborate carvings on the stones, your mind wonders about what it must have been like when the priests conducted their rituals here, offering the freshly ripped-out hearts of winners – or was it losers? – of every ball game, as a sacrifice to the sun to feed it, so that it could retain its fiery energy.

Pyramid of the Moon

The Pyramid of the Moon is smaller to that of the Sun. It was built later, around AD 300 on a rectangular base measuring 150 m (495 ft) long and 120 m (396 ft) wide, rising in four stages to the top at 35 m (116 ft). Stairs on its south flank go up to the top. It's an easier climb and with just as commanding a view.

The Plaza of the Moon is peppered with the ruins of a dozen temple platforms where religious ceremonies were believed to have been conducted. Both the symmetrically arranged Plaza and the Pyramid of the Moon combine to make up one of the best-proportioned complexes in the archeological zone.

achieved by the Teotihuacanos in the building of the city-complex is striking and is still obvious in the structures that remain. Each facade is 40 m (130 feet) wide and is built in the *talud-tablero* style as manifested in the pyramids which have sloping (*talud*) and upright (*tablero*) features. The most important ruins of Teotihuacan are the ones that are still intact: Pyramids of the Sun and Moon, La Ciudadela, Palace of the Jaguars, Temple of the Feathered Shells and the Palace of the Quetzalpapaloti.

La Ciudadela

La Ciudadela is a vast walled square measuring 154 sq m (1,656 sq ft) with platforms topped by pyramids. Its name means citadel but La Ciudadela was not a fortress in the strict sense of the word. It seems to have been a nerve center for the entire city, for here was where the supreme ruler lived and on either side of the citadel's main pyramid – the Temple of Quetzalcoatl – are blocks of ruins

Cathedral in Cuernavaca harking back to the 16th century.

Mariachi band in Cuernavaca.

showing rooms and residential patios where the administrators were probably housed. The Temple of Quetzalcoatl dedicated to the plumed serpent-god has carved stone walls showing distinct patterns of huge serpent heads.

Palace of the Quetzalpapaloti

Even more outstanding is the **Palace of the Quetzalpapaloti**, which belonged to members of Teotihuacan's elite, believed to be priests who were the custodians of the nearby Pyramid of the Moon. Carved square pillars surround a patio, signifying a residence at that time. It also served as a place of religious ritual.

Here are found some of Teotihuacan's best preserved murals portrayed on bas-reliefs showing quetzales (the rare tropical bird of central America) and the papaloti (butterfly).

Behind the Palace of Quetzalpapaloti is the **Palace of the Jaguars** which shows paintings of jaguars in headdresses and other symbols pertaining to water and fertility. Below the Palace of Quetzalpapaloti sits the **Temple of the Feathered Shells**, built between AD 200 and AD 300. Its altar is elaborately designed with shells, flowers and birds.

On the fringes of the archeological site are the ruins of apartment complexes where more murals have been found. At Tepantitla, priests in ritual

Shady spot to while the time away.

costumes are shown spilling water and seeds from their hands while at Tetitla, the murals depict jaguars, quetzales and the rain god Tlaloc.

Moreloa and Cuernavaca

Morelos, one of Mexico's smallest states, was named after Jose Maria Morelos y Pavon, a priest and member of Miguel Hidalgo's War of Independence rebels. When Hidalgo was executed, Morelos took over as leader of the movement.

Cuernavaca, capital of Morelos, is the country's oldest resort. Only 82 km (51 miles) from Mexico City, it is a popular tourist destination because of its history and proximity to the Distrito

Federal. Dubbed the "city of eternal spring", Cuernavaca lies 1,538 m (5,045 ft) above sea level and was a choice vacation spot for the elite of Mexico City since the days of the Hapsburg Emperor Maximilian who established a summer retreat here in 1865. Alas, the city is not as cool as before and a burgeoning population and a growing industrial satellite complex to the south may have something to do with it.

Still, it makes a great weekend escape thanks to its cleaner air and verdant surroundings. So much more pleasant is Cuernavaca that many *capitalanos* from Mexico City have moved here to live, commuting daily to the federal capital to work.

Long before the Spanish Conquest,

The Legend of Popocatepetl

Popocatepetl, the
'mountain that smokes.'

Once upon a time there lived a powerful Aztec king who had an only daughter, the beautiful Iztaccihuatl. As the Aztec king was ageing, his enemies conspired to get rid of him and take over his kingdom. The king called up young, brave warriors from all over his land and declared to them: "I offer my daughter in marriage, and also my kingdom, to him who conquers my enemies."

Among the warriors was Popocatepetl, the bravest of the lot, who was already in love with Iztaccihuatl and she with him. He promised her that he would return in victory and marry her. Popocatepetl set off. Time passed and there was no news. One day, the king passed the temple of the sun and overheard his daughter crying out to Quetzalcoatl, the Aztec god: "Oh god Quetzalcoatl, father of our town! Popocatepetl has not returned. Protect him and help him defeat the enemies of my father. Oh great Quetzal-coatl, if you help Popocatepetl, I promise to go to the grand temple and light a sacred fire in your honor. I also promise that if he does not return, I shall climb up the roof of the temple and jump off!"

Mortified upon hearing this, the king regretted having sent Popocatepetl off to war and to his certain death. He immediately sent for two soldiers with instructions to find Popocatepetl and get him to return immediately. The king said to let Popocatepetl know that he could have his daughter's hand in marriage even if he had not fulfilled the condition of defeating his enemies.

The two soldiers left on their quest. After

Cuernavaca was an important center for the Aztecs who built pyramids here and in nearby Tepoztlan. Its original inhabitants, the Tlahuica Indians, named it Cuauhnahuac which aptly described its exact location: "Place on the outskirts of the forest".

Cuernavaca is small and compact, characterized by many colonial buildings and several wealthy *colonias* (suburbs) dotted with large houses with swimming pools. Until the mid-1980s, the town had only 380,000 people. Today the number has grown to nearly a million, swelled by an influx of Mexican City residents who moved here after the devastating earthquake of 1985.

The heart of Cuernavaca is the tree-shaded **Plaza de la Constitucion** where Indians from nearby villages gather daily to sell eye-catching handicrafts, spilling over to the smaller but just as

several days, they met the rest of Popocatepetl's army who had returned from being defeated in a battle. The king's emissaries asked after Popocatepetl and one of the men replied: "He is dead! He died after having killed many enemies. Yacatzin was with him and saw him die." The king's emissaries brought Yacatzin to see the king who asked him if Popocatepetl said any last words. "Yes," said Yacatzin, "he died while whispering the name of Iztaccihuatl."

The king made Yacatzin promise not to tell the princess of Popocatepetl's death. He would break the news to his daughter himself, he said, and try to console her. Alas, the king could not find the right words to comfort his grieving daughter. One day, covering her face with a white veil the way brides do, the princess slipped away unnoticed, never to be seen again. Like a floating white cloud, she climbed to the summit of a mountain to lie down and dream of marrying Popocatepetl.

In the meantime, Popocatepetl, whom Yacatzin had mistakenly thought was dead, returned. The warrior had only been hurt and despite having to bear the shame of defeat presented himself to the king with only the thought of Iztaccihuatl in mind. He was told that the princess had disappeared, It was Popocatepetl's turn to grieve. He set off in search of her, scouring towns and valleys. One day, a villager told him that he had seen a woman in white going up a mountain. The villager said that he had tried to go up the

mountain himself, but each time he did so, there was a storm and he had to retreat.

Popocatepetl located the mountain and began his ascent. There was no storm. He finally reached the summit and there lying on the mountain, was Iztaccihuatl, asleep forever. The tormented Popocatepetl knelt down next to his beloved Iztaccihuatl, swearing to keep a perpetual vigil by her side. Soon, it started to snow and before long, the bodies of Iztaccihuatl and Popocatepetl, lying close together, were covered in white.

After that, the mountain where Popocatepetl had lain, was frequently seen spouting smoke and fire as proof that his love for Iztaccihuatl would never be extinguished. Both lovers had fulfilled their promise to be with each other in eternity.

The names of Popocatepetl and Iztaccihuatl are Nahuatl in origin. Nahuatl is the language of the Aztecs and Popocatepetl means "mountain that smokes" while Iztaccihuatl means "woman in white". For some time, the Aztecs would celebrate two days of festival every August in memory of the two lovers who were regarded as symbols of fertility. The Aztecs would ascend the mountains bearing gifts and flowers. Today, the festival is no longer held but people still swear that they can see the human forms of the volcanoes. And, even in the pastry shops you can find on sale a sweet roll made in the shape of a volcano and covered in sugar icing in honor of the two sweethearts.

147

shady Jardin Juarez next door, both of which make up the zocalo. Lined up in the zocalo waiting to shine shoes are the *limpiabotas* while gaily uniformed *mariachi* bands stand by, ever ready to strike up a tune for a fee.

Cuernavaca is lively and cosmopolitan thanks to the presence of a large foreign student population enrolled in the city's 17 language schools. And each day on sidetrips from Mexico City,

Cuernavaca receives a steady stream of tourists who come specifically to glimpse the city's imperial past.

Of this, there are a few vestiges left. The most important is the **Palacio de Cortes** on Calle Salazar, one block southeast of the zocalo. Now the Museo de Cuauhnahuac, it contains exhibits documenting the history of Mexico from the pre-Hispanic era to modern times. The imposing stone palace with parapets

A vestige of the imperial past is glimpsed at the Palacio de Cortes.

and a watch tower, resembles a fortress, a look tempered only by its arched front balconies. Its construction took ten years, from 1522 to 1532 and Cortes had it built on top of an old pyramid of Cuauhnahuac which he had destroyed. Parts of the pyramid base are still visible on the museum floor, particularly at the entrance.

The double-storey palace was Cortes's retirement home. Adorning a wall on its second floor is a mural painted by Diego Rivera, said to be among his most outstanding works. The 1920s mural depicts the conquest of Mexico and was a gift to the people of Cuernavaca by the then US ambassador to Mexico, Dwight Morrow.

Walk three blocks west of the mu-

seum and you will come to the 16th-century **Catedral de la Asuncion** at the junction of Hidalgo and Avenida Morelos. Looking like a fortress because of its soaring high walls and built also by Cortes, the Cathedral is said to be one of Mexico's oldest. It was completed in 1552 and contains a collection of paintings of some note. Believed to be the work of a Japanese convert who had settled in Cuernavaca in the 17th century, the paintings revealed the persecution of early Christian missionaries in Sokori, Japan. If you are visiting Cuernavaca on a Sunday, do not miss the *mariachi* mass held in the Cathedral at 11 am when bands play hymns adapted to *mariachi* music.

From the Cathedral, stroll across

The 16th-century Capilla de Nuestra Senora de la Asuncion in Tepotzlan.

Avenida Morelos to visit **Jardin Borda** (Borda Gardens), the official residence of Emperor Maximilian (open Tuesday-Sunday 10 am-6 pm, admission: N$2). The gardens boast fountains and pools surrounding the 18th-century mansion built by silver baron Jose de la Borda who had made his fortune from mining in Taxco. In 1866, Maximilian and his wife took over Jardin Borda.

Walk half a block south of Jardin Borda to the **Ayuntamiento** or Palacio Municipal, a cluster of government offices housing some of Cuernavaca's most important paintings. The murals, painted on the walls of the rectangular building overlooking a courtyard, detail phases of Mexican life and history. Among them are scenes that document the life of Maximilian in Cuernavaca. The most talked about painting perhaps is a canvas that shows the emperor riding a horse in the grounds of his vacation retreat, Casa del Olvido, while an Indian woman, the famous La India Bonita, his paramour, smiles from behind a tree. The Palacio Municipal is open Monday-Friday 8 am-6 pm, with free admission.

La Casa del Olvido (House of Forgetfulness) in outlying Cuernavaca was so named because the emperor was said to have forgotten to build quarters for his wife, Carlota, although he did not forget to include a small house that La India Bonita was said to have occupied.

Officially named La Casa de Olindo, the complex has been turned into the

Tiled courtyard of a Santa Monica convent in Puebla.

Museo de la Herbolaria y Jardin Botanico. The herbalarium cum botanic garden includes many of the trees and herbal plants that Maximilian grew for use as medicine. Take a stroll in the garden to discover the kinds of traditional plants the Indians used to treat digestive problems, colds, coughs and other ailments. Such alternative medicine is still being practiced by Indians today and many of the leaves and roots of the same plants are sold in Cuernavaca's market along with healing images.

Cuernavaca is a good place to shop for handicrafts as many Indians from surrounding villages come to the zocalo and to the Mercado de Artesanias just outside the Palacio de Cortes, to spread out their wares on the ground. Colorfully painted wooden masks, woven rugs, bags, *serapes* and leather goods, offer a wide choice. There are also stalls in the zocalo selling silver jewelry from Taxco.

If you wish to brush up on your Spanish before heading elsewhere, Cuernavaca would be a good place to do so. Its language schools are a favorite of non-Spanish speaking diplomats about to begin a posting in Latin-America. The best part about studying in Cuernavaca is that you can study on a weekly basis, resume travelling and return to pick up where you had left off. West of Cuernavaca is the thermal resort of **Cuautla** (an hour's drive on Highway 160), popular for its *Los Balnearios* (mineral baths).

About 6 km (4 miles) south of Cuautla is the town of **Auenecuilco**, birthplace of Emiliano Zapata, the legendary revolutionary general whose peasant amry sought land reform under the slogan *Tierra y Libertad* (Land and Freedom).

Tepoztlan

Remnants of Aztec civilization in Morelos are alive and well at the picturesque village of **Tepoztlan**, only 24 km (15 miles) from Cuernavaca. It was here that the Aztecs built the pyramid of Tepozteco high up on a 2,113 m (6,930 ft) mountain that overlooks the scenic valley of Tepoztlan which is itself over 1,524 m (5,000 ft) high.

Tepoztlan is special. It has a certain magic and mystical allure, attributed to the belief that the serpent-god Quetzalcoatl was born here over 1,200 years ago. It was in any case, the ceremonial site for the worship of Tepoztecatl, the god of *pulque* (a liquor made from the maguey plant and drunk by the Nahua Indians) who was also their god of fertility and harvest. Tepoztecatl is still wildly remembered every year on 8 September when pilgrims come to drink *pulque* and to watch the folkloric Chinelo dancers perform.

At other times, most people flock to Tepoztlan to visit the remarkably well-preserved pyramid of Tepozteco. Perched on the edge of craggy cliffs rising 3 km (2 miles) above Tepoztlan and clearly visible from the village center, the pyramid seems to beckon you up.

Take the challenge and you will be rewarded with a wonderful vista of Tepoztlan and the surrounding valley. The climb takes one to two hours. You don't have to be fighting fit but it's a fairly exhausting trek up steep boulder-strewn ridges.

The 10 m (33-ft) high Tepozteco pyramid is rectangular with steep steps that reach up to a platform at the top. Because of its structure, it is believed to have been an Aztec temple for sacrifices and the elevated location was just perfect for such sacred ceremonies.

Yet, according to another school of thought, the pyramid could also have been an observation post built by the Tlahuica Indians to guard over the valley. If it was, they certainly chose the right spot as it has commanding views of the region. Whatever its purpose, one thing was clear: the pyramid managed to remain intact over the centuries only because it was so difficult to reach.

Sunday is the best time to visit Tepoztlan as it is market day and Indians from surrounding villages pour into town to sell their handicrafts in the small village square and on the main road. Typical of the region are hand crafted clay objects in the form of animals and houses.

The Indians also converge to worship at the 16th-century **Capilla de Nuestra Senora de la Asuncion** right on the town square. The chapel is noted for its archeological museum located at the rear. The museum houses pottery and clay figures from the various pre-Hispanic civilizations in Mexico including objects from Teotihuacan. Artifacts from around Tepoztlan trace the history of the region from the time of the Olmecs to the arrival of the Spanish. The museum is open Tuesday-Friday, 10 am-2 pm and 4 pm-6 pm, Saturday and Sunday 10 am-6 pm, admission: N$3. Adjacent to the chapel is a former Dominican Convent (the ex-Convento Dominico de la Navidad) built in 1559 with well preserved religious frescoes decorating its corridors (open Wednesday-Sunday 9.30 am-5 pm, free admission).

Xochicalco

More significant pyramids may be found at the sprawling archeological site of **Xochicalco**, an hour's drive from Cuernavaca. Its Nahuatl name means Place of Flowers and although Xochicalco now sits in rather desolate surroundings, you can somehow picture the grandeur of this ceremonial center in its heyday from AD 650 to AD 900 as you pick your way amid the partially restored ruins.

Xochicalco was a focal point for the Toltecs who also built it as a fortress and

trading center. Over the centuries it was invaded by succeeding waves of pre-Columbian cultures – the Olmec, Mayan, Zapotec, Mixtec and Aztec – each of which left traces of their occupation on the monuments. One of the most important structures in Xochicalco, the still-intact **Pyramid of the Plumed Serpent**, for instance, shows carved reliefs of the Toltec serpent-god Quetzalcoatl in snake and bird forms but with a priest wearing a Mayan headdress amidst the coils.

Xochicalco's importance waxed as that of Teotihuacan's waned. The latter declined around AD 700 just when Xochicalco was beginning to flourish and at the time of the Spanish arrival, Xochicalco served as a tributary to the Aztec empire of Tenochtitlan. It was at Xochicalco that the Zapotec, Maya and Gulf Coast tribes met to correlate their calendar systems.

Indeed, Xochicalco's underground observatory has been recognized as an astronomical and engineering feat. The Aztecs kept track of the sun through a tiny aperture letting in light through the roof of a pyramid, using their calculations to verify their calendar. For a tip, the warden of the pyramids will unlock the gates that lead through a series of tunnels into the observatory to view the shaft of light.

Apart from the Pyramid of the Plumed Serpent and the observatory, the other structure of significance in Xochicalco is the **ballcourt**. Situated next to the Pyramid of the Plumed Serpent and with two rings instead of the usual single ring, conjecture has it that teams vied with each other for the honor of being sacrificed to the Toltec sun-god atop the pyramid where right after the game the winners' hearts would be ripped out to feed the sun's energy.

Puebla

Welcome to **Puebla** and imagine yourself transported to Spain, for Puebla is, without a doubt, one of Mexico's most Hispanic cities. Indeed, a walk down Avenida Reforma, the principal thoroughfare, somehow evokes the feeling of strolling down a street in Barcelona or Madrid.

Puebla owes its intensely Spanish character to several families from Toledo who settled here in 1531 and proceeded to model it after their old hometown including introducing the making of the distinctive Talavera pottery which has become one of Puebla's most important industries.

Puebla, the capital of Puebla state set at an altitude of 2,230 m (7,315 ft), was, until it was overtaken by Guadalajara in the 19th century, Mexico's second largest city. Today, with a population of over one million, it ranks as one of the country's most interesting cultural and architectural centers.

Taking only two hours to travel by road from Mexico City, Puebla is also a popular destination for day trippers from the capital city.

Founded in 1531 under the auspices of Bishop Julian Garces of Tlaxcala, Puebla was named Cuidad de los Angeles (City of Angels) to rival neighboring Cholula as a religious center, and later renamed Puebla de los Angeles. Because of its profusion of churches, one for every day of the year, Puebla could well be dubbed the "city of churches". Most of them are highly ornamented with carved facades and decorated with beautiful hand painted ceramic tiles.

The choice of churches and museums to see in Puebla is simply dizzying. Each has its own striking character on the outside and possesses its own special art treasures within. You could spend days exploring the various churches but there are two churches that are a must in your itinerary.

The Church of Santo Domingo on Avenida Cinco de Mayo, three blocks north of the zocalo, the heart of Puebla, is a true masterpiece of Mexican Baroque architecture. Its simple exterior belies what awaits the visitor within, especially its exulted Capilla del Rosario (Rosary Chapel). What a dazzling piece of work! Its walls, ceilings and dome are richly decorated in gilded carvings filled with cherubic angels and saints. No inch is left uncovered except the lower part of the walls which are themselves embellished with pretty tiles.

The **Cathedral**, facing the zocalo, is the other church in Puebla that must be seen. From the outside, it looks forbidding with its almost black, stark exterior. But inside, the church is elaborately decorated with multiple gilded domes and a central altar. A choir with gigantic organ pipes from France and Germany dominates and if you are inside the church at the right time you might hear divine music emanating from the pipes.

On the outskirts of Puebla, just over a mile northeast of the zocalo is the historic hill of **Guadalupe**. From the hill's two forts (Loreto and Guadalupe), the Mexicans successfully defeated French invading troops on 5 May, 1862. The battle of Cinco de Mayo is re-enacted every year in celebration of the occasion. You can learn more about the invasion at the Museo de la Intervencion housed in the Fuerte de Loreto.

If one of your main reasons for coming to Puebla is to shop for ceramics, you will not be disappointed. Almost every street in the city center is lined with shops offering a selection of the attractive hand-painted Talavera pottery for which Puebla is justly famous. Buy them as decorative plates, vases, tiles or practical tableware for the home. They are not cheap but are unquestionably beautiful and well worth the price and effort to lug home (or ship) as mementos. Onyx, attractively carved into animal shapes, fruits and ashtrays,

is the other Puebla craft you can bring home.

A visit to Puebla is not complete without trying the famous *mole poblano* (chocolate sauce) that goes with Mexico's traditional *pollo con mole* dish (see " *Cuisine* Chapter). Although Oaxaca lays claim to producing the best *mole* sauce, it was said to have been invented in Puebla by a nun in the kitchen of the Santa Rosa Convent, now the Museo Artesanias del Estado de Puebla, a 15-minute walk north of the zocalo. A tour of the museum's typical Puebla handicrafts includes the kitchen.

From Puebla, you can glimpse, on a clear day, its two permanently snow-capped volcanoes, located 45 km (28 miles) away: **Popocatepetl** (5,452 m/ 17,887 ft) and **Iztaccihuatl** (5,286 m / 17,343 feet), Mexico's two highest peaks after Pico de Orizaba (5,700 m/18,701 ft) in Veracruz.

For a peerless view of the majestic volcanoes, go to pine forested **Tlamacas**, nestled (3,962 m/13,000 ft) high between the two mountains. If you are fit, you can hike up Popocatepetl in eight hours. Iztaccihuatl, however, can only be climbed with the right mountaineering equipment. Tlamacas has lodging facilities and guides for hire.

Cholula

The small town of **Cholula**, with a population of 40,000, set at over 2,134 m (7,000 ft) above sea level, 10 km (6

Indian market in Toluca.

miles) west of Puebla, is noted for its churches which the Spanish built upon shrines sacred to the Indians. Until the arrival of the Conquistadores, Cholula was a religious center dedicated to the worship of Quetzalcoatl and was equal in power to Teotihuacan.

However, Cortes considered Cholula's pagan temples a hindrance to the Christianization of new Spain so he had them destroyed and ordered a church to be built on every one of them. Though some 400 shrines are believed to have existed, there are only 39 churches in Cholula. The most visited church is the **Santuario de Nuestra Senora de los Remedios**, built atop a shrine to the rain god. Unknown to Cortes, the shrine was itself sitting upon the Great Pyramid (said to have been the world's biggest) dating back to AD 100 and buried beneath it were five more pyramids.

Excavations have only revealed part of the Great Pyramid, the ruins of which can be seen sprawled across a huge mound. Eight kilometers (5 miles) of tunnels burrowed beneath, reveal earlier layers of the structure. Go on a guided tour of some of these tunnels – it's fascinating.

Cholula has several other churches worth visiting. Top of the list, near the zocalo, is the **Capilla Real** with its 49 domes, the **Church of San Francisco Acatepec** with its beautiful tiled facade and **Santa Maria de Tonantzintla**, noted for its exuberant three dimensional Indian stucco decorations. The last two churches are a couple of miles south of Cholula.

Desierto De Los Leones

The main attraction west of Mexico City is **Toluca**, renowned for its centuries old Indian market the town is only an hour's drive on Highway 15. Twenty-five kiometers (16 miles) along the route, you can make a detour to a 4,940-acre national park with the enchanting name of **Desierto De Los Leones** (Desert of the Lions). Swirling mists early in the morning add a mystic touch to this scenic pine forested park that was named after a 17th-century former Carmelite convent located in its midst. The sprawling gardens of the convent are now the venues of concerts and exhibitions on Sundays. Trails offer pleasant walks in the forest, a popular picnicking ground for Mexico City residents on weekends.

Toluca

On first acquaintance, **Toluca** (Lugar del Dios Tolo – Place of the God Tolo) does not impress. At its outskirts, every road in this city of nearly half a million seems to converge into one another and it is heavily congested with traffic. It's worse on Fridays when the weekly *tianguis* or Indian market is held – the prime reason for visiting Toluca.

Spread over several blocks, the market has been taking place every

Magnificent stained-glass panels at the Cosmo Viral Jardin Botanico.

week for centuries. It's chock-a-block full of Indians from surrounding villages who pour in to trade or to buy. It's a cacophony of sounds as vendors shout out the virtues of their wares but it is also a feast for the eyes, as an assortment of fare competes for your attention.

There are live chickens, pigs, mountains of fruit, vegetables, household items, clothes and the ubiquitous cooked food stalls. Handicrafts too are available in a bewildering variety and from nearby Indian villages – *rebozos* (women's shawls) from Tenancingo, pottery and trees of life from Metepec, *serapes* from Tianguistengo and woven baskets, earthenware, carpets, embroidered textiles and other items from elsewhere. And remember, it's definitely *de rigueur* to bargain.

Despite its madhouse atmosphere on its outskirts, Toluca surprises with its quiet, almost stately center, dominated by the **Plaza de los Martyrs** which is flanked on its south side by the town's 19th-century **Cathedral** and 18th-century **Santa Veracruz Church**.

However, the main object of interest is the vast **Cosmo Viral Jardin Botanico** (Cosmic Glass Botanical Garden) with its glass-stained panels by Leopoldo Flores. The garden is located a block east from Plaza de los Martires. Dedicated to Japanese explorer and botanist, Eizi Matuda, who in 1955 designed a herbolarium for the state of Mexico, the garden also has a Japanese rock garden and shrine.

Guerrero

The state of Guerrero takes its name from General Vicente Guerrero, another hero of the War of Independence. It is one of Mexico's most visited states, thanks to its proximity to Mexico City and the presence of four main attractions – the silver town of Taxco, the caves of Cacahuamilpa and the world famous coastal resorts of Acapulco and Zihuatenejo/Ixtapa.

159

High diving thrills of La Quebrada.

Taxco

Taxco is picture-postcard perfect. Snuggled in a mountainous pocket of Guerrero, the town is truly a slice of Spain with steep, winding cobblestone lanes (*callejones*), colonial buildings with iron-laced balconies and orange tiles and a generous sprinkling of plazas and patios overflowing with flowers.

The Spanish arrived in 1529 looking for tin but found rich deposits of silver instead. Except for two periods of lull when the silver ran out, Taxco always wore

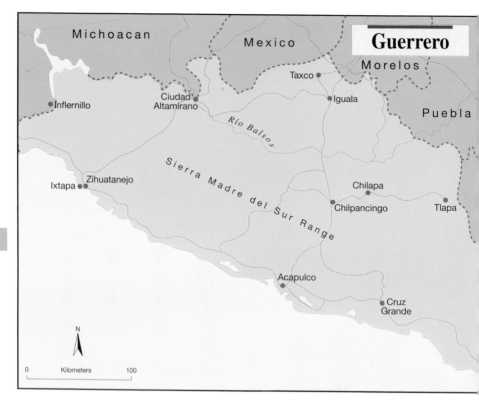

an air of prosperity which it still retains today. A pleasant climate of between 14°C (57°F) and 27°C (80°F), its elevated setting at 1,754 m (5,756 ft) and a colonial atmosphere have made Taxco, with a population of 45,000, a very attractive tourist town and one of the most popular for day trips out of Mexico City.

Although the Aztec king, Moctezuma I had been in control of the area around Taxco since 1455, it was only in the 1530s that Taxco started to develop, when at the behest of Cortes, the Spanish came to hunt for tin.

Even then, it was not until the 18th century when Joseph de la Borda struck one of the richest veins of silver, that Taxco boomed. The Frenchman, in Taxco to assist his miner brother, made the discovery in 1734 by accident when his horse tripped while they were travelling and dislodged a stone, uncovering the silver. The town benefitted from Borda's wealth. He changed his name to Jose and in gratitude to God, went on to build, between 1751 and 1758, the majestic **Iglesia de Santa Prisca** with its intricate Churrigueresque facade and soaring 40 m (130-ft) baroque twin tower that has become Taxco's best known landmark and one of Mexico's finest churches.

Apart from the Santa Prisca located just across from the zocalo, Borda also built several mansions including Jardin Borda in Cuernavaca which became

Taxco's best known landmark, the majestic Iglesia de Santa Prisca.

Maximilian's summer retreat. Borda's largesse was so great that legend has it that he offered to pave the road from Veracruz to Mexico City with silver coins if the Pope agreed to visit Taxco.

Borda's success spurred on other prospectors to try their luck in Taxco, but when the silver ran out again, they left. Taxco bounced back again in 1932 when William Spratling, a retired American academician arrived. He saw a future in the abandoned mines which still yielded some ore and so set up a workshop to make silver jewelry, recruiting

Taxco's youths as his apprentices.

Spratling's creations were a hit and his apprentices graduated to setting up workshops of their own. There are some 300 of these today turning out the range of very fine silverwork you see in all the town's shops. The shops start to appear along the highway on the approach to Taxco and all the items are very tempting, although some of the designs tend to be a little on the conservative side.

If you do decide to buy silver, remember to look for the number 925 which should be stamped on the jewelry as an indication of its authenticity (indicating 0.925 degree of purity). Items without the stamp may be *alpaca*, or silver-plated jewelry – not the real thing, but pretty nonetheless.

As a result of Spratling's sojourn in Taxco, his house, now the **Guillermo** (Spanish for William) **Spratling Museum** has become an attraction. Located behind the Santa Prisca church, the main object of interest in the three-storey house is the pre-Hispanic art collection that Spratling had amassed. The museum is open Tuesday-Saturday 10 am-5 pm, Sunday 9 am-3 pm.

There are two other houses worth visiting: **Casa Humboldt**, one of Taxco's oldest colonial homes built in the 18th century and noted for its Moorish façade and **Casa Borda** constructed in 1759. Casa Humboldt on Calle Juan Ruiz de Alarcon, 10-minutes' walk east of the zocalo was the residence of the German explorer and naturalist Baron Alexander von Humboldt.

A couple of blocks northwest is Casa Borda lived in by none other than Jose de la Borda. The curiously built house has two storeys at the front and rises up five storeys at the back. It is now the City Hall or Palacio Municipal.

Taxco is always bustling especially on weekends when it is crammed with sightseers. The center of town, the **Plaza**

Blue haven in the Bay of Acapulco.

Borda or zocalo, is packed with visitors and townsfolk. The nearby square on which the Santa Prisca stands is awash with worshippers and the *callejones* leading off from the zocalo are lined with Indians selling baskets, wooden masks, bark paintings and leather. Most of the silver is sold in shops.

To unwind, you might consider a stay at the luxury resort of **Monte Taxco**, accessible by cable car or road. The 34-m (110-ft) high hill resort on the outskirts of Taxco offers a breathtaking view of Taxco and its surroundings.

Artisan's market in Taxco.

For something totally different, drive or take a taxi to the wondrous Grutas (caves) de Cacahuamipa, popularly called **Las Grutas**, 20 miles from Taxco. They may be lesser known but the Cacahuamilpa caves can rival the Carlsbad Caverns of New Mexico.

An illuminated 2-km $(1^1/_4$-mile) long walkway allows you to stroll deep into the 30 m (100-ft) high caves to admire the bizarre sculpted limestone galleries. It's an awesome experience indeed. The caves are open daily from 10 am-5 pm, with hourly tours at N$15.

Acapulco

The resort of **Acapulco** spells fun and frolic for many sunseekers. For over 40 years and despite competition from newer and flashier purpose-built mega-resorts like Cancun, Ixtapa and now Huatulco, Acapulco has never quite lost its magic.

The reason may stem from Acapulco's split personality. One half of its famous Bay of Acapulco is breath-takingly studded with gleaming hotel blocks that reach dizzy heights; the other half is a contrasting world of sprawling narrow streets crammed with old shops, houses and people but brimming with local color and charm.

While some holidaymakers never venture beyond modern Acapulco to take a peek at its poorer but decidedly more ornate historic half, it is the sights,

In Taxco, houses are tucked into steep hills.

sounds and smells of both these two worlds that collide and blend to make a visit to Acapulco so special.

Long before Acapulco made a splash on the international tourist map, it had already appeared as an important name on sailing charts back in the 16th century. After setting foot in Tenochtitlan and establishing himself in Mexico in the 1520s, Hernan Cortes discovered the natural harbor of Acapulco.

He established it as a port of call for the "*naos*" or Spanish trading galleons that sailed from Manila in the Philippines and China bringing with them precious silks, ivory, porcelain and spices from the Orient.

From Acapulco, the cargo travelled by land to Mexico City from where it continued to Veracruz to be loaded on ships bound for Europe. As gateway to the Orient, Acapulco prospered but it was jealously eyed by English and Dutch pirate ships. To ward off possible pirate attacks, **Fort San Diego** was built in 1616 on a strategic hill commanding a view of the Acapulco Bay. The star-shaped fort still stands where it was rebuilt in 1776 when a powerful earthquake reduced Acapulco to shambles.

Although the fort did not have to prove its invincibility against the pirates, it strength was tested in 1810 when it held out as the last bastion of Spanish defense for four months against the rebel forces of Jose Morelos in the War of Independence. The Revolution of 1810 which cut trade ties between

Cliff Divers of La Quebrada

Cliff divers start their training young.

It was sheer poetry in motion. The young man, free-falling with arms and legs spread out, suddenly curled up his knees, hugging them and tucking in his head. Then in a split second, he stretched himself tautly like a sheath to slice, head first, into the water. This was no ordinary dive from a pool springboard. It was a death-defying leap over two rows of sharp, jagged cliffs into the swirling waters of a rocky inlet in the Pacific Ocean.

Welcome to La Quebrada, where men known as *clavadistas* (cliff divers) risk their lives to jump off towering cliffs into the sea five times a day – for the thrill of it as well as for some hard-earned cash. Spectators have to pay N$5 each to watch the dives from a terrace overlooking the cliffs.

It's a dangerous stunt but the *clavadistas* are skilled. And they have honed their precision-timed jump into the rock-strewn water into an art. The divers have been entertaining crowds since they made their debut in 1934. Many of them have been doing it since the age of eight – that's when training first starts and the boys work their way up the cliffs.

The dives are nail-biting performances to watch. The *clavadistas* first pray at a shrine before they hurtle off the towering 46 m (150-ft) high cliffs, and if they are scared they certainly don't show it. Calmly and coolly, they take their places atop the cliffs, limbering up and flexing their muscles as they contemplate the drop below them studying the waves as they crash onto the rocks.

They have to assess how far out they should

Spain and Mexico also signalled the decline of Acapulco as a port city.

Acapulco slipped into obscurity for over a century before it rose to prominence again – this time as a resort for the jet-set. The comeback began in 1927 when a paved road to Mexico City made Acapulco accessible to wealthy Mexicans who found this spot of the Pacific Coast to their liking. Luxury hotels were soon built to cater to a burgeoning crowd of vacationers.

After the Second World War, Acapulco became a rest and recreation center for American troops. But it was the 1960s film *Fun in Acapulco* in which rock star Elvis Presley portrayed a G.I. having a frolicking time with a bevy of beauties that rocketed the resort to fame.

Acapulco's glamor image has not lost its shine since then. The all-year sunshine resort is still attracting "norteamericanos" by the planeloads. And it's got all the excitement that any-

jump to avoid hitting the sides of the cliffs. They must also time their jump to hit into an incoming wave which increases the depth of the usually shallow water in the inlet. The moment of entry must be precise or the *clavadistas* might find themselves hitting razor-sharp rocks on the sea floor instead.

The first man moves into position, breathes deeply; just when he sees a wave coming in, he takes the plunge. He descends gracefully but as if pulled into a vortex. The water turns foamy just as he hits it; he disappears and you wonder: did he make it?

After what seems a long time, his head emerges to the relief of the crowd who are clearly thrilled. He promptly climbs back up to the cliffs for another go. At night the performances are even more spectacular with the divers carrying torches as they leap.

The best spot to view the spectacle is on the terraces of the bar and restaurant of the Hotel El Mirador, which is perched atop almost the entire length of the cliffs. (View from the bar is N$30 including two drinks).

The performance times can be erratic but generally they take place at 1 pm and at 7.30, 8.30, 9.30 and 10.30 pm in the evening. La Quebrada is a short steep walk from the zocalo in Acapulco's old quarter. The cliffs are located along the coast where the Peninsula de las Playas juts out to sea.

---

one out to have a good time could possibly ask for. There are restaurants, cafes, bars, discos, nightclubs and fashionable boutiques, all concentrated along **La Costera**, which follows the outline of Acapulco Bay. There's even a market for T-shirts, hammocks, *serapes* and other Mexican handicrafts.

Acapulco is for the dedicated nightbird as the resort hardly ever goes to sleep. The action in discos and nightclubs revs up late at night and lasts through to the early hours of the morning. Some of the discos border on the fantastic. Bocaccio, for instance, is housed in a building that resembles a work of modern art. And patrons can program personal messages on an electronic screen. Another, called Fantasy, features laser lights, confetti and a dance floor with floor-to-ceiling windows overlooking the Bay of Acapulco.

Restaurants too are dressed up in different themes to attract patrons. Many offer dining with a view on open air terraces that overlook the bay. A variety of cuisines are available and seafood (try the *huachinango* or snapper) features on most menus.

The 16-km (10-mile) Acapulco Bay where the luxury hotels are concentrated offers a cornucopia of watersports delights from sailing and jet-skiing to parasailing and deepsea fishing. Land sports in this city of 1.3 million include tennis and golf. For something more traditional, take in the excitement of *jai alai* or the melodrama of bullfights between December and March.

The Bay of Acapulco is actually a string of beaches each stamped with its own character. If you are coming in from the airport, you will first glimpse **Playa Icacos** where the deluxe hotel strip begins, followed by the more crowded **Playa La Condesa** where the sand is finer and the surf more powerful. To the west of La Condesa is a stretch of gay beach. Driving along the city's main avenue of Costera Miguel Aleman (or La Costera) you soon leave behind the

The tempting waters of Acapulco.

"gringoland" of high-rise condominiums and luxury hotels to arrive at the "afternoon" beaches of **Playa Hornos** and **Hornitos**, so-called because they are bathed in the warm rays of the afternoon sun. The setting is more local in flavor with less crowded beaches and more Mexican families who prefer the budget-priced hotels in this area.

A mile or so farther along La Costera will bring you to the **Malecon**, which marks the beginning of Acapulco's old colonial quarter and its downtown area. La Costera continues to do a loop around

sidewalks of streets running parallel to the esplanade as they tuck into fresh clams and oysters served in a half-shell on a bed of ice. The shellfish disappear so quickly many of the sidewalk restaurants open only for lunch. Indulge also in a *ceviche* (marinated raw fish) or enjoy a freshly caught fish grilled over an open fire. Then take a walk to the zocalo set between the sea and the Cathedral. This is where the townsfolk gather to sit on benches to chat or simply to pass the time. The **Mercado de Artesanias** (arts and crafts market) off the zocalo offers lower-priced handicrafts than those on La Condesa.

Quiet though the old quarter may be, it offers two attractions which should not be missed. The first is the spectacular heart-thumping leaps executed over jagged cliffs by intrepid young men – the *clavadistas* or cliff divers in La Quebrada (see box). The other is the historic Fort San Diego, a relic of Acapulco's illustrious colonial past.

Set on a hill that overlooks the Bay of Acapulco, the fort has been turned into a museum with displays tracing the development of Acapulco as a port and its role as a middleman between the Orient, Mexico and Spain. Among the more interesting displays are the old cannons, some exquisite collections of porcelain vases, replicas of Chinese ships and the nao, silk, hemp and other 19th-century trading items. The fort is open Tuesday-Sunday 10.30 am-4.40 pm, with an admission fee of N$10.

For a more authentic flavor of a

the jutting Peninsula de las Playas that curves round to hug the Playa Larga and the old harbor to return as Avenida Adolfo Lopez Mateos to downtown Acapulco. The atmosphere and more placid pace of life here in the old city are far removed from that on La Condesa but therein lies its charm.

Join the locals before noon on the

Acapulco, the sun-seeker's paradise.

Mexican resort head 11 km (7 miles) northwest of Acapulco to **Pie de la Cuesta** (Foot of the Hill), a once sleepy fishing village that has awakened to the potential of tourism.

Seafood restaurants and small hotels offering budget accommodation line its main beach. The waves are too high for swimming but it's a good place to watch the sun set. You can swim or waterski in the mirror-flat waters of Coyuca Lagoon nearby. Or simply relax on the sand and play back in your mind the exploding helicopter scene in

port to Puerto Marques on an adjacent bay. A hill separates the two bays and the climb up **La Carretera Escenica** (Scenic Highway) affords tantalizing glimpses of what awaits you at the summit – a magnificent sweeping view of the entire Acapulco Bay.

Puerto Marques itself is a small village tucked in a bay between two small peninsulas. Sailboats come here to shelter and it's popular for waterskiing and sailing. A popular spot for swimming and snorkeling is **Isla de la Roqueta**, a tiny island off Playa Caleta on the Peninsula de las Playas. Apart from the coral, the main attraction here is the submerged Virgin of Guadalupe statue. Glass-bottom boats are an alternative for those who can't dive.

Zihuatenejo

More sun, sand and sea await in quiet, unpretentious, friendly **Zihuatenejo**. It is just the place to get away from the madding crowd, although it is not too far off from Acapulco, in neighboring Ixtapa, 11 km (7 miles) west. Indeed, Zihuatenejo and Ixtapa on Mexico's sparkling Pacific Coast are a unique twin destination. But there is nothing alike about them.

The fishing village of Zihuatenejo, with only a population of 40,000, wrapped around the lovely Bahia de Zihuatenejo still retains a bit of its former sleepy self which accounts perhaps for its enduring charm while Ixtapa is an

Rambo II that was filmed here.

Or just wander around to take a peek at village life – children playing in hammocks, a revivalist group on the beach preparing for baptism in the water or village folk doing a bit of housekeeping in their backyards. For a panorama of the Bay of Acapulco, drive out 18 km (11 miles) east towards the air-

Golfing is a major past-time at the many resorts.

international resort with hotel after high-rise hotel soaring skyward on 39 km (24 miles) of beachfront lining seven picturesque coves.

Both have helped each other grow while visitors have the best of both worlds to enjoy: top class golfing, yachting and sophisticated night time entertainment in Ixtapa and a village atmosphere, good beaches and inexpensive shopping for handicrafts in Zihuatenejo.

In contrast to Ixtapa, Zihuatenejo has charm and history. It was an international port during the Spanish colonial era and was linked with Acapulco as one of the ports of call in Mexico for the *nao* sailing from the Philippines loaded with precious silk, spices and porcelain from the Orient. The goods

bound for Spain were then transferred overland to Veracruz and reloaded to ships sailing to Europe.

Fishing was also the main livelihood for Zihuatenejo's villagers and even today, the bounty of the sea is still being harvested to supply Zihuatenejo's waterfront restaurants with fresh seafood daily.

The village has remained very small, comprising some 20 cobblestone streets fanning out from **Paseo del Pescador**, its primary thoroughfare lining the main beach of **Playa Principal**. On the shores of Playa Principal are numerous *palapa* (thatched-roof) restaurants offering seafood and a marvelous vista of Zihuatenejo's boat lined pier.

The famous Acapalco sunset.

Enjoy a tranquil night-time stroll here or come early in the morning to watch fishermen wade out to sea to throw their nets while flocks of pelicans gather around hoping for a meal. If angling is your sport, you can hire a boat to take you out to do your own fishing, for the Pacific coast is rich in big game fish such as marlin and tuna.

From Playa Principal, you can walk northeastward to **Playa Madera** and **Playa La Ropa**, two more beaches comprising the Bahia de Zihuatenejo. Take a taxi from town if you do not fancy steep climbs as La Ropa is located at the base of a hill. Over the years, the increasing popularity of Zihuatenejo has resulted in small hotels and bungalows popping up on the hills beyond Playa

Madera and La Ropa where there's better swimming than on Playa Principal. What's more, they offer spectacular views over the Bahia which you can enjoy on your walk or drive. And on La Ropa, parasailing, jetskiing, sailing and other watersports are available.

The best swimming, however, is at **Playa las Gatas**, the last beach on the Bahia on the east, accessible on foot from La Ropa or more easily by boat from Zihuatenejo's pier. Las Gatas was the royal playground for the ancient Tarascans who once inhabited the region. One of the kings built a breakwater to keep out the high waves to create a lagoon in which his daughters could swim safely. It is this very lagoon that is Las Gatas' main draw while a coral reef

Sun, sand and sea at La Quieta beach in Jxtapa.

that grew around the breakwater provides the prime spot for snorkeling in Zihuatenejo. *Palapa* restaurants provide deckchairs for lounging, serve seafood and rent out jetskis. The N$6 boat trip to Las Gatas (last boat back is at 5 pm) gives a wonderful view of Zihuatenejo

Bay. Apart from the beaches, you can visit a newly opened archaeological museum which is open from Tuesday-Sunday, 12 noon-7 pm. It traces the pre-Hispanic and colonial history of the coast around Zihuatenejo. Or shop for handicrafts in the Mercado de Artesanias

and jetskiing on the beaches of the hotels. There are scores of restaurants to choose from for fine dining while discos and bars provide a different kind of action in the evening.

Ixtapa was conceived as a purpose built mega resort by Fonatur, Mexico's tourist authority, to bring in mass tourists to the country's Pacific coast. Like Cancun, Ixtapa was chosen by a computer which was asked to pick a spot with easy access to North American markets, good weather, tropical vegetation and quality beaches. When Ixtapa was selected, it was nothing more than a coconut plantation. Today, it has 20 luxury hotels spread out over 5,000 acres of broad boulevards and greenery and it is still growing.

Most of Ixtapa's hotels cluster around **Playa del Palmar**, occupying individual alcoves. Some have been built on different levels into the hills and offer magnificent views. While the computer was spot-on in choosing Ixtapa for its scenic beauty, beaches and weather, it erred on one score: it picked a locality that often has high waves and a strong undertow which makes swimming definitely dangerous.

Safer swimming can be done on **Isla Ixtapa**, an island with a nature reserve, a short boat ride from Ixtapa's Playa Quieta or an hour from Zihuatenejo's pier. Buses and taxis shuttle back and forth between Ixtapa and Zihuatenejo so you can move between the two contrasting worlds of sun, sand and sea with ease.

near the waterfront. Other than that, there is little else to do in this laid back place. But that is precisely the magic of Zihuatenejo which keeps visitors coming back.

There is plenty to do, however, in neighboring **Ixtapa**: golfing at the 18-hole Palma Real Golf Club, tennis on its courts, waterskiing, sailing, parasailing

Jalisco

Jalisco is one of Mexico's most colorful states in the central part of the country, bordering on the Pacific Coast. Like Oaxaca state, Jalisco is quintessentially Mexican. This is the home of *tequila*, the *mariachi*, the *Jarabe Tapatio* (Mexican Hat Dance), the *sombrero* and the *charro* (Mexican cowboy). And it is the birthplace of one of the country's greatest muralists, Jose Clemente Orozco. Jalisco offers craft towns, the world famous resort of Puerto Vallarta on its Pacific coast, and Guadalajara, one of Mexico's most fascinating cities.

Guadalajara is a city rich in culture and tradition.

Guadalajara

Guadalajara, the capital of the state of Jalisco, deserves all the praise that has been heaped upon it, for it is in one word, simply fabulous. Everything here is on a grand scale – its churches, its monu-

Jalisco

San Sebastián

Bahía
de
Banderas

Arroyo Reparito

Mismaloya

Puerto Vallarta

Río Cuale

Mascota

Yelapa

Llana Grande

Talpa de Allende

Mirandilla

Río Tuita

El Tuito

Río Tomatián

Cuautla

Tomatián

Río San Nicolás

Pacific
Ocean

Bahía
Chamela

Chamela

La Huerta

Río Purificación

N

Tenacatita

Cihuatián

0   Kilometers   50

Melaque

Bahía
de Navidad

ments, its parks and plazas. Yet it is not difficult to get around this big and beautiful city – Mexico's second largest with a population of over three million – for most of its sights are concentrated in the city center and an efficient bus system ensures its outlying attractions are within easy reach. Little wonder it has attracted a large North American retiree colony concentrated especially around nearby scenic **Lake Chapala** (where D H Lawrence lived and wrote *The Plumed Serpent*), an hour's drive to the south.

Guadalajara occupied its present site in 1542 after having been moved thrice from previous its locations since 1532 when it was first founded by Spanish strongman Nino Beltran de Guzman. The latter called Guadalajara and the surrounding areas *La Gran Espana* (Greater Spain). Guzman's gross mistreatment of local Indians, however, led to his dismissal and he was replaced by the more amenable Perez de la Torre who renamed the area *Nueva Galicia* (New Galicia).

In 1821, after Mexico became independent, the name Jalisco was adopted. This is a derivative of Xalisco, one of the Chimualhuacan Indian kingdoms that had existed in the area before the arrival of the Spanish.

Guadalajara, as the hub of Jalisco, thrived right from the start and today ranks high in commercial importance to Mexico City. Several overseas consulates have offices here and the presence of a sizeable foreign population including many students enrolled in the city's

Keeping out the afternoon sun with the sombrero.

universities has given Guadalajara a sophisticated and cosmopolitan stamp.

It is a city rich in culture and traditions. You can watch flamboyant Ballet Folklorico dances or attend a philharmonic concert on Sunday at **Teatro Degollado** or hear typical Jaliscan music on the **Plaza de Armas** on Thursday and Sunday evenings. You can catch a Fiesta Mexicana show of *Jarabe Tapatio* and folk dances at any of the city's top hotels or take in anything from jazz and classic guitar recitals to flamenco and ballet at numerous other venues throughout the city.

More traditional fare is dished up every evening when the *mariachis* entertain at their very own square – the **Plaza de los Mariachis** – where you can sit

Riding through the city in a calandrias.

under parasols and pay (N$2 a song) to be serenaded. And in a rodeo ring behind **Parque Agua Azul**, you can be enthralled by the fancy rope work and horsemanship of Jalisco's best *charros* in their smart cowboy outfits as they perform in their weekly Sunday rodeos.

At the heart of Guadalajara lies the **Cathedral**, a stupendous sight with its massive dome and yellow-tiled twin Gothic towers. It sports a mix of six architectural styles, the result of its lengthy period of construction between 1561 and 1618 and part reconstruction in 1848 when its present towers were added on after the original ones had been flattened by an earthquake.

The Cathedral is richly decorated inside with Tuscany style pillars and art treasures donated by King Ferdinand VII of Spain. It contains the image of La Virgen de la Nuestra Senora which is highly venerated in Guadalajara and a painting of *The Assumption of the Virgin* reportedly done by Murillo in 1650. Four huge squares lie on each side of the Cathedral and they are always bustling with people and activity. Facing the Cathedral, on its east side is **Plaza de los Laureles,** dotted with laurel trees.

To the south is the **Plaza de las Armas** with its ornate kiosk of statues and lamps brought in from Paris. Opposite this verdant plaza is the **Palacio del Gobierno**, built between 1643 and 1774, a delightfully florid building of different styles embellished with stone cannons and armored knights on top. The Palacio

Entertainment at the Plaza Tapatia.

was the venue for Hidalgo's landmark 1810 decree abolishing slavery. Inside, over a stairway is a fantastic mural of Miguel Hidalgo by Jose Clemente Orozco in 1937 capturing the passion of the padre's fight for justice for the people.

To the Cathedral's north is the **Plaza de los Hombres Ilustres** with its statues of Jalisco's famous sons some of whom lie buried under the circular Greek style monument, the Rotonda de los Hombres Ilustres, just behind. On the east side of the Plaza is the **Museo Regional de Guadalajara**, converted from the baroque style San Jose seminary which was completed in 1700. Among the museum's exhibits are archeological artifacts, Spanish and Mexican paintings, regional arts and crafts and Em-

peror Maximilian's carriage.

Facing the Cathedral's east side is the lengthy **Plaza de la Liberacion** ending at the fabulous Teatro Degollado. The theater has been remodelled several times since its completion in 1856. A frieze of *Apollo and the Nine Muses* adorns the top of the theater's colonnaded entrance. Inside is a vast expanse of mural-decorated ceiling. Home to the Guadalajara Symphony, the theater hosts other performances, notably, the Ballet Folklorico on Sundays.

Beyond the theater is the impressive **Plaza Tapatia**. It is decorated with a row of fountains on one side stretching to the historic Instituto Cultural de Cabanas; on the other, it is lined with a pedestrian mall flanked with shops and

The Teatro Degallado in Liberdad Plaza is regarded
one of the best 19th-century theaters in Mexico.

eateries and great open spaces filled
with sculptures, tabachin trees and park
benches extending all the way to
Mercado Libertad.

The massive **Mercado Libertad** is
nothing to look at from the outside, but
inside, it is a hubbub of activity. The
market's three levels offer restaurants,
fruit and vegetables, cheese, fresh meat,
fish, handicrafts, hardware and household goods. Hunt for bargains here from
the hundreds of stalls offering ceramics,
baskets, guitars and *serapes* and also try
the typical Mexican dishes.

Outside the market, *calandrias* or horse drawn carriages await to offer a leisurely, romantic tour of the city. You can also find *calandrias* by the side of the Museo Regional.

Across from Mercado Libertad on Calzeda Independencia, Guadalajara's main artery, is the **San Juan Dios** church, at the hub of the city's old quarter where the Guadalajarans have fun and laughter in simple restaurants and bars. It is very *tapatio* (typically Guadalajaran), as they would say. Next to the church is the **Plaza de los Mariachis** which takes on a romantic glow when lit at night. Here you can dine or drink and be serenaded by the merry music of the *mariachis*. Again, it's very *tapatio*.

Don't miss a truly Guadalajaran institution either – the splendid **Instituto Cultural de Cabanas** which houses the best works of one of Mexico's finest muralists, Jose Clemente Orozco. His frescoes are splashed on the walls and ceiling of the institute's chapel with the most spectacular piece, the *Man of Fire*, decorating the central dome. His works from the old Museo Orozco have been moved here and you can see more of them, including sketches, if you roam about in the institute's 23 courtyards. The institution is open from Tuesday-Saturday, 10.15 am-6 pm, with an admission fee of N$6.

The building had served, since its completion in 1810, as an orphanage until 1980 when it was resurrected into a cultural center for concerts and theater performances. But old habits die hard and you will often hear it being referred to by its original name of Hospicio Cabanas. For an astonishing Guadalajaran phenomenon, take a 15-minute bus ride to the end of Calzeda Independencia to Parque Mirador where you will find yourself staring out to a canyon, the **Barranca de Oblatos**, plunging 674 m (2,211 ft) deep right on the outskirts of the city. You can watch the Cola de Caballo (Horse Tail) waterfall cascading down the canyon from Parque Dr Atl (take the Ixcatan bus on Avenida Alcalde), or go on exploratory treks on the canyon floor.

Zapopan

Zapopan, once a separate Indian village and now a suburb of Guadalajara 6 km (4 miles) from the center, is a very special place. It is the site of the impressive 18th-century **Basilica de Zapopan** where the image of Nuestra Senora de Zapopan (Our Lady of Zapopan) resides. The glass encased image of the Virgin is the object of feverish veneration by a million pilgrims every year on 12 October. At 5 am on this day, thousands of chanting and stomping Indian dancers in traditional costumes lead the six-hour dramatic procession carrying the doll-sized image of Our Lady of Zapopan from Guadalajara's Cathedral to the Basilica, followed by thousands of devotees.

In front of the Basilicia stands a

The National Spirit of Mexico

Agave plants, from which the famed tequila originates.

Tequila, a clear potent liquor, is synonymous with Mexico and has long been considered its national drink. There's more to the making of tequila than most fans of the drink would realize. For one thing, the agave plant that yields the pineapple-like fruit from which the magic liquid is extracted to make tequila, is but one of 197 varieties. It is the special blue-leaved Tequilana Weber Azul agave plant that thrives on the soil and climatic conditions of Tequila, a town in Jalisco, about 48 km (30 miles) from Guadalajara.

What's more, the precious fruit – the crown of the agave plant – is considered ripe for harvest only after eight to ten years of painstaking cultivation. During this period, the shoots of the plant are constantly pruned to allow the crown to grow while diseases and pests have to be kept at bay.

Each year, the stem growing in the center of the agave plant is removed to prevent the fruit from flowering in spring, a move that also ensures all the plant's natural sugar is stored in the crown.

When ready for harvest, the shoots of each agave plant are cut away and the huge 68 kg (150 1b) crowns sitting in the middle are collected and brought in truckloads to the tequila plants based in Tequila. It's a fascinating trip to Tequila where you can view the beautiful agave dotted landscape stretching as far as the eye can

see and where tequila plants welcome visitors who come to see how the beverage is made.

It all starts with the arrival of the agave crowns which are first cut and shredded then cooked in steam vats for up to 14 hours. The pulp is then pressed and the extracted juices are cooled to a desired level of sugar concentration before they are ready for fermentation. This is a process that takes up to 32 hours. Once the sugar in the agave juices has been converted into alcohol, distillation follows.

It involves two stages: distilling the alcohol in the fermented juices first to 50 percent proof (25 percent alcohol) and then to 110 percent proof (55 percent alcohol). The tequila is then stored for four months after which it can be bottled and sold or kept for further ageing. The longer tequila is left to age, the more full-bodied and smoother, and of course the more expensive, it becomes. There are several types of tequila. Pure tequila is the white liquid normally associated with the drink; it's strong and can be imbibed neat or mixed. Amber -colored tequila is blended. It has a pleasant aroma and flavor that makes it a good mixer.

Tequila *reposada* is one grade up. It is slightly greenish-gold in color, the result of having been aged – for at least 120 days in oak vats that give it its special color and taste. It's smooth on the palate. But the finest tequila is the unmistakable *anejo*.

Anejo tequila is aged, for a minimum of two years, in white oak barrels that impart a distinctive mellow flavor and aroma, and it should be savored neat. The longer the *anejo* has been aged, say connoisseurs, – the more exquisite it is, with some of the very best spending up to seven years stored in wood.

Drinking Tequila

Aficionados drink it straight, sprinkling some salt on a wedge of lime and biting into it after each sip. That's the short cut.

Traditionally, however, the drinking of tequila involves four steps. First, salt is placed on the top of your wrist. You lick it, bite into a piece of lime and then take a gulp of pure tequila and lick more salt. Foreigners unused to the taste of the heady brew can drink margarita instead, a cocktail made from tequila, lime juice and orange liqueur, which is shaken before it is served in a salt- rimmed or salt free glass. *Salud*!

Tequila processing plant.

statue of Pope John Paul II and a child, commemorating the papal visit to the church on 30 January, 1979. The church grounds also house the fascinating **Museo Huichol** where the colorful beaded and yarn woven handicrafts of the Huichol Indians who live in isolated villages in Jalisco are on sale and display. The museum is open Monday-Friday 10 am-1 pm and 4 pm-7 pm, Saturday and Sunday 10 am-1 pm.

A short 30-minute drive or bus ride from Guadalajara are two of Jalisco's most intriguing craft towns. The first to be reached is **Tlaquepaque**, a fashionable little town that has cashed in on its craft traditions. Leading off from its main plaza are a number of streets where you can spend several enjoyable hours browsing in crafts stores and galleries.

But first, drop in at the **Museo Regional de la Ceramica y los Artes Populares de Jalisco** at Avenue Independencia 237, for an inkling of what the town has to offer. There is plenty, from ceramics and glassware to papier-mache animals and textiles. The museum is open Tuesday-Saturday, 10 am-4 pm, Sunday, 10 am-1 pm.

Diagonally opposite the museum is a glass factory where daily glass-blowing demonstrations are conducted. While in Tlaquepaque do not miss a meal at the Restaurant Sin Nombre (Restaurant With No Name) at Madero no. 80, a delightful place in a garden setting with an exquisite menu.

Tonala is the next craft town, 10 minutes from Tlaquepaque. It is less

The Mexican struggle for independence is depicted in Guadalajara's many murals.

touristy and more down to earth than Tlaquepaque with prices to match its less glorified status. But, it is a big manufacturing base for ceramics and glassware and you are likely to pick up good bargains there.

Puerto Vallarta

Despite rapid development, hot and humid **Puerto Vallarta** on Jalisco's Pacific coast is still a gem of a resort that has not lost its luster. Huddled around the 40-km (25-mile) Bahia de Banderas against the backdrop of the rugged Sierra Madre, Puerto Vallarta combines the beauty of the cobalt blue Pacific coast with the luxury of resort beach

hotels and the charm of an old fishing village turned colonial town.

It was known as Puerta Las Penas before it was renamed Puerto Vallarta in 1918 in honor of Ignacio L Vallarta, a governor of the state of Jalisco during the Mexican Revolution who contributed greatly to the modernization of the state and of the village itself.

But it was only in 1964 when John Huston picked it as his film location for *Night of the Iguana* starring Ava Gardner and Richard Burton, whose torrid off-screen romance drew international headlines, that Puerto Vallarta was put on the tourist map of the world.

As the *paparazzi* flocked in to report and take pictures, Puerto Vallarta's fame grew. Soon, tourists started to arrive to

A riot of color in the flamboyant folk dance.

gawk at where it all took place. Hotel developers followed and inevitably, Puerto Vallarta was transformed. Today, tourism has become its major industry and the resort's population has burgeoned to a quarter of a million.

It offers a bit of everything for everyone. Apart from fine beaches and extensive watersports facilities, there is good shopping, great art galleries, excellent seafood and an active nightlife.

Although more and more hotels and condominium blocks have stretched out on the bay on one side of Puerto Vallarta while on the other, hotels and private homes have taken over the hills, the development of the resort is nowhere near that of Cancun, and like Acapulco, it offers the best of both worlds

– the old and the new. The old is still very much the same. It is cut into two by the Rio Cuale with both sides making up the heart of Puerto Vallarta with its cobblestone streets and old houses. Old men riding pack mules on the streets are not an unusual sight.

The center of town is the spacious **Plaza de Armas**, north of Rio Cuale, fronted by an open air amphitheater and a series of Roman-like arches facing the sea. Behind the plaza towers the attractive **Templo de Guadalupe**, topped with a crown and the scene of the town's many festivals.

Beyond the plaza stretches the **Malecon**, the lively seaside boardwalk lined with restaurants, bars and nightclubs. A mile beyond the Malecon, the

The Music of the *Mariachis*

The mariachis make distinct Mexican music.

Mariachi music is unmistakably stirring, vibrant and catchy. The smartly dressed *mariachis* in their *charro* costume and the merry music which they make, have become, like the wide-brimmed *sombreros* which they also wear, one of Mexico's best-known symbols.

The *mariachis* were said to have originated in Jalisco in the mid 19th century as wandering minstrels made up of farming folk who banded together to entertain at country gatherings.

They sang mostly haunting ballads lamenting lost love or songs of heroic horsemanship. It was only when groups of *mariachis* moved to Mexico City in the 1920s to entertain that they became a hit and the music they played soon became instantly recognizable as the country's national sound. *Mariachis* and their music have kept up with the times ever since they first appeared on the scene more than 100 years ago. The band started off with a harpist and several guitarists strumming the *vihuela* (small five string guitar).

Six string guitars were later brought in. Then, as the harp (used to produce bass sounds) proved too awkward to carry around on their assignments, the *mariachis* replaced it with a bigger *vihuela* that was specially invented. Looking like an outsized guitar and dubbed the guitarron, this instrument has since become the mainstay of every modern *mariachi* band.

In the 1920s, trumpets which had been introduced from Europe were added and they soon became indispensable for producing the grand flourishes that have made *mariachi* music so distinctive today.

The number of people making up a *mariachi* band appear to vary from region to region but typically it consists of eight musicians: three violinists, two guitarists, two trumpeteers and the guitarron player. Any number can sing with the rest providing the back up.

Even the uniforms the *mariachis* wear have undergone transformation. The peasant style loose pants, shirts and neck scarf which the early musicians wore were discarded in favor of the smart rodeo style outfits sported by the stately *charros* (cowboys) of Jalisco.

The modern *mariachis* certainly look stun-

beach is lined with high rise hotels and condominiums, a classy marina and newly developed Nuevo Vallarta with more condominiums and time share apartment blocks.

South of Rio Cuale is the traditional – and more enchanting – part of Puerto

Vallarta, which represents the town as it was before the boom began in the 1970s. Much of the action is concentrated around the beach with the uninviting name of **Playa de los Muertos** (Beach of the Dead). But the golden sand beach is anything but uninviting. It is lined with

ning in their smart, well-fitting riding pants with silver studs running down the sides, frilly shirts and embroidered jackets. Cowboy boots have replaced the leather *huaraches* on their feet while the huge *sombrero* which they wear for the head, adds a flamboyant touch.

Where do you find them? You will often hear them first before you see them, so loud and stirring is their music. The *mariachis* can be found wherever there's a need for entertainment – in restaurants, nightclubs, country fairs, in open plazas, even in churches. And the *mariachis* provide the rousing background music for bullfights and *charreadas* (rodeos).

Two cities are literally the home of the *mariachis*: Guadalajara in Jalisco where the music was born and Mexico City where they established their fame.

The Plaza de los Mariachis is the place to go in Guadalajara to be romantically serenaded as you sip a margarita or dine at a parasol-shaded table, while in Mexico City you can shop for the finest sounds at **Garibaldi Plaza**, a mind-boggling *mariachi* mart.

From as early as 5 pm until the wee hours of the morning, *mariachi* bands at Garibaldi Plaza strike up their music hoping to be heard and hired, making the venue one of Mexico City's liveliest places to be at night.

You can wander from group to group to pick the best music for hire – for one song or more.

You will also spot *mariachi* groups hanging around the roadside near the Garibaldi Plaza as they wait for cars or pick-up trucks to drop by to hire them for private parties. Ah...the *mariachis*...what would Mexico's music be without them?

Perpetuating the Aztec myths at festivals.

hotels with *palapa* (thatched roof) terrace restaurants offering marvelous views of the sunset. Behind the beach is the oldest part of town, filled with art galleries, *taquerias*, numerous sidewalk fondas offering *mariscos* (seafood), modest hotels, restaurants and bars.

One of the best ways to enjoy Puerto Vallarta is to take a stroll along the deserted Playa de los Muertos late at night while the rest of town is in full swing. The rush of waves on the shore and the twinkle of lights on the surrounding hills lends a romantic touch.

Beyond the Playa de los Muertos on the southern curve of Bahia de las Banderas, are more resort hotels and private villas hugging the hills. Dotted along the bay here are Puerto Vallarta's most beautiful beaches. There are five in total – Playa Gemelas, Mismaloya, Boca de Tomatlan, Playa de las Animas and Yelapa – but the most well known and still the most outstanding is **Mismaloya** where the *Night of the Iguana* was filmed. The road leading to

Mezcal

In almost every town and village in Oaxaca state, you will find shops selling *mezcal*, a spirit made from the sap of the *maguey* plant. Unlike tequila which comes from only a particular *maguey* plant, *mezcal* can be made from different species of the plant. However, the processes for making and ageing *mezcal* are the same as those for tequila.

During the bottling stage, a *gusano* (worm) and a *orpechuga* (chicken breast) may be added to give the *mezcal* a more distinctive flavor. Sometimes, fruit flavors such as peach are added which ends up making the *mezcal* taste more like a liqueur. *Mezcal* can also be bought plain and unadulterated. It is drunk like tequila.

Mismaloya climbs up the hill behind the Bahia de Banderas, offering a magnificent vista of the ocean and coast.

Ten km (6 miles) later, it descends into a little cove where a huge hotel, La Jolla de Mismaloya stands on one side of the beach with private houses studded on the slopes behind it. On the other side of the beach are *palapa* restaurants and a hill leading up to the film location site, now in ruins.

You can climb up the hill to where only the shells of buildings now stand, but it is not easy as the path on the way up is overgrown with weeds. But you can go half-way up the steps that Ava Gardner's character in the film used to run down to the beach to swim in the sea with her beach boys. The place may have changed since the filming, but you can still hear the clicking of iguanas in the bushes and the sea where they swam

The thrills and spills of charros on horseback at Tlaquepaque.

Tlaquepaque is an intriguing craft town only a short drive away from Jalisco.

is as tequila clear as ever.

Pick your own spot on the beach outside the *palapa* restaurants which serve superb seafood and a range of exotic cocktails – try the *coco loco* – to put you into a tropical mood.

Just off Mismaloya, about 15 min-

utes by boat, is **Los Arcos**, a National Underwater Park, located around a series of three arches where snorkeling is excellent. Another way to enjoy Puerto Vallarta is to go on a cruise. Two types are offered: a three-hour sunset cruise and an all-day cruise of the coastline.

Michoacán

Mexico's garden state – that's what Michoacán is, thanks to its lush vegetation made possible by an abundant annual rainfall and well-drained fertile valleys fed by Rio Lerma and Rio Balsas. Michoacán is more than just pleasing to the eye; it is also one of Mexico's most traditional states where ancient customs like the making of centuries old handicrafts and the Festival of the Dead (see box) are kept alive and perpetuated in pockets of Indian mountain villages, that are home to the Purepechans or Tarascans.

Occupying a mountainous area of 96,213 km (37,155 sq miles) that covers part of the Sierra Madre Occidental, Michoacán enjoys a climate that ranges from temperate to tropical. From the attractive highland town of Patzcuaro at 2,743 m (9,000 ft) above sea level to the coastal resort of Playa Azul, there is plenty in the state to keep you pleasantly occupied.

Church of San Augustin overlooking the courtyard of Morelos' birthplace.

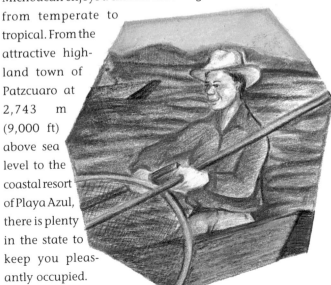

193

Morelia

Morelia is the capital of Michoacán and if you travel on Highway 15 from Mexico City, you will be greeted after a drive of four hours by the 253 graceful arches of the city's 18th-century aqueduct system and **Las Tarascans**, a fountain of three Tarascan Indian maidens, which looks even more splendid at night when it is fully illuminated.

The Highway continues to become Morelia's main street, **Avenida Madero**,

sandstone used in its elegant buildings has given Morelia a softer touch.

Originally named Valladolid and settled by many families from the Spanish city of the same name, it was renamed Morelia after Mexico gained independence, in honor of Jose Maria Morelos de Pavon, a native son and parish priest who played a major role in the Mexican War of Independence.

Morelia is a small city of nearly half a million people, with cool, spring like weather, thanks to its 1,829 m (6,000 ft) high setting. It's a city made for walking since everything of interest is within a short distance from each another.

Occupying pride of place on **Plaza de los Martires**, the heart of Morelia on Avenida Madero, is the city's immense twin towered **Cathedral** and intricately-carved facades that are a mix of architectural styles (herreriano, baroque and neoclassical) – the Cathedral took a century to build from 1640 to 1744.

Visit the Cathedral in the morning when the sun's rays filter through its dome's multiple windows lighting up the interior with a magical glow. The Cathedral's unique treasures include the Cristo de la Sacristia (Christ of the Sacristy) a figure of Christ made from corn paste and orchid sap, the gigantic 4,600-pipe organ and a silver baptismal font.

Facing the Cathedral on the opposite side of Avenida Madero is a line of handsome colonial buildings now turned into hotels and restaurants with wrought-iron balconies, carved pink tinted facades and arches, some Moorish

which is oh-so-Spanish with its colonial buildings on one side and the massive and magnificent 17th-18th century Cathedral on the other.

Indeed, Morelia, founded in 1541, was designed along the austere lines of Madrid in Spain but the rose-colored

The Colegio de San Nicolas in Morelia, where Morelos studied.

in style. Join the *Morelenses* as they sit under the arches for a drink or a meal (delightfully inexpensive for a city) and watch the world go by.

As a city dedicated to Morelos, it is not surprising to find two museums named after him. In fact, they were his homes where he was born and raised. A 10-minute walk south of the Cathedral at the corner of Garcia Obeso and Corregidora, next to the Church of San Augustin is the **Museo Casa Natal de Morelos** where Morelos was born on 30 September, 1765. Used partly as a public library and a Cine Club, two of the rooms display some manuscripts and other Morelos memorabilia. An eternal flame in a corner of a courtyard burns in his memory.

Two blocks farther down Garcia Obeso and one block east on Avenida Sur 323 is the **Museo Casa de Morelos**, an old Spanish brick house where Morelos lived for many years. It offers a more comprehensive exhibition tracing Mexico's independence history, Morelos' role, and some personal memorabilia including the household goods used by his mother. You can also take a peek into his simple bedroom.

For an idea of where Morelos studied, visit the noisy **Colegio de San Nicholas,** two blocks west of the Cathedral, on Avenida Madero Poniente. The Colegio is one of the oldest universities in the Americas, established in 1540. This was where Miguel Hidalgo, Mexico's father of independence taught and

Hotel Catedral, colonial elegance in Morelia.

became Morelos' mentor, and later inducted him into the core rebel group fighting for freedom from Spain.

A few steps around the corner of the Colegio is **Nigromante** where the historic **Palacio Clavijero** stands. The Palacio now houses the city's tourist office and a library. Enter the latter to view the lovely interior of the former Jesuit college that was founded in 1660.

On the right side of the palace is the **Mercado de Dulces** (Market of Sweets) where you can indulge in *ate* (fruit pastilles typical of Michoacán) and the myriad variety of candy and tantalizing chocolates that the Morelenses have a weakness for.

For an understanding of Michoacán's past from pre-historic and pre-Hispanic times to its present day cultures, drop in at the **Museo del Estado** which is open Monday-Friday, 9 am-2 pm, and 4 pm-8 pm, weekends and public holidays until 7 pm. The museum is opposite the pleasant Jardin de las Rosas. The Jardin is only a block's walk up Nigromante.

Three blocks east of the Museo del Estado, on Avenida Morelos Norte and a block past the landscaped Plaza del Carmen, is the **Museo de la Mascara** where you can view the variety of masks used for the many dances of Michoacán. It is open Monday-Friday, 10 am-2 pm, weekends and public holidays, 10 am-6 pm. The museum is next to the Casa de la Cultura, which occupies the ex-Convento del Carmen, where you can

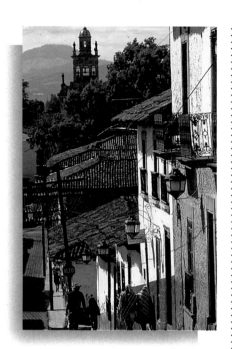

Cobblestone streets of the picturesque town of Patzcuaro.

watch typical Michoacán dance and music performances.

Morelia is a delightful place to shop because of the rich variety of handicrafts made in the state of Michoacán and the best place to see, and buy, what's available is the **Casa de las Artesanias** in the ex-Convento of San Francisco on Plaza de Valladolid, a 15-minute walk east of the Cathedral.

There's a general display and sale of different types of handicrafts on the ground floor: clay figurines from Ocumicho or decorative colorful pottery from Capula and Patamban. Upstairs, tiny shops specialize in crafts from individual towns and villages in Michoacán, offering occasional demonstrations of how they are made: beautifully crafted

guitars from Paracho, masks, embroidery and *rebozos* from Tocuaro and copperware from Santa Clara del Cobre.

Patzcuaro

Nestled in the Sierra Madre Occidental at an elevation of 2,134 m (7,000 ft) is Patzcuaro, a picturesque town of 65,000 people, located 3 km (2 miles) from serene Lake Patzcuaro and an hour's drive west from Morelia. Both the town, the lake and the surrounding villages are enclosed by pine forested mountains which give the area the ambience of a country resort, a feeling which is enhanced by a cool climate with temperatures averaging 16°C (60°F).

You will enjoy many pleasant hours walking the cobblestone streets of colonial Patzcuaro, wending your way through Indian handicrafts stalls and open-air food stands and touring the scenic countryside. The home of the Tarascan Indians, whose original name is Purepeche, Patzcuaro owes its unique character to the wonderful mélange of its Indian cultural heritage with its Spanish architectural legacy.

Patzcuaro served as the capital of the Purepeche Indian kingdom for nearly two centuries before the Spanish arrived and exploited them. Ethnically and linguistically, they differed from the other groups found in Mesoamerica. The Aztecs called them Michoaques and the place where they came from, Michoacán, means "place of lakes".

The 16th century Biblioteca Gertrudis Bocanegra.

The Spanish were the ones who named the Purepechans Tarascans. The story goes that the Purepechans called the Spaniards "*tarascos*" or sons-in-law as many of them took the Purepechans' young daughters as wives. It was a derogatory term but the Spaniards thought it referred to the Indians themselves and began calling them as such.

The peace loving Purepechans had surrendered without a fight to the Spaniards when they arrived in Michoacán in 1529. However, the head of the Spanish troops, Nino de Guzman, was a cruel man who tortured and killed many Indians while forcing others to work under harsh conditions in gold mines around the area.

The barbaric acts of Guzman did not go unnoticed for King Carlos V of Spain sent a team to investigate. Among the members was a priest by the name of Vasco de Quiroga who reported Guzman's savagery and had him returned to Spain in 1536. Quiroga stayed on to try to undo the harm that Guzman had wrought upon the Indians.

At the same time, the diocese of Michoacán was founded and Quiroga was nominated bishop. He was a humanitarian and highly popular. Quiroga also encouraged each Purepechan Indian community living on the shores of the lake to specialize in a craft so they could earn from it, thus freeing them from being tied to the mines. The crafts have survived today making Patzcuaro and its surroundings great places to shop.

In 1540, Quiroga declared Patzcuaro the capital of Michoacán. It grew into an important colonial town with many elegant buildings that have given Patzcuaro a strong Hispanic flavor.

Despite its attractiveness, Patzcuaro and its lake have not been invaded – thank goodness – by the impact of mass tourism, although it is a favorite destination, especially on weekends, with Mexican families from nearby Jalisco and Mexico City.

Patzcuaro is centered around its two tree-shaded main plazas – bustling **Plaza Gertrudis Bocanegra** and the bigger, more stately **Plaza Vasco de Quiroga** a block away, both named after the town's most illustrious citizens.

A statue of Quiroga towers above the plaza named after him. On Sundays, artists display their works in the usually quiet square which is surrounded on all sides by arcaded Spanish 17th-century colonial buildings that have been turned into charming middle-of-the-range hotels and restaurants. Enjoy pleasant dining, either indoors or outside, on the sidewalk under the arches.

Gracing her own plaza and gazing down on the hustle and bustle surrounding her is the statue of Gertrudis Bocanegra, one of Mexico's heroines in the War of Independence who was shot in 1817 in Plaza Quiroga, for her role in the struggle.

More modest colonial buildings housing budget-priced hotels, surround Plaza Gertrudis Bocanegra. Instead of dining you can hunt for souvenirs, for crammed under the arches of the hotels on its west side, are a cornucopia of Indian stalls selling handicrafts, candy and music cassette tapes.

More artisan products may be found in the **Mercado de Artesanias** leading from the north side of the plaza. On Fridays, the plaza itself turns into a colorful Indian market when Tarascans from the environs of Patzcuaro pour in to display and sell their wares.

Although Patzcuaro is extensive, stretching all the way to the lake shores, the places of interest are concentrated downtown, near the two plazas. On the north of Plaza Gertrudris, next to the Mercado de Artesanias is the 16th-century **Biblioteca Gertrudis Bocanegra**, once the church of San Augustin, which contains an impressive mural by Juan O'Gorman documenting Patzcuaro's history. The Biblioteca-Gertrudis is open Monday-Friday 9 am-7 pm, and Saturday 9 am-1 pm. Its neighbor is the ex-Convento San Augustin, now **Teatro Emperador Caltzontzin**, which houses more murals upstairs. In its main halls, the walls and ceiling of the theater are studded with unusual hat motifs.

For an insight into the arts and crafts of Michoacán, drop in at the

Museo Regional de Artes Populares, formerly the Colegio de San Nicolas Obispo, two blocks east of Plaza Quiroga. Beautiful old lacquerware, ceramics, copperware and embroidered work are displayed. Here too may be found a statue of Christ made from corn paste and orchid sap, a uniquely Indian work of art.

In the museum grounds are the ruins of a pre-Columbian Indian village and pyramid dating back to the 12th century. The village is open Tuesday-Saturday 9 am-7 pm, free on Sundays, 9 am-3 pm.

Shoppers will enjoy the **Casa de los Once Patios** (House of 11 Courtyards), first used as a hospital and then as a Dominican nunnery. Spread over the many courtyards in the building, found in a cobblestone alley a block off Plaza Quiroga are shops specializing in each regional handicraft ranging from Paracho guitars and copperware from Santa Clara del Cobre to Uruapan lacquerware and ceramics from Tzintzuntzan. If you have a guide with you, he will point out many items of interest left intact from the Convent days, including the bathrooms used by the nuns.

But the single most important building in Patzcuaro that was the brainchild of Vasco de Quiroga is the **Basilica de Nuestra Senora de la Salud**, three blocks

Paracutin Volcano

The Paracutin Volcano. Note the church spire that was not covered by volcanic ash.

As the villagers of Angahuan tell the story, it all happened rather inexplicably some 50 years ago and without a single casualty. On the tranquil morning of 20 February, 1943, a farmer was, as usual, ploughing his cornfields. Suddenly, at 3.15 pm, the ground beneath his feet started to shake and a column of fire and lava shot out into the sky. The startled farmer tried to stop it by shovelling earth over the jet of molten lava. It got worse and he fled back to his village.

Bells of alarm rang out. Some villagers hurriedly packed their belongings to leave the same day. As more lava, fire and rocks flew out, other villagers followed suit in the next few days and quickly emptied Paricutin. Soon, villagers from neighboring San Juan Parangaricutiro also moved out as lava flowed towards their village.

Thus was born the Paricutin volcano which continued to spew lava and rocks for the next nine years until, as suddenly as it had started, it stopped on 6 March, 1954.

Today, the volcano rises above a landscape which was once flat. The village of San Juan Parangaricutiro is buried underneath a rubble of lava rocks at the foot of the volcano with only the spires of a church sticking poignantly out. There is no trace of Paracutin itself; it had been completely engulfed.

You can make a fascinating trip on foot or horseback to the church to view the ruins and landscape and go on to ride across the crater of

east of Plaza Gertrudis Bocanegra. Quiroga's original plan was to build a church with five naves laid out like the palm of a hand with each nave representing Michoacán's cultures and races and the central nave or palm, the Catholic church. A series of earthquakes aborted his plan and only the basilica, which was the central nave, was completed in 1603. The church houses the Virgen de la Salud enclosed in a glass case with a crescent moon before her. The moon signifies that the Virgin is

above all things and the image itself is venerated as a miracle figure attributed with powers of healing.

In 1540, Quiroga encouraged the Tarascan Indians to make an image of the Virgin. They did, fashioning it out of cornstalks and orchid sap. When several miracle cures occurred among the Indians, Quiroga transcribed at the feet of the Virgin the words "Salus infirmorum" (Healer of the Sick). Since then, the faithful have been making their way to the basilica to pray to the image for cures.

the volcano which bubbles away innocently these days. The trek starts from Angahuan where there is no shortage of guides with horses for hire. The roundtrip cost is variable but you can bargain it down to N$30 for a ride to the volcano, N$15 to the church.

As you walk or ride past Angahuan village, you will notice fields of lava which the villagers will tell you destroyed their once fertile earth where few crops can now be cultivated. You then enter a park of pine trees. The church spires are now visible rising eerily above the land-scape. The ride takes you past more lava fields and then great boulders of volcanic rocks as you approach the church.

Only one church tower is intact, the other was destroyed. The altar however was saved and the image of San Juan was quickly salvaged and now resides in San Juan Nuevo (an hour from Uruapan) where the San Juan Parangaricutiro population set up their new home. The image is highly revered as a saint for curing the sick. The zocalo which faced the church is covered with volcanic rocks but its layout can be discerned. It takes about an hour to ride or walk to the church. From there, it's another two hours to the volcano, including riding across its crater.

The Paricutin Volcano certainly makes an excursion you will not easily forget.

In 1737, the Virgin was declared Patzcuaro's patron saint. 8 December marks the feast day of the Virgin and sees thousands of pilgrims from all over Mexico paying homage, some crawling on their knees from the approach road to the basilica, all the way to the altar.

Lake Patzcuaro

Little seems to have changed in the villages on the islands in Lake Patzcuaro

Janitzio Island in Lake Patzcuaro.

where people still fish in the lake with their traditional butterfly nets and speak their Purepechan dialect. A thin veil of mist covers the lake early in the morning, breaking up only when the sun's rays pierce through to reveal scores of feeding egrets and herons and the rounded outlines of the Sierra Madre rising above the lake.

Lake Patzcuaro is 88 km (55 miles) in circumference and is one of Mexico's highest lakes. There are five islands in the lake and several villages dotted along its shores. Slow *lanchas* (boats) ply daily between the islands and Patzcuaro's docks providing a wonderful opportunity to sightsee on the lake.

Take the *lancha* to **Janitzio**, its biggest island, a little bit too touristy per-

Shops in Tzintzuntzan selling local handicraft produced in
traditions of ancient times.

haps, but undeniably beautiful. The boats depart as soon as they are filled, but they ply from 7 am - 5 pm daily. The round trip fare is N$6.50.

From afar, as the boat chugs across the mirror calm waters towards it, Janitzio looks like a typical Mediterra-nean village with stepped adobe houses and orange-tiled roofs rising on its slopes. A giant statue of Morelos with his right hand raised resting atop the island, spoils the otherwise idyllic picture.

As the boat encircles the island for an all round view, there are opportuni-

onto the lake. Other types of fish caught in the lake are *charrales*, a delicious finger sized anchovy-like fish that is eaten deep fried, and *mojara*, a sort of snapper which is grey in color and fried in fillets.

Walk up the stepped alleyways of Janitzio to the statue of Morelos for a peerless view of the lake and its surroundings. You can climb up inside the statue (which is decorated with murals depicting Spain's history and Morelos' role in it) and go right up to its raised hand for a higher view.

As you wander up and down the alleyways, little shops flanking the passageways will catch your eye with the numerous artisan products of the area: lacquer trays, wooden handicrafts, masks, tiles and souvenir butterfly nets. There is the church of San Jeronimo to visit and more views to enjoy from the churchgrounds overlooking the rooftops of Janitzio's houses where you may glimpse Purepechan women hanging out the day's washing to dry.

Tzintzuntzan

ties to snap pictures of Patzcuaro fishermen in action flipping their enormous butterfly nets to catch *pescado blanco*, a transparent white fish that is a Patzcuaro specialty. You can try the fish fried in batter or grilled at any of Janitzio's numerous restaurants for half the price on to that the mainland, and with a more picturesque view to boot, looking out

Enchanting little Purepechan Indian villages are scattered around Lake Patzcuaro, most of them practising ancient handicraft traditions introduced since the days of Quiroga.

Among the more popular villages is one with a delightfully sounding name that trips off your tongue – **Tzintzuntzan**, the "Place of Humming-

Mural in a 16th century monastery in Tzintzuntzan.

birds" in the Purepeche dialect. Tzintzuntzan was for some time the capital of the Purepeche kingdom, which at the height of its power built Las Yacatecas, a series of ceremonial pyramid temples that have recently been restored and may be visited. Tzintzuntzan also served as a religious base for Quiroga, when he was first made Bishop of Michoacán, before being moved to Patzcuaro in 1540.

Today, the 3,000 inhabitants of Tzintzuntzan have established a reputation for making carved furniture, handpainted ceramics and straw figurines. Across from the main village square where most of the craft shops are concentrated is the **Templo de San Francisco** on whose grounds are some

Natives of Michoacan.

Bustamente animal sculpture.

gnarled olive trees that were said to have been planted by Quiroga.

South of Tzintzuntzan, in the former 16th-century copper mining center of **Santa Clara del Cobre**, scores of ateliers turn out wonderfully handcrafted copper pitchers, pots, urns and other kitchen utensils and decorative items. And 10 km (6 miles) north east of Tzintzuntzan in the bigger town of Quiroga that takes its name from the humanitarian priest, you can shop for lacquerware, leather craft, *serapes* and woollen sweaters.

Uruapan

West of Morelia and an hour's drive away is **Uruapan**, the salad bowl of Michoacán. Blessed with fertile soils and ample rainfall that make it one of Michoacán's – and Mexico's – richest agricultural areas, cool, temperate Uruapan at 1,711m (5,613 ft) high, aptly means "place of eternal spring" in the local Purepeche dialect. Although a profusion of flowers, fruits and trees is grown here – among them, orchids, lemons, strawberries, pine and cedar – Uruapan's specialty are avocadoes of which it produces nearly half of the world's output each year.

Your impression of Uruapan, with a population of 200,000, and its surroundings is one of verdant greenery everywhere you turn, the result of its well watered location on the east bank

Tzintzuntzan pottery.

of the Rio Cupatitzio.

Indeed, the town houses a unique national park (Parque Nacional Eduardo Ruiz) where the Rio Cupatitzio begins. The forested park has several waterfalls gushing out from underground springs creating many pools in which it's possible to swim. Popular with Uruapan families especially on weekends, the national park is ideal for picnicking and nature walks and is open daily from 8 am-6 pm, with an entrance fee of N$10.

More and grander waterfalls may be seen at **Tzararacua**, 10 km (6 miles) from Uruapan. Jets of water from the Rio Cupatitzio plunge 27 m (90 ft) into a pool of water in a park- like area of trees and flowers. Apart from some churches containing valuable cane figures made

by the Purepeche Indians, such as the 16th-century **La Magdalene Chapel**, Uruapan is a craft town famous for its hand painted lacquerware. The **Museo Regional Huatapera**, used originally as a hospital when it was completed in 1533, showcases Michoacán and other Purepeche handicrafts that are also available in Uruapan. The museum opens from Tuesday - Sunday, 9.30 am - 1.30 pm and 3.30 pm - 6 pm)

If you are energetic and enjoy adventure, make a memorable sidetrip from Uruapan to the Paricutin volcano which made its appearance under mysterious circumstances only 50 years ago. The 2,824 m (9,266 ft) high volcano is accessible from the Purepeche village of **Angahuan**.

Waterfall in Parque Nacional Eduardo Ruiz in Uruapan.

Guanajuato, better known as the Bajío, is made up of two states – Guanajuato and Queretaro. Set at least 304 m (1000 ft) high on Mexico's central plateau north of the volcanic corridor, the Bajío harbored rich deposits of silver, gold, iron, lead and zinc which accounted for much of the region's prosperity. It is also blessed with fertile soil conducive to growing wheat, corn and fruit trees. But the Bajío is more than just a grain belt and mining center; it is fondly referred to as the cradle of independence for it was here, nearly two centuries ago, that the struggle to break away from ruling Spain was born.

The movement owes its success to four splendid colonial cities which today still stand out above the rest in the land – Guanajuato, San Miguel de Allende, Dolores Hidalgo (all in Guana-juato state), and Quere-taro.

Courtyard of a colonial-style restaurant in Queretaro.

The Bajío

211

Guanajuato

Guanajuato is a city that takes the breath away.

Perched 2,029 m (6,656 ft) high in the middle of a dry, rocky valley on the edge of a ravine surrounded by mountains that form a dramatic backdrop, your first impression, from a distance, is that of a mirage especially after having travelled across a bare, almost inhospitable landscape to get there. The craggy terrain prompts you to wonder: how could a city be carved out of such land? The Tarascan Indians must have had the same thought for they named it Guanaxhuato after the wild frogs that inhabited the area.

The answer, however, lies underground, for beneath Guanajuato were incredibly thick veins of silver that made the city one of the world's biggest pro-

ducers of the shining ore. With the money, the silver barons could tame the rugged territory, honing out of the peaks and hills a city filled with magnificent churches and colonial houses. The result is a bit of a jagged jigsaw puzzle of a city where streets suddenly disappear into tunnels, then re-surface, and where some lanes are so narrow that the inhabitants of houses can literally reach out to one another.

Indeed, on one such lane – the city's narrowest – romantically called the Callejone del Beso (Street of the Kiss) two lovers, so the story goes, were able to exchange kisses and conduct their courtship across their almost-touching balconies despite the disapproval of their families over their relationship.

The jumble of underground passages, narrow alleys and steep streets gives the city a delightful touch albeit in a chaotic sort of way – a nice contrast to the more staid charm of the other colonial cites in the Bajío.

Guanajuato, with a population of 75,000, is the capital of the state of the same name. It earned its place in history as the country's "cradle of independence" for it was here that the first stirrings and agitation of independence from Spain began. The first wave of settlers to Guanajuato was triggered by the discovery of silver in 1548. The deposits were so abundant that Guanajuato contributed nearly a third of the world's silver for the next 200 years.

Despite its wealth, all was not well in Guanajuato as most of the silver barons reaping the riches were Spanish-born. They luxuriated in their fine mansions whilst the Indians slaved in the mines for a pittance.

The fountainhead of resentment was a growing, affluent and influential criollo (creole) class made up of Mexican-born Spanish landowners and some miners, in Guanajuato and neighboring Queretaro. Not only did they dislike the overbearing, arrogant Spanish, but they also felt that it was time that Mexicans ruled themselves.

Hostility against these colonial overlords came to a head in 1808 when Napoleon invaded and occupied Spain. Mexico was thrown into a state of political confusion. Taking advantage of the situation, the independence movement group felt the time was ripe to strike. A series of meetings disguised as literary discussions took place and plans were drawn up for rebellion.

Somehow, the authorities got wind of the group's activities and a meeting on 13 September 1810, in a house belonging to a member, Miguel Dominguez, was broken up. Despite the setback the group pressed on and three days later, in Dolores, a parish priest and the leader of the dissident group, Miguel Hidalgo, defiantly shouted out his now famous "Grito" or cry of independence, rallying the rebels together for the attack. Dolores was the first to fall in the revolt; other towns in Guanajuato followed suit as one by one they also succumbed – San Miguel de Allende, Celaya, then Guanajuato.

Go on a thrilling, scenic tour of Guanajuato by the local bus as it travels on the city's main streets which dip into dark subterranean passages, then emerge above ground, affording glimpses of well-preserved antiquated buildings and leafy parks.

Romanesque facade of Teatro Juarez.

These underground passages were built when the Guanajuato River – the cause of the city's flooding problems in the past – was drained and covered. It's not an exaggeration to say that the tour may come across as a bit of a roller-coaster ride. Because of the confusion of interlocking streets, do not drive here.

In any case, it's easy to move around Guanajuato on foot if you make a point of staying near the city center around the main square, **Jardin de la Union**. The Jardin is the place to be in the evenings when musicians come out to play or sing, and performers to dance. You can sit out on the terrace of a restaurant to take it all in while dining or enjoying a drink.

Opposite the Jardin is the **Teatro**

Juarez sporting a Romanesque facade on the outside and a distinctly Moorish design inside. Next to the theater is the **Church of San Diego** boasting a Churrigueresque exterior.

Two blocks west of the Jardin along Obregon is the ocher-colored **Basilica de Nuestra Senora de Guanajuato**, fronting the Plaza de la Paz. The Basilica's simple exterior might disappoint but its stunning interior definitely won't. The jewel to be seen here is the beautifully wood-crafted image of Nuestra Senora de Guanajuato, the city's patroness, mounted, appropriately, on a silver base – a gift from King Philip II to Guanajuato in gratitude for the city's contributions to Spanish coffers.

Walk behind the Basilica along

Guanajuato has narrow, winding streets.

Aguilar till you reach the corner where it intersects with Positos. Here rises the splendid **La Campania**, completed for the Jesuit order in 1765 and noted for its dome and an Aztec sun painted in the middle of it, to woo Indians into the church. La Compania is next to the University of Guanajuato whose youthful population adds to the city's zest.

Farther west along Positos is the house where Diego Rivera was born and where a collection of his works is on display. Four blocks west of Rivera's museum on the other side of Positos is perhaps Guanajuato's most important historical attraction – the **Alhondiga de Granadita** or Granary, turned fortress, prison and now a museum.

The massive structure, completed in 1808, took a decade to build and its solidness was the reason why the Spanish, hounded by Miguel Hidalgo and his rebels, chose to hold out here. The Alhondiga was in fact the last place to surrender to the rebel troops in the War of Independence.

It was a spectacular surrender. On 28 September, 1810, while 20,000 rebels besieged the fortress, an Indian miner known as El Pipila stormed the door of the Alhondiga and set it on fire, allowing the rebels to rush in to slaughter the Spanish soldiers and royalists hiding there. But, a year later, the Spanish captured the rebel leaders in Chihuahua. Four of them – Hidalgo, Allende, Jimenez and Aldama – had their heads cut off and these were hung in cages in barbaric display on the four corners of

A room in Diego Rivera's house.

the Alhondiga for 10 years. The Alhondiga served as a prison for 100 years before it was turned into a museum in 1967. Exhibits on display, including some murals by Chavez Morado, trace Guanajuato's history.

To best appreciate the spread of Guanajuato and its topography, take a scenic ride by bus from Hotel Central behind the Alhondiga on Juarez up the Carretera Panoramica to **Hormiguera Hill** where the Pipila monument stands. Dedicated to the miner who set the Alhondiga ablaze, you get quite a view of Guanajuato from here, you can also climb up inside the statue (N$1) for an even loftier vista.

Return to the city center on foot, down a cobblestone alleyway (leading

Courtyard in a San Miguel De Allende house.

from the statue) that winds past picturesque houses perched on the hilly slopes.
The walk takes you back to Calle Sopena
facing the Jardin de la Union.

Dolores Hidalgo

Lying almost equidistant between
Guanajuato and San Miguel is the attractive town of **Dolores Hidalgo**. Originally named Dolores, the name Hidalgo
was added in 1824 in honor of Mexico's
father of independence, Miguel Hidalgo,
who declared war on Spain here with his
"Grito de Dolores".

The rather quiet town of only 40,000,
but the town has a provincial air about
it, bursts into revelry every year on 15

and 16 September, to celebrate Independence Day.

A pretty flower-filled main square,
the Jardin, with its statue of Hidalgo,
dominates. Huddled around it, are rows
of restaurants, a tourist office and municipal office, cafes and banks.

The main reason for coming here
for most visitors – including Mexico's
presidents who turn up on each anniversary of the war to repeat Hidalgo's
proclamation – is to see the church where
he made his cry before his congregation
and to visit the house where he lived.
Another is to shop for the floral-pat-
terned blue-and-white pottery for which
Dolores has long been famous. The
church where Hidalgo preached and
uttered his cry is the impressive

Parroquia de Nuestra Senora de Dolores with its towering pink twin spires. It flanks the Jardin on the north and is adjacent to the tourist office. Its interior is noted for its beautiful baroque altars.

Hidalgo's home, the **Museo Casa Hidalgo**, is a graceful building at the corner of Morelos and Hidalgo streets, one block southwest of the Jardin. The house, lovingly tended to like a shrine, contains Hidalgo's personal memorabilia as well as documents tracing the history of the independence movement. It is open from Tuesday-Saturday, 10 am-6 pm, and Sunday 10 am-5 pm.

San Miguel De Allende

Magnificent churrigueresque facade of Church of San Francisco.

Lively, elegant **San Miguel De Allende** is a museum-piece of a colonial town with a population of 50,000. Set at an altitude of over 1,829 m (6,000 ft), its salubrious climate and charming ambience have made it a magnet for a growing resident community of North Americans. It's easy to see why when you wander about the city, soaking up its somewhat arty atmosphere.

No one is in a hurry here. There are art galleries and churches to visit, arts and crafts shops to browse in and walks to enjoy in the surrounding countryside.

It was precisely this leisurely lifestyle that first drew artists and writers to settle down here. Their presence spawned the development of art schools and colleges. For a while, a bohemian atmos-

phere prevailed. Then young foreigners came to study Spanish, drawn by San Miguel's reputation as a trendy artists' colony and language schools soon sprouted. There's now a distinct cosmopolitan air that reigns over the city.

Founded as San Miguel in 1542, de Allende was added in memory of the city's most illustrious son, Ignacio Allende who joined Miguel Hidalgo's independence cause.

A statue of the sword-wielding Allende on horseback occupies pride of place in one of the city's plazas named after him – **Plaza Ignacio Allende**.

The plaza, newly tiled over and made into a little park, is the site of three ancient churches – the Templos de la Salud, Loreto and Oratorio de San Felipe

Neri. **La Salud** boasts a churrigueresque exterior with a carved figure of La Immaculada, the Immaculate Virgin surrounded by saints. The church is topped with a blue and yellow tiled dome. The chapel of **Loreto** is part of the bigger Oratorio de San Felipe Neri next door. Patterned after a chapel in Italy's Loreto where the Virgin Mary was said to have lived, there is a main altar with a glass-enclosed image of the Virgin. While tiles from Spain, China and Puebla decorate the floors and walls.

The chapel, however, is eclipsed by its bigger and grander neighbor, **San Felipe Neri**, with its many towers and domes. The 18th-century church has Indian touches in its architecture, in its baroque facade for instance and Indian-style doorway. The life of San Felipe Neri, who founded the Oratorio Catholic order in the 16th century is depicted in a series of oil paintings within the church. Behind Plaza Allende is the **San Francisco Church** on the corner of San Francisco and Juarez streets, bordering on a small park. It is noted for its 18th-century Churrigueresque facade and the image of St Francis of Assisi at the top. On the edge of the park is a statue of Christopher Columbus.

There always seems to be a festive air about San Miguel especially around the leafy square of **El Jardin**, the town's zocalo, one block west of San Francisco Church. Locals and tourists hang out on the benches of El Jardin by day and night, to chat and gossip, to hear *mariachi* bands playing in the garden's musical

kiosk, to eat at the roadside stalls dotted around the plaza or even to have their shoes shined.

Rising majestically above El Jardin on Calle Umaran just opposite is the spectacular **Parroquia** or Cathedral, its handsome mock-Gothic spire soaring towards the sky. It's San Miguel's major landmark and it is visible for miles around. If you have the feeling that it also looks somehow like a French cathedral, you are right. La Parroquia was designed in the 19th century by an Indian mastermason, Zeferino Gutierrez, who took his inspiration from postcards of French Gothic cathedrals.

Also on Umaran, 100 yards on La Parroquia's left, is the house where Ignacio Allende was born. Now a museum, the **Museo Historico de San Miguel de Allende** documents the history of San Miguel, the life of Allende and the independence movement.

Take a walk on streets leading off from the Parroquia and the Jardin and you will see some of the best of San Miguel's colonial architecture reflected in the *posadas*, restaurants, art galleries and government buildings. They all sport the same look: laced iron-grille balconies and windows and pastel-colored walls exteriors, with spacious open-air garden courtyards within.

Don't miss the art galleries or arts and crafts shops housed in fine buildings that usually enclose a courtyard cafe. The pottery, brasswork, silver jewelry and weavings are of excellent quality. The prices are high but at least

Miguel Hidalgo

Mural of Miguel Hidalgo.

priest of the local church. He became very active in the community. He promoted the arts by setting up a music band and he introduced the making of crafts such as tiles and pottery for which Dolores is famous today. He also taught the community to produce silk and grow grapes to make wine. Hidalgo won many hearts for his work and it was this popularity, particularly among the Indians and the *mestizos*, that was an important factor in the success of his campaign for independence. He was only drawn to the cause for independence after meeting with Ignacio Allende (after whom San Miguel was named). But once he was fired up, he lost no time to agitate for freedom from the Spanish. He became leader of the independence movement and plotted the moves that led to his uttering the cry of independence in Dolores.

This brought him under the Inquisition again and caused him to be excommunicated on 13 October 1810, but Hidalgo was not to be cowed. He charged the Spanish for not being true Catholics themselves as they had exploited and pillaged Mexico shamelessly. On 19 October, Hidalgo signed a decree putting an end to slavery in Mexico. Hidalgo organized more forces in the north, moving as far as Zacatecas and Chihuahua. Hidalgo placed a former student of his, Jose Maria Morelos y Pavon, to gather support in the south.

But alas, Hidalgo was finally captured and shot dead on 30 July, 1811 in Chihuahua. His head was brought back to Guanajuato where he had claimed his first victory over the Spanish. For ten years, the head was hung in a cage on one corner of the Alhondiga along with the heads of three other comrades in arms – Allende, Aldama and Jimenez – which were hung on the other corners. Hidalgo, however, did not die in vain. The gruesome display of heads, intended by the Spanish as a warning to others, in fact kept alive Hidalgo's vision for a free Mexico and spurred others to finally achieve it in 1821.

Miguel Hidalgo was born on 8 May, 1753, in Guanajuato. His parents were *criollo* (creoles), that is, Mexicans of pure Spanish descent. Hidalgo studied at the Colegio de San Nicolas Obispo in Valladolid, which was renamed Morelia, and after he was ordained a priest in 1778, he taught at the same college where he was later appointed rector. Hidalgo was a rather unconventional padre, who questioned the infallibility of the Pope and did things such as gambling, reading banned books and keeping a mistress.

He was brought before the Inquisition in 1800. Although nothing was proved against him, he was transferred in 1804 to Dolores, as

you are sure you are not getting duds. And nothing can be more pleasant than taking a break from shopping to sip coffee or have lunch in the shady court-

yard in full view of a church tower.

The language schools and art colleges are in the southwestern part of the city from the Jardin. Many of the language schools, like the Instituto Allende, are housed in colonial buildings that reek with atmosphere.

Las Bellas Artes, a five minute walk west of the zocalo, is the city's most famous art college for it was here that muralist David Sequeiros was enrolled. While it's possible to take up short art courses, Spanish-language enrollment requires a minimum of a month. It's an immersion program involving a stay with a family, cultural activities and excursions to nearby places of interest.

There are a number of markets in San Miguel and you can pick up a wide range of handicrafts. There are woollen *serapes*, bags, rugs, ponchos and even Guatemalan crafts.

San Miguel is lively in the evenings too. The problem is deciding where to go as many restaurants, cafe-bars and pubs offer music and ambience. String combos strumming Latin-American songs and Andean-style bands playing pan-pipes and flutes comprise the main fare. As for food, you will notice that seafood is popular here although San Miguel is nowhere near the coast.

Take a stroll out to the "suburbs" of San Miguel encircling the city. Its narrow steep streets are lined with colonial houses and hotels, painted in pink and white. On some street corners, old ornate fountains stand. Occasionally, you may pass by pack donkeys led by an Indian on his way back to a village.

From here or at the edge of the city at a spot called **Trece Cruces** (Thirteen Crosses) there is a clear view of San Miguel, its skyline of church steeples glistening in the sunshine. Gazing upon the city at your feet, you realize how well deserved is San Miguel's status as a national monument. Long may it remain that way.

Less than a 30-minute drive or bus ride from San Miguel en route to Dolores Hidalgo are a couple of hot springs at **Taboada**. The pools' naturally-heated mineral waters are healthy for the skin and they provide a welcome soak if you are here in the cool mornings.

Queretaro

Queretaro is an attractive city steeped in history and political intrigue. Its skyline of church spires and glittering tiled domes, pleasant open air garden plazas and pastel-colored colonial buildings lend a touch of old-world charm.

In the old city center, a stroll in the *andadores* or pedestrian alleys flanked by houses with iron-laced balconies and windows overflowing with flowers gives you a feeling of having stepped back in time to perhaps the early 19th century when Queretaro was at the center of one of Mexico's turning points in history.

The city played a crucial part in the War of Independence for it was from here that word reached Miguel Hidalgo and his rebels that their plan to overthrow the Spanish yoke had already been found out-resulting in his hasty delivery of the "*Grito*" on 16 September, 1810, in Dolores.

Statue of La Corregidora, Queretaro.

The person who gave the word was Dona Josefa Ortiz, known as La Corregidora for she was the wife of El Corregidor, the mayor. It was at their house that Miguel Hidalgo and his rebels often met to plot their revolt.

When their conspiracy was discovered, launching a hunt for the rebels, the mayor locked his wife in a room where she managed to whisper through a keyhole about the impending fate awaiting the rebels to a sympathizer who sped off to inform Hidalgo.

Since then, Queretaro, the capital of Queretaro state, vies with Guanajuato for the title of Cunha de Independencia (Cradle of Independence). In 1848, Queretaro was the venue for the signing of the Treaty of Guadalupe which gave over half of Mexico to the United States as a prize of the latter's victory in war.

It was also here that Emperor Maximilian gave in to Benito Juarez's forces in defeat. His trial was held at the **Teatro de la Republica** in the city center and he was ordered to be shot on the outskirts at **Cerro de las Campanas** or Hill of Bells (now a park) on 19 June, 1867. A chapel was built on the spot where Maximilian fell but it is eclipsed by a giant statue of Benito Juarez.

Queretaro's pivotal role in politics continued into the 20th century. Mexico's Constitution was drawn up and signed here in 1917. And the country's ruling Institutional Revolutionary Party (PRI) saw it fit to mark its formation in Queretaro in 1929.

Before the Spanish arrival, Queretaro was settled by the Otomi Indian tribes in 1446 and was later absorbed into the Aztec empire. But it was the occupation of the city by the Spanish who came in 1531 that gave Queretaro its distinctive stamp that is still seen today.

Queretaro has a population of just under half a million and it enjoys a mild climate thanks to its altitude of 1,842 m (6,042 ft). It has clean streets, few tourists and no gringo community, making it a very pleasant – and truly Mexican – city to visit.

At the center of Queretaro is **Jardin Obregon**, a spacious square filled with plants and benches where locals sit out on Thursday and Sunday evenings to hear band concerts and at other times simply to relax. Overlooking the Jardin Obregon is the **Church of San Francisco** with its attractive dome made up of tiles brought in from Spain in 1540.

Five minutes southwest of Jardin Obregon is the **Church of Santa Clara** fronted by the Neptune Fountain which boasts a breathtaking Baroque interior that contrasts sharply with its 1797 neo-Classical design by Francisco Eduardo Tresguerras, Mexico's best known architect. Also sporting a tiled dome but sited away from the center is the **Church of Santa Cruz** on Independencia, a 15 minute walk east of Jardin Obregon.

The monastery next to the church, the **Convento de la Santa Cruz**, was embroiled in many of Queretaro's historical events. During the War of Inde-

pendence, Spanish troops used it as a hiding place. For four months in 1867, before he surrendered, Maximilian turned the Convento into his military headquarters and after he was tried, he was held here before being shot.

One of the most remarkable miracles associated with the Convento is the growth of a tree from a stick planted into the ground by a friar in 1697. The thorns on the branches of the tree resemble crucifixes and the tree is said to be the only one of its kind in the world. Now there are more trees in the courtyard where the first one grew and visitors are allowed to wander into the monastery to have a look at them. The convento is open Monday-Friday, 9 am-2 pm and 4 pm-6 pm, and Saturday and Sunday, 11 am-6 pm.

La Corregidora is fondly remembered by Queretaro. The main street in the city is named after her and her statue stands prominently in the **Plaza de la Corregidora** diagonally opposite Jardin Obregon. Just a stroll away from her statue is La Corregidora's former house, now the **Palacio de Gobierno**, on Plaza de la Independencia, in which the room where she was locked is now used as a conference hall. The Palacio is open daily, from 7 am-9 pm.

Queretaro has two fine museums, both converted Conventos. The **Museo Regional** occupies the former monastery of the Church of San Francisco next door. Its wide range of exhibits covers the entire gamut of Mexican history from the prehistoric, colonial, independ-

An aqueduct in Queretaro.

ence and imperial eras to the revolution and post-revolutionary periods. It is open Wednesday-Saturday, 10 am-6 pm, Tuesday and Sunday, 10 am-3.30 pm.

The exterior architecture of the **Museo de Arte de Queretaro** (the former San Augustin Convento one block south of Santa Clara Church) has a rich Baroque facade studded with angels and gargoyles. Learn more about the architecture of the ex-Convento and 16th and 17th-century European and 19th-century Mexican paintings by browsing inside the museum.

Queretaro's amazing aqueduct still brings in water to the city 248 years after it was built. The impressive 28-m (93-ft) high arches number 74 in all and took the Spanish a good nine years to com-

plete. You can get a better idea of this piece of Spanish engineering marvel by strolling down **Calzada Zaragoza** where the aqueduct stands (a five-minute walk east of the Santa Cruz convent). A lookout at the beginning of Zaragoza gives you an overall perspective of the aqueduct. Facing the lookout is a square containing the tombs of La Corregidora and her husband. Behind the tombs is a shrine to the couple.

When in Queretaro, don't forget to try the famous sorbets of Neveria Galy at 5 de Mayo 8, off Jardin Obregon, especially the *nieve limon*, made from lemon juice and local red wine. If shopping for gems is on your list, Queretaro is the place to find good quality opals, amethyst, topaz and onyx.

The Gulf Coast

The Gulf Coast states of Veracruz and Tabasco present a distinct face. Tropical and swampy, low-lying and humid, intensively farmed, punctuated with big ports and massive oil industry installations, they are populated by lively, extrovert people whose demeanour is quite a contrast to that of the circumspect citizens of the plateau or the taciturn inhabitants of the Indian highlands. This is apparently nothing new: the puritanical Aztecs regarded their coastal contemporaries as licentious.

Local boy with a hefty catch.

This vivacity is as it should be, since for many years this coast was Mexico's welcome to the world – until the advent of air travel and superhighways. Being the coastal region closest to the capital and facing North America and Europe, it received Mexico's visitors through the port of Veracruz. By the same token, and by its low-lying topography, this was also Mexico's vulnerable flank, the place where Spanish, French and American invaders landed.

225

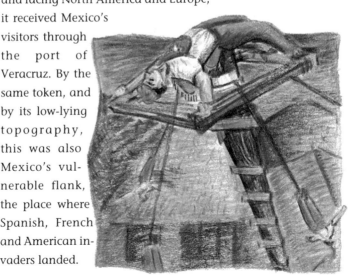

Remnants of ancient civilizations.

It was Cortes who established the first Spanish foothold at Villa Rica de la Vera Cruz which became today's great port of Veracruz. In this region, the Olmecs created the first high civilization of ancient Mexico and left mysterious massive stone heads. Later the Totonacs built upon Olmec culture and some 180,000 of this Indian people survive today. They are famed for their Voladores (see box) and the Pyramid of the Niches at El Tajin.

Today's Veracruz and Tabasco states are highly productive. Oil is king in this region, for most of Mexico's massive reserves are found offshore in the Bay of Campeche or onshore in southern Veracruz and Tabasco. Industrial development has been rapid and extensive in this area since these huge oilfields were discovered in the early 1970s, with refining and processing centered on the cities of Coatzacoalcos and Minatitlan.

Then there's agriculture. With both fertile, well-watered lowlands and cool highlands, Veracruz is a leading producer of a wide range of crops including sugarcane, potatoes, beans, chilli peppers, pineapples, oranges, vanilla, coffee, corn and cocoa.

Since 60 percent of Tabasco is made up of lagoons, swamps and rivers, and it gets rather more rain than it would wish – like 5 meters (16 ft) annually in some places – the state is quite happy to have found black gold for its living in addition to cocoa farming, cattle ranching and fishing.

Voladores

The flying Voladores.

Without doubt the most dramatic and most bizarre of Mexican folk traditions is the *The Dance of Those Who Fly*. Originated by the Totonac Indians of Veracruz, it has achieved international fame due to daily performances in tourist resorts like Acapulco, but this strange phenomenon is properly not a circus act at all but a solemn religious rite dating back well over a millennium. Despite that, the fliers – *Voladores* in Spanish – have today become little more than a money-earning spectacle even in the Totonac heartland at Papantla and El Tajin, where visitors thrill at their acrobatic antics.

In white blouses and scarlet pantaloons, with flimsy tasselled helmets on their heads, five men climb up a 20-m (66 ft) high pole. Reaching the small platform on top, four of them attach a rope to their waist and sit to face the fifth who dances, beats a drum, and plays a *puscol* (wooden flute) upon the poletop a little higher.

Suddenly, at his signal, the four roped men launch themselves backwards, fling out their arms, and begin rotating round the pole as if flying. Like figures in an aerial merry-go-round, they make 13 hair-raising revolutions as their ropes unwind from the pole-top, until they near the ground, at which time they jerk themselves upright and land on their feet.

What's it all about? Opinions vary widely, since the rite spread all over Mexico and changed its meaning with each location, arisen a compendium of beliefs has. Take your pick.

The man on top represents the Sun, the pole is the Tree of Life, the fliers are the four elements of Earth, Fire, Air and Water. Four men circle 13 times, which makes 52 revolutions, the same number as the planet makes around the sun to complete a sacred "century" in the old Mesoamerican calendar.

It's a fertility rite in which the birdmen invoke the four corners of the universe as they fly round and bring sun and rain down to earth when they land. The fliers are reborn warriors and sacrificial victims who pay homage to the gods in the heavens and plead for the sun's blessing. The *Valadores'* hovering between heaven and earth is a symbol of harmony between man and gods.

Traditionally the Totonacs performed the rite on St Francis's Day. A tree was ceremonially chosen, cut down and made into a pole. Pole and dancers were blessed at a church.

With a mixture of Christian and pre-Hispanic ritual blessing, most notably by the placing of a live turkey into the pole hole to be ritually sacrificed by crushing, the pole was set up before the church. Today the chief celebrations at Papantla occur during the Corpus Christi festival each June.

Regular performances take place in the town of Papantla and at El Tajin next to the Pyramid of the Niches. They tend to occur around midday, or whenever enough people have gathered to make it a paying proposition. A collection is taken from the crowd afterwards, when everyone is suitably awed and satisfied. For the fliers, it's a job these days. The Papantla men are formed into several groups which also tour and ply for hire, and they even have a trade union.

Carved helmeted giant Olmec head – ancient rulers, warriors or ballplayers?

Northern Veracruz state is characterised by farmlands, oilfields, beaches and Totonac culture. Oil was discovered at Poza Rica ("Rich Well") in 1930, propelling a new industrial city, but its extraction has little affected the peaceful character of the coast around Tuxpan, where miles of white sand beaches entertain local people, or nobody at all.

Tuxpan is a pleasant fishing town which has a museum of Totonac and Huastec artifacts and a Mexico-Cuba Friendship Museum resulting from Fidel

Castro's sojourn here in 1956 while planning the Cuban Revolution.

The major attraction in the north is the civilisation of the Totonacs, a people who have populated this area for at least 1,500 years and were the first Indians that Cortes encountered upon landing. Their most important archeological site is at El Tajin, near Poza Rica, where the Pyramid of the Niches rises. This temple structure is unique in form. Square-based, composed of seven tiers which rise to a height of 25 m (82 ft), it is honeycombed with 365 large square niches, one for each day of the year.

This temple is the major monument uncovered of the Gulf Coast Classic Period which extended from AD 600 to AD 1200. Stumbled upon in 1785 by a Spanish official and cleared a few decades ago, the site underwent extensive excavations in the early 1990s.

El Tajin

El Tajin was one of the most important regional capitals of the Classic Period, and was influenced by its Olmec predecessors in the same area and its Teotihuacan contemporaries on the plateau nearby.

The Totonac urban center spreads over 10 sq km (45 sq miles) and contains more than a hundred mounds, some on a flat site, others upon an acropolis, and it is only partly excavated.

The Pyramid of the Niches was the most obvious relic when the site was discovered in dense jungle. The niches are reckoned to be altars in which offerings were made.

There are also numerous ball courts at El Tajin, the most outstanding being the **South Ball Court**, which is adorned with splendid carved reliefs showing ball game players and the attendant human sacrifice. Scholars think that the ball game originated here, and the fact that at least eleven courts have been found at El Tajin is convincing support for the theory.

In its late phase, the site came under Toltec influence, when those people were the dominant force on the plateau. It was shattered by barbarian invasion around AD 1200 and abandoned.

The Totonacs were farmers and traders, much given to floral decoration and phallic fertility rites. They were eventually defeated by the Aztecs who coveted the produce of their tropical lands. The Totonacs were forced to pay heavy tribute in quetzal feathers and jaguar skins, such that when Cortes stepped onto their lands, they soon allied with the Spanish against the Aztec oppressor. For this they received preferential treatment in the early colonial days which helped them survive as a culture better than many other ancient peoples.

Papantla

Papantla, "place of birds", is today's Totonac center, a market town surrounded by vanilla growing estates, very

The Olmecs

Inseparable from the image of the Gulf Coast states of Veracruz and Tabasco are the great stone heads left by the Olmecs. Carved out of basalt, varying in size up to 3 m (10ft) high and almost equally broad, each with distinct and somewhat negroid features, all of them helmeted, they are both the motif of the region and something of a mystery. Who do they represent? What was their purpose? How did they get there?

We do know a fair amount about the Olmecs though, and research regularly uncovers more. They were the first major civilisation of Mesoamerica, emerging well over three millennia ago and reaching their height between 1200 and 400 BC.

The Olmec world holds a special place in the sweep of cultures that rose and fell in Mexico before the Spanish conquest. Because of their early achievements in art, politics, religion, science and economics, the Olmecs stand as a "mother culture" to all the civilisations that came after.

Towards the end of the second millennium BC in southern Veracruz, the typical Mesoamerican society of small village life gave way to a stratified society of city states with ceremonial centers, adorned with pyramids and palaces, built around plazas tiled with mosaics. Where petty chiefs had claimed obedience,

kings now held sway, attended by richly clad warriors and courtiers; their political organisation and technical capability were such as to enable the building of great stone monuments; fine sculpture and mural painting took the place of cottage crafts. Instead of shamanism, high priests governed elaborate rituals and constituted an intelligentsia; they recorded the motion of the stars, studied the mysteries of time and space, gaining an esoteric knowledge that raised them above other mortals.

The Olmecs also practised ritual sacrifice, played a ceremonial ball game, and invented glyphic writing. All these things laid the pattern for all subsequent Mesoamerican civilisations, from the Mayas to the Aztecs. In confirmation of their widespread influence, Olmec relics have been found throughout Mesoamerica.

Artists of Excellence

As artists, the Olmecs excelled in making exquisite figurines, carved out of basalt, serpentine and jade or moulded from clay. The figurines were often of supernatural creatures that were part human, part jaguar, reflecting the dominant cult of the jaguar god, probably a facet of the supreme rain deity. Olmec jade sculpture is the finest and most frequently found formed

near Poza Rica and El Tajin. Vanilla beans and figures fashioned out of vanilla pods are sold to visitors. Totonac Indians grace the town in their traditional white cotton, the women in colorfully embroidered blouses. Death-defying *Voladores* (fliers) perform their dare-devil feats, for a fee up a pole in the cathedral close, as they do at El Tajin's ruins [see *Voladores* box].

Forming the zocalo's south wall, the cathedral has a remarkable carved facade depicting Totonac history and

culture. Papantla comes most alive during the Festival of Corpus Christi in June, when the *Voladores'* flight frequency increases dramatically.

Jalapa

Jalapa (or Xalapa) is the capital of Veracruz, a university town of colonial origins lying in the foothills of the Sierra Madre Oriental. Its old streets are charmingly crooked, cobbled and steep, with

into Mesoamerica, often of humanoid figures with enigmatic mask-like faces, or with cat-like features. Olmec artists also made many lively little figures of odd subjects like bald-headed babies and bearded wrestlers, dwarfs and hunchbacks.

On a riverine plain that spreads along the Bay of Campeche, four Olmec centers rose to prominence, enriched by key resources. **San Lorenzo** exploited fine clay for the making of pottery. **La Venta** had rubber, salt and tar. **Laguna de los Cerros** and **Tres Zapotes** controlled the basalt quarries. The name we have given them reflects the prevalence of rubber in their region: Olmec means "Rubber People" in the Nahuatl language of Central Mexico.

As to the great carved, helmeted heads, of which 16 have been found, some scholars interpret the unique monuments as idealised warriors or ballplayers, others see them as stereotyped images of universal ancestors, and still others argue that their individual features indicate portraits of rulers.

Whatever they represent, the broad-nosed, short-faced physiognomy does reflect a physical type of Mesoamerica, and African influence is discounted as highly unlikely. It is theorized that the stones were pulled on sledges and rafted down rivers to get them from the Tuxtla Mountains to their sacred sites.

walled gardens decked in flowers. The newer parts have wide avenues and parks, and the whole town overlooked by craggy peaks.

Jalapa has an excellent Museum of Anthropology concerning the Olmec, Huastec and Totonac cultures of the coastal region. The town's name is immortalised in its world-famous *jalapena* peppers. Mexico's highest mountain, **Pico de Orizaba**, a dormant volcano of 5,760 m, crowns the Sierra to the west of Veracruz city, close to the motorway

from Mexico City and Puebla. A beautiful snow-capped cone, its slopes present little difficulty to experienced climbers, who can follow well-worn trails (access from Tlachichuca) and use rest huts on the climb towards the final icy challenge of a crevasse-creased glacier.

After that, or even if you're just motoring down to Veracruz, a stop at the brewing town of **Orizaba** is requisite. Here you can sample the very fine Dos Equis and Tres Equis beers of the Moctezuma Brewery (guided tours, free drinks). Nearby natural springs account for this industry. A notable oddity is Orizaba's **Palacio Municipal**, a 19th-century cast-iron structure imported from Belgium.

From Orizaba the trunk road descends to the lushness of coffee and sugarcane plantations and the colorful flower-growing district of Fortin de las Flores before rolling across the plain to the sea at Veracruz.

Veracruz

Veracruz is Mexico's premier port, a steamy city of one million inhabitants, lively and fun-loving, which is why *capitalinos* are known to drive all the way down from their austere plateau to the coast just for Saturday night. Once ocean liners eased into the docks in stately manner, but now Veracruz lives largely from cargo traffic and industry, plus tourism. Popular with Mexicans, it's easy to reach from Mexico City and cheaper than Acapulco.

The inhabitants are known as *jarochos*. A convivial bunch, they crowd the city's zocalo nightly, but anytime is a good time to go to the **Plaza de Armas**, which is the heart and soul of Veracruz. Lined by cafes and restaurants within whitewashed colonnades, the square is good for breakfast, lunch or dinner, and offers the best show in town – wonderful for people watching and catching the city's musical kaleidoscope.

It gets especially lively at night when the Municipal Orchestra blare its trumpets. Then the *marimba* men and *mariachis* ply for trade, and the guitar trios belt out Veracruz's most famous song, *La Bamba*, with its seagoing refrain: "*Yo no soy marinero, soy capitan, soy capitan...*" ("I'm not a sailor, I'm a captain, I'm a captain...")

Everybody goes to the Plaza de Armas, as they have been doing ever since it began as the walled heart of the city – conquistadors, pirates, slaves, viceroys, traders, invaders, sailors, tourists. One was Sir Francis Drake, national hero to the English, marauding pirate to the Spanish.

Veracruz used to be the only Gulf port for the Spanish colonial trade with Europe; in the old days Spanish galleons took away silver and gold to the Old World and brought back livestock and luxuries. Today in the zocalo, tourists mingle with the *jarochos* and a myriad of vendors and buskers – lottery ticket sellers, trumpeters, kids hawking chewing gum, guitarists, Indian boys selling hand-rolled cigars, harpists, domino players, shoeshine boys.

Seafood is the first choice at Veracruz – shrimp, octopus, oysters, red snapper. Pass the day over a *cafe con leche*, the fine old La Parroquia tiled cafe, situated just off the zocalo is a Veracruz institution.

The city's premier historical sight is the old fortress of **San Juan de Ulua**, located on an island in the bay. The fort was progressively from the 16th to 18th centuries. What good it ever did is debatable, as a whole series of marauders, invaders and usurpers have entered Mexico via Veracruz, from Drake to Maximilian.

Within the city there's the 16th century **Baluarte de Santiago**, the last remnant of nine forts which used to form part of the city walls. On the zocalo stands the fine old **Palacio Municipal**, with its entire courtyard intact.

Ruins of Zempoala

Immediately to the north of Veracruz lie the Totonac ruins of **Zempoala**, with some partly reconstructed pyramid temples dating from just before the Spanish conquest, when Zempoala was the Totonac capital. Cortes picked up his first allies here after landing nearby. Just to the south of Veracruz begin the beaches, with Mocambo as the leader. These are very popular with less affluent Mexicans who flock down from the capital for holidays and weekends.

Going south from Veracruz, the first touristic site is **Tres Zapotes**, an ancient Olmec ceremonial center with one large basalt head. Next, up in the Tuxtla Mountains from which the Olmecs quarried their basalt, are the old colonial towns of **Santiago Tuxtla** and **San Andres Tuxtla**.

Santiago Tuxtla has the largest Olmec basalt head ever found in its main plaza; the Cobata head, which is 3 m (10 ft) high. San Andres Tuxtla is a pleasant cigar-making town. The scenic attractions of this area are San Martin Volcano and Lake Catemaco which overlook one another.

Temple of Inscriptions at Parque La Venta, Tabasco.

Tabasco

Tabasco has a pretty hot and greasy reputation: Tabasco chilli sauce, swamps, oilfields, and petrochemical industries. Tabasco was prized for its cocoa when the bean was used as money in Mesoamerica and when chocolate was a European luxury food during colonial times. Shaded cocoa groves continue to flourish in Tabasco's watery world. There's not much here for the tourist apart from the Olmec archeological site of **La Venta**, whose most important finds were lugged to the state capital of Villahermosa. Outside this large modern city, at **Parque La Venta**, many splendid Olmec relics are displayed in a beautiful forest park with zoological gardens populated by deer and alligators, including three great basalt heads and other fine sculptures. In town, the **Regional Museum of Anthropology** has a good collection of Olmec and Maya artifacts.

Villahermosa is an affluent and well laid-out city which reflects the region's oil wealth and a commitment to urban excellence, with its broad boulevards, parks and cultural institutions.

North Central Mexico

Highway 15 from Nogales, Arizona on the US border to Tepic is one of the more popular routes travelled by those going south in Mexico by way of car. Covering three states – Sonora, Sinaloa and Nayarit – the highway passes through the forbidding Sonoran desert and agriculturally rich lands of Hermosillo, before descending to the scenic coastal highway bordering the Pacific Ocean offering tempting stops at resorts such as Bahia San Carlos, Mazatlan and San Blas. Each has its own special character and charm.

Barranca Del Cobre as seen from El Divisidero.

Bahia San Carlos, which has been literally invaded by American retirees lured by its warm weather and beautiful beaches, offers good deep sea fishing and diving.

Mazatlan

Mazatlan is a resort on a bigger scale thanks to its striking location on a peninsula that juts out like a finger into the Pacific Ocean.

Waiting for a passenger at Chacahua Lagoon in Puerto Escondido.

Legend has it that Mazatlan was a base for pirates along the Pacific coast who found its coves and inlets perfect hiding places to bury their treasure. It's these same coves that woo sunseekers to Mazatlan today, earning it the rank of 5th most popular destination in Mexico.

Despite increasing tourism, Mazatlan remains an important shrimp port supplying tons of the crustacean to the United States, Canada and Europe. Deep sea fishing is also big business. Indeed, Mazatlan is widely acknowledged as one of the world's most important deep sea fishing capitals.

San Blas, not to be confused with the El Sufragio/San Blas railroad junction, is a fishing village that has started to attract travellers who find its secluded beaches and surrounding jungles filled with exotic bird and plant life an irresistible combination.

Barranca Del Cobre

But, however magnetic these beach destinations may be, they cannot match a natural wonder that for many travellers is the chief reason for wanting to visiting northwest Mexico: the Barranca Del Cobre, a fabulous gorge that cuts across the rugged Sierra Madre Occidental. After rising from the Pacific coast, it dissects the state of Sinaloa in the north and carves out the midriff section of the state of Chihuahua in northcentral Mexico, to end at the cattle ranching center of Chihuahua.

Dubbed Mexico's Grand Canyon, the spectacular **Barranca Del Cobre** (Copper Canyon) is often compared to Arizona's Grand Canyon, but it is four times bigger and 85 m (280 ft) deeper.

The canyon is named after one of the copper mines that used to be mined in the area. The canyon rim itself lies at an average altitude of 2,438 m (8,000 ft) with magnificent gorges plunging down sharply below. The maximum drop is a breathtaking 3,700 m (12,140 ft) from the top of the Mohinara Mountain down to the canyon floor.

The canyon is a lush, fertile terrain dotted with farms, lakes, hotsprings, rivers and pine forests and studded with caves that are the homes of the semi-nomadic Tarahumara Indians. Its climate varies. On the canyon brink, it is temperate with snow in winter, while in the mountains the summits are permanently snow-capped and it is semi-tropical on the canyon floors.

The longest rail bridge through the Copper Canyon.

Train ride through the Copper Canyon

A 644-km (400-mile) rail track from the sugarcane centre of Los Mochis to Chihuahua snakes through the canyon, providing a convenient means of access to many of the villages and towns along the route. **Los Mochis** is situated just south of Bahia San Carlos.

The Chihuahua/Pacifico Railway took 76 years to build and was consid-

ered an engineering marvel when it was completed in 1961. It ploughs through 88 tunnels of the Tarahumara range of the Sierra Madre Occidental, and crosses 37 bridges. The 14-hour train ride is dramatic and deservedly ranks among the world's most scenic rail journeys. But the best way to enjoy the canyon is to stop at one of the points along the rim – Creel is recommended – and stay a few days to trek, go horseback riding, visit the caves of the Tarahumara Indians or simply to relax and take in the beauty of the natural wooded surroundings.

The train leaves Los Mochis at 6 am or Chihuahua at 7 am and takes 14 hours to complete – without delays. Choose to start from Los Mochis if you don't want to miss the best scenery.

Mountain village in the Sierra Madre.

However, the train from Chihuahua tends to pass through this area in the dark if it is delayed. Take the more comfortable and less-prone-to-delays first-class *vistotren* rather than the *mixtotren* which leaves an hour later from both stations, and ask for a seat on the right-hand side for the best views.

A surprisingly good box breakfast is included in your fare (N$70 to Creel). You can buy your ticket a day in advance from the Viajes Flamingo travel agency at Hotel Santa Anita in Los Mochis, or after 5 am on the day of departure from the train station itself.

The train pulls out of Los Mochis just as the sky turns into a pink glow from the slowly rising sun, trundling past flat farming lowlands. The first

stop is **El Surfragio/San Blas**, 48 km (30 miles) away, the junction at which the Chihuahua/Pacific Railway connects with the Pacific Railroad that follows the shoreline of the Gulf of California to the US border.

More lowlands come into view with cacti making frequent appearances. In the marshy areas, flocks of black herons feed while farms begin to stir to life as villagers milk their cows.

La Fuerte

Thirty-two kilometers (20 miles) later, the train calls in at **La Fuerte**, 81 m (264 ft) above sea level to load up more cargo and passengers. La Fuerte was established as a mission station outpost in 1564 and was an important silver mining center. Mule trains carrying bags of silver destined for Spain plied El Camino Real (the Royal Road) that linked this quaint colonial town to **Los Alamos**. The train picks up speed and at the next stop of **Loreto**, 305 m (1,000 ft) high, the climb up the canyon begins in earnest, just three hours after leaving Los Mochis. It is also the start of the most spectacular scenery.

The train crosses the first – and the longest – of its bridges over the Rio Fuerte, then its longest tunnel running along the walls of a forested canyon and shortly after, its highest bridge (close to the Sinaloa/Chihuahua boundary when you have to wind your watch an hour forward). From then on, the canyons soar higher and higher, completely encircling the train as it climbs up the Tarahumara Range.

As you stand in between the carriages looking out of the half-open doors for an unrestricted view into the canyon, you will be able to glimpse boulder strewn riverbeds below the track and the towering craggy cliffs with vertical walls closing in on the canyon and note the sheer drop from the edge of the track to the canyon floor as it crosses the bridges.

The picturesque views pass by so fast and furiously that you have to be quick with your camera to capture the best shots. At times the topography flattens out and pine trees and flower meadows skirting bubbling streams appear. These lush views are all very reminis-

cent of European alpine scenery.

Just before **Temoris**, look out to the left side of the train for a view of a waterfall, then go back to the right side as the train dips into a tunnel to do a 180° loop and you will see the same waterfall again. A vast semi-circular track filled with railway cars appears below as the train slowly clambers up above Temoris.

Bahuichivo is the next stop, a favorite destination for tour groups. The heart of the Barranca Del Cobre can be reached in five hours by truck from Bahuichivo. Two more stops are made at **Cuiteco** and **San Rafael** before the all important **El Divisidero** is reached, where passengers are allowed to disembark for a full view of the Copper Canyon. The panorama of vertically converging gorges is truly awe inspiring. The station is a hubbub of activity with food stalls and Tarahumara Indian women in colorful costumes selling handwoven baskets and pottery.

Fifteen minutes later, the train is on the move again. In another hour, a few minutes after **Pittoreal**, it does a 360° loop and the track which the train has just travelled over appears clearly below. One hour later, eight hours after leaving Los Mochis, the train arrives in Creel, a popular base for excursions into the Copper Canyon.

The only other stop of interest after Creel, before the train completes its run at Chihuahua, is **Cuauhtemoc**, home of the blue-eyed and blond Mennonites. They are a sect of Protestant Germans

Sonora

Arid desert in Sonora.

Sonora is a contradictory place. Mexico's second largest state, it has one of the lowest populations. Formed largely of arid desert and rugged mountains, it is a leading agricultural producer. For centuries neglected and ignored by the capital as a barbaric land, the state provided two presidents who were instrumental in creating modern Mexico: Obregon [1920-24] and Calles [1924-28]. A haunt of outlaws and bandits, it produced Alvaro Obregon who took a leading part in the drafting of the Constitution of 1917, considered the legal bible of the modern Mexican nation.

Sonora is the home of the Yaqui Indians and other tribes who long resisted the white man. The nomadic indians of the north knew the Spaniards as warriors, predators and despoilers of their land.

The daring and persistent Jesuits eventually gained their trust, not without considerable martyrdom, then the fathers had to protect their missions and converts from the Spaniards who sought slave labor. After the 1767 expulsion of the Jesuits, the Yaquis resisted the brutal usurpation of their lands right up to the 1930s, when President Cardenas granted them a large reservation.

Little was easy in Sonora until the coming of irrigation in the mid-20th century. Since the building of a series of dams, the southern wedge of the state has become highly productive in cotton, wheat, soybeans and vegetables.

Recently tourism has made its mark, with coastal resorts like Bahia Kino and Guaymas attracting thousands of US motorhome vacationers. Fishing the Gulf of California has always provided a living.

Sonora's desertscape is most marked in the Desierto de Altar at the head of the Gulf, which is carpeted with sand dunes. In the national park wilderness area around Pinacate Volcano, moonscape takes over – volcanic craters, lava flows and cinder fields. Wildlife abounds in the northern sector: puma, deer, antelope, wild boar, Gila monster, wild sheep, quail, red-tailed eagle. Sonora, is so near the United States, but just so different and wild.

who found their way to Mexico in the 1920s after fleeing to Russia and Canada many years earlier to escape religious persecution in Europe. They have preserved their distinctive way of life and still wear the same black and white costume of their ancestors.

Creel

Creel, poised 2,286 m (7,500 ft) high on the rim of the Barranca Del Cobre, is well positioned for exploratory trips into the canyon. It is a small village of 9,000 people with a strong Indian character, thanks to the presence of a large community of Tarahumara Indians who live in its surroundings. Indeed, many of the colorfully dressed Indians often make an appearance in Creel's zocalo and many of their handicrafts – mainly pottery, baskets and woven belts – may be bought in Creel's stores.

The Tarahumara Mission Store run by Catholic missionaries is recommended as the money made from the sale of handicrafts, photos and books about the Tarahumaras is ploughed back to help them. The store is open daily, 9.30 am-1 pm and 3 pm-6 pm.

Around the zocalo are two churches and the Sala de Arte with an excellent photographic display of Tarahumara Indians and a small exhibit of their crafts. Concerts are occasionally held here. Leading off from the zocalo is the main street flanked with hotels, grocery stores, souvenir shops and pharmacies.

Lumbering has long been Creel's main industry but tourism is catching up and the presence of nine hotels, most of them offering various excursions into the canyon, testifies to this. Venturing into the canyon is the main reason that people come to Creel.

Excursions

Dotted around Creel are lakes, pine forests and beautifully sculpted cliffs which are easily appreciated on a drive along the main highway. A mile from Creel

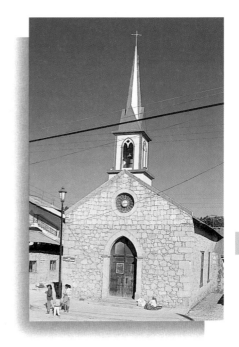

Church in Creel.

241

are the cave homes of the Tarahumara Indians set in the lush countryside park of **Arareko** which they use for pasture. The Indians will open up their homes for visits and photography for a tip of a few pesos. Past the caves are whole stands of grey rock formations each topped with a smaller rock earning the area the name of *Valle de Hongos* (Valley of Mushrooms). Another 8 km (5 miles) along the highway will bring you to **Lake Arareko** surrounded by walls of yet more mushroom-shaped rocks.

Two waterfalls are accessible from Creel, the smaller **Cusarare Falls**, just 23 km (14 miles) away, with a drop of 30 m (100 ft) and the more spectacular **Basaseachic Falls** which have the second highest drop in the world after An-

The Tarahumaras

Tarahumara women and children.

They call themselves Raramuri, "the footrunners", but as with several other native names they could not pronounce, the Spanish corrupted it to Tarahumara.

The Tarahumara Indians have a reputation for being swift runners and on the rim of the Copper Canyon, you sometimes come across Tarahumaras breaking into a run. Long distance running is common among nomadic tribes worldwide as it is often the chief means of getting from one place to another in the absence of other forms of transport. Despite the introduction of the horse and the pickup truck in recent times, many Tarahumaras in remote areas still rely on running to get about. What's more, they can out do a horse easily in the inhospitable terrain.

Apart from running, many ancient customs of the fleet footed Tarahumaras have survived making them one of the most traditional of Mexico's native tribes.

Conjecture has it that they originated from Asia during the Ice Age before the Bering Straits cut the land continents of Asia and America into two. There are some 60,000 Tarahumaras today, living a semi-nomadic existence spread out in the deep canyons and on the rim.

The Tarahumara women wear attractive colorful full skirts and pleated loose blouses, a *koyera* or cloth band wrapped around the forehead and espadrille-style leather sandals or *akaka*. The men's costume is even more distinctive. Taking the place of pants is a *tagora*, a breech cloth that is wrapped around the waist, with the back longer than the front and held together by a wool girdle, a full sleeved shirt, a *koyera* for the head or sometimes a bandana, and *akaka* for the feet.

The Tarahumaras live off the land: when there are no rains, crops fail and they suffer. Thus, ceremonies like rain dances still play an important role in their lives. The Indians, however, still blame crop failure on the Spanish who seized their best lands when they arrived to look for gold. Their dislike and suspicion of the white man, which persists today, led to the Tarahumaras isolating themselves even further. This accounts for the survival of many of their traditions.

Assimiliation into Christianity

The only white men the Tarahumaras did not reject were the Jesuit missionaries who arrived in their midst in 1607. They faced resistance at first because they came at the same time as the conquistadores and were associated with them. However, both the missionaries and the Tarahumaras found they had much in common. The Indians' caring and sharing nature and their respect of the individual were similar to the Christian teachings of the missionaries who established missions throughout the canyon territory to carry out their work.

Before long, the Indians embraced Christianity. They did so with such enthusiasm that despite the expulsion of the Jesuits from Mexico in 1767 on the order of King Charles III of Spain and the closing down of their missions, the Tarahumara still practise many of the religious ceremonies which the Jesuits introduced. However, these were reinterpreted and integrated with native rituals and symbolism.

The result is a rather unique celebration of some Christian events. An example is Holy Week when they stage processions in which pharisees and soldiers take part. Those representing the pharisees are painted white and carry white flags; the soldiers bear red flags.

To the Tarahumaras, the pharisees also symbolize the hated *chabochis* (white men) who came to take their lands. In the dances of the fiesta, the pharisees are shown to be in authority until they are conquered by the soldiers in the classic case of good triumphing over evil.

The pharisees are also represented as the partisans of Judas who appears in their festivities as a straw figure. Dressed like a *chabochi*, he is the target of jeering and meets his fate by being burned or pierced through by arrows. The Tarahumaras complete their Holy Week festivities in church on Holy Saturday with the *pascol* in which they dance, with bells jangling around their ankles, to the music of violins and flutes.

The *pascol* represents the Resurrection. At noon, bells peal and a small bird is released signalling the time for the pharisees to die. They roll on the floor, hitting the straw figure with their wooden swords then get up to run out of the church screaming, knocking down wooden arches which obstruct a cross and tearing decorative feathers on their heads. The death of Judas follows and the fight between the pharisees and the soldiers ensues. For this fiesta and others, the Tarahumaras consume their favorite corn brew called *tesguino*.

Inside a cave home of the Tarahumaras.

Caves in Arareko Park.

gel Falls in Venezuela.

Basaseachic is reached after an extremely bumpy four hour truck ride and a 90-minute walk, but the view of the waterfalls cascading down 246 m (806 ft) into a lake below more than compensates for the arduous journey.

Another highly recommended excursion is a trek to a pool of hot springs on the floor of the **Recohauta Canyon**. The trip starts with a bumpy 90-minute ride through pine forests to the brink of the Recohauta Canyon which offers a majestic view of towering cliffs dropping in a V-shape into Rio Tararecua.

A track takes you in about an hour down 305 m (1,000 ft) to the boulder-strewn river. Loose stones on the path make the walk a little treacherous, so be careful. Another ten-minute scramble over the huge boulders along the river will bring you to the beautiful Recohauta hotsprings. Cascades of hot water gush out into a pool from the side of the canyon creating mini waterfalls beneath which you can stand for a body warming shower in the cool air.

Soaring high above the canyon floor are fantastically shaped cliffs, one shaped like a lioness' head, another like a Saint Bernard, others resembling human figures. What an awesome feeling it is to sit right there on the bottom of the canyon and be dwarfed by the cliffs. Without a doubt, time spent exploring the bowels of the canyon is the best means of appreciating the majestic grandeur of Mexico's canyon country.

Recohauta hot springs.

In pre-Hispanic times, the north of Mexico was the land of the Chichimecs. A semi-nomadic people beyond the pale of civilisation, the chichimecs occasionally attacked and invaded the developed cultures to the south like the Toltecs and Aztecs, much as the barbarian tribes of ancient Northern Europe such as the Huns, Vandals and Goths, attacked the Roman Empire.

The Spanish conquerors paid little heed to the territory, and took two centuries to subdue the Chichimecs.

The northern frontier lands, barren, dry, rocky, sparsely populated and immense, were long neglected by the dominant and distant central region, and became the domain of cattle ranching *caudillos*, bandits, cowboys and rustlers like Pancho Villa.

In this century, the independent spirit of the northerner was the driving force of the Revolution, producing not only Villa but a succession of national leaders: Madero, Carranza,

Largely barren lands of the north east.

247

Silverware is available in many upmarket shops in Monterrey.

Obregon and Calles. Yet the Mexican north, despite its modern industrial development, is still in some ways a barbarous territory, lacking the cultural unity that a dense population and a rich colonial culture gave the rest of the country as far north as the Zacatecas silver routes.

The settlement of the northeastern provinces of Nuevo Leon, Coahuila and Tamaulipas, the "Second Conquest of New Spain", was carried out by later generations of conquistadors beginning in the second half of the 16th century, when the whole area was named the Nuevo Reino de Leon (New Kingdom of Leon), and ending in the course of the 18th century with the colonization of Texas. Especially after the annexation of Texas by the United States in 1848, the northeast territory's history hung on the fortunes of leading cities like Saltillo, Ciudad Victoria and Monterrey.

Despite the importance of Monterrey in particular in Mexico's national economy, and the existence of colonial relics in many places, the northeast remains a land for lovers of the wild and the desolate, for hunters and hikers rather than for tourists and culture buffs.

Monterrey

"It happened in Monterrey, a long time ago" goes the song. Founded in 1596 and named after the then viceroy, the Count of Monterrey, this town was once

North East Mexico

Del Rio
Ciudad
Acuna

Eagle
Pass
Piedras
Negras

UNITED STATES
OF AMERICA
(TEXAS)

N

0   Kilometers   100

Laredo
Nuevo
Laredo

Monclova

Nuevo
Leon

McAllen
Brownsville
Reynosa
Matamoros

Coahuila

Monterrey

To Torreón
Parras
Saltillo

Linares

Concepción
del Oro

Zacatecas

Tamaulipas

Gulf of
Mexico

Real de
Catorce
Matehuala

Ciudad
Victoria

Soto La
Marina

San Luis
Potosí

To Zacatecas

Ciudad
Mante

Tampico

Aquascalientes

San Luis
Potosí

Río
Verde

Ciudad
Valles

Veracruz

Jalisco   Guanajuato   Querétaro

Hidalgo

To Guadalajara

The wild desolation of the frontier lands became the domain of cattle ranchers and cowboys.

a quiet colonial city of leafy plazas and mellow mansions, the center of a sheep-ranching economy. By contrast Monterrey today is the proud industrial engine of the north and Mexico's third largest city. Monterrey's romance today lies only in the minds of Mexican modernisers who prize it as a model of the nation's industrial future. Sometimes called "the Pittsburgh of Mexico", steel and beer are the big industries here. After all, if you work in a red hot steel mill all day, or all night, you're going to need a lot of ice cold beer to cool you down afterwards.

Monterrey, almost encircled by the craggy peaks of the Sierra Madre Oriental, a backwater until the railway reached it in 1882, burgeoned thereaf-

ter to reach its current population of some 3 million, a city of high rise commercial buildings whose heroic centrepiece the massive public square of the Gran Plaza, recently emerged the demolition of several city blocks.

Understandably nicknamed the Macro, the Gran Plaza is surrounded by some of the best of Monterrey's architecture, old and new. For example, the modern **City Hall** and the old one with its 16th-century courtyard. Above all towers the **Beacon of Commerce**, a laser lighthouse that beams green shafts over the city at night, built by famed modernist architect Luis Barragan.

The **Cathedral** is also situated on the plaza, a useful employer of local labor in that it was begun in 1600 and not completed until two and a half centuries later. It has a baroque facade and a Catalan bell tower.

The finest example of colonial architecture is the **Obispado** (Bishop's Palace, built 1788), situated on a hill overlooking the city, which is set against the Cerro de la Silla mountain.

The palace church shows battle scars from the US invasion of 1846, when it was a fort. Pancho Villa and his men also bored it with gunshots in 1915 whilst evicting the old regime. Now, the Regional Museum of Nuevo Leon it depicts the state's history.

After seeing the sights, thirst-quenching at the **Cuauhtemoc Brewery** is in order. It's Mexico's biggest and oldest and produces the pilsner-type Tecate and Carta Blanca beers and the rich brown Bohemia beers. Tours are conducted from Tuesday to Friday.

The brewery also houses a museum of art, the Baseball Hall of Fame (Mexican division), and a sports museum highlighting the northern Mexican male's favorite diversions: boxing, football, rodeo and bullfighting. And, naturally, there is a Museum of Beer.

Apart from the mountains, the Monterrey region's primary scenic attraction is the **Grutas de Garcia**, a series of large cave chambers with interesting formations of stalactites and stalagmites. Located high in the Sierra del Fraile, they are reached by a cable-car. Also close to the city are the **Barranca de Huasteca**, a dramatic 300-m (98-ft) deep canyon, and the **Cascadas Cola de**

A vendor exhibiting an Aztec carving.

Caballo (Horsetail Falls), a 25 m (82 ft) high waterfall whose narrow form resembles a horse's tail.

Coahuila

Coahuila, though a much larger state than Nuevo Leon, has far fewer inhabitants, and is given over to wilderness and vast ranches. It is also noted for wine production. Its capital Saltillo is only a fifth the size of Monterrey, but it is also a manufacturing center for vehicles and textiles.

Situated 160 m (525 ft) up in the parched Sierra Madre, only an hour's drive west from its big counterpart, Saltillo is a much more relaxed and stately place with several colonial monuments. Its 18th-century **Cathedral of Santiago** is rated the finest in the north, hewn in an eclectic mix of styles from the Romanesque, Churriguersque, Baroque to the Plateresque.

The city is famous for its excellent *serapes,* whose weaving can be observed at some mills, e.g. El Saltillero. Leather goods and silverware are other specialities. *Mariachis* pop up at night in the town center.

If you take the railway due south from Saltillo for about 100 km (62 miles), you come to an old curiosity of the northeast, a silver-mining ghost town. Lying in San Luis Potosi state, famed for its silver, **Real de Catorce** is the boarded up remains of a once wealthy town of 40,000 people whose population decamped early this century after the silver price slumped.

Now inhabited by a few hundred souls, it stands high up in a narrow valley, regaled in dry mountain air and with splendid views. It can be reached by a road tunnel formed of old mine shafts. The surrounding mountains are a prime source of the hallucinogenic cactus, peyote, prized by the Huichol Indians and made famous in Carlos Castaneda's books.

Tamaulipas

Tamaulipas stretches along the northeast coast, with the industrial towns of Nuevo Laredo, Reynosa and Matamoros on the US border and the industrial port city of Tampico in the south. In between, the population is sparse, except at the state capital, Ciudad Victoria where cotton, maize and sugarcane are grown, and cattle are raised. **Ciudad Victoria** has a pleasant zocalo and a venerable colonial hotel. At nearby **Vicente Guerrero Dam**, there is good bass fishing and winter duck hunting.

The coastlands are flat and formed largely of seawater lagoons with fishing villages. They extend almost 500 km (311 miles) down to **Tampico**. "Tampico, Tampico, on the Gulf of Mexico" goes a lesser known song, but there isn't really much to sing about here unless you like steamy smelly ports, and this one is Mexico's second biggest, complete with oil refineries which process the crude from offshore and from oilfields to the north and south. The main attraction of this area is inland from Tampico, the Huastec country, or Huasteca, spreading over southern Tamaulipas, eastern San Luis Potosi and the northern Veracruz states.

Huasteca

The Huastecs were the dominant Indian people of this region, at the time of their apogee from about AD 800 to AD 1200. Their language is related to Mayan, giving rise to the theory that Mayan peoples once inhabited the whole Gulf Coast until the intervention of the Olmecs in the middle section. The

A contrast of parched dryness and green forests.

Huastecs had ceremonial centers and were skilful potters and carvers but little remains of their ancient culture.

Tamuin, between Tampico and Ciudad de Valles, is the most important site, with stone platforms and some frescos which are possibly concerned with the cult of Quetzalcoatl, the Plumed Serpent. Some of the characteristics of this important cultural figure of late Mesoamerican history were Huastec. The Huastecs, much given to phallic rites, have a carnal reputation which displeased the puritanical Aztecs, whom they fought with. Huastec warriors regaled in fearsome filed and colored teeth.

Probably one million Huastecs lived at the time of the conquest but they were soon decimated by disease and enslave-ment. Today about 100,000 live on in the center of their old domain, to the south of Ciudad de Valles, which has the **Museo Regional Huasteca** and is a center of archeological and ethnographic research. Many Huastec women still wear colorfully embroidered traditional dress with tree of life symbols. Huastec ceremonial dances also invoke fertility.

Tamazunchale is a town with the Sunday market crowded with Huastecs; the town also specialises in butterflies. South of the Tropic of Cancer, the area is lush with bamboo and banana groves. In the oil refining industrial city of Ciudad Madero, adjacent to Tampico, the **Museo de la Cultura Huasteca** is worth a visit.

The central route from El Paso/Cuidad Juarez on the US Mexican border to Mexico City is a less travelled road than the shorter Gulf Coast route or scenic Pacific Coast highway. Still, the three states that make up this part of North West Mexico have a magic of their own.

Chihuahua

The Church of Santo Domingo in Zacatecas.

It is Mexico's biggest state and its capital, **Chihuahua**, where many men walk about attired in cowboy hats, boots and jeans, has a touch of the wild west. Chihuahua's suburbs are sprawled over such rugged territory that they seem to have been carved out of some kind of no man's land.

Indeed, the region's wilderness provided an ideal refuge for War of Independence leader Miguel Hidalgo who fled here before he was betrayed, captured and executed in 1811. And in 1864, Chihuahua served as a base for President Benito Juarez when he retreated here to

Pedestrain mall of Calle Libertad.

escape from invading French troops led by Emperor Maximilian.

The vastness of Chihuahua made it suitable for cattle ranching which, along with silver mining and timber, helped the state to grow wealthy. But not all was well beneath the veneer of prosperity as the cattle lords held sway over a feudalistic system.

After the turn of the century, the exploited *campesinos* unable to take it any more, exploded into rebellion and joined the 1910 Mexican Revolution led in the north by the legendary Pancho Villa whose mansion in Chihuahua is one of its main visitor attractions today.

Peace now reigns over the city of 800,000, but Chihuahua is still best remembered for its role in the country's revolutionary history and as the birthplace for the Chihuahua toy dog which is hardly ever seen on its streets today.

Chihuahua has a fine baroque Cathedral on Plaza de Armas and a pleasant city center dominated by the pedestrian mall of Calle Libertad where you might occasionally spot Tarahumara women in their colorful dresses or the more severely outfitted Mennonites in black and white.

But its principal attractions are linked to politics. You can visit, for instance, the cell where Hidalgo was imprisoned before his execution. Now part of the post office on Juarez, behind Calle Libertad, it is connected to the Palacio Gobierno whose walls are decorated with murals by Pina Morales tracing Chihuahua's history.

Quinta Luz, the home of General Francisco Villa, better known as Pancho Villa, is of course the main draw. Located in the suburbs, his elegant mansion is now the **Museo de la Revoluccion** where exhibits trace the history of the Mexican Revolution and the role of Pancho Villa and his ragtag contingent of peasants, cowboys and *bandidos*. There is an amazing display of weaponry and the 1922 Dodge Brothers car in which Villa was assassinated on the morning of 20 July 1923 while driving in Hidalgo del Parral, is also on display. The bullet holes punctuating the bodywork of the car are clearly visible. The museum is open daily from 9 am-1 pm and 3 pm-7pm.

If you are not making a visit to

Young amigos.

Casas Grandes, you can pop in at a superb pottery shop opposite the museum for some very fine samples of Casas Grandes pottery.

Hidalgo Del Parral

Located in the southern part of Chihuahua state close to the border with Durango, the mining town of **Hidalgo del Parral's** main claim to fame (some would say, notoriety) is the fact that Pancho Villa was gunned down here, in a plot hatched by a group of intelligentsia. Pancho Villa was buried here until recently when his body was removed to Mexico City. There is a museum cum library dedicated to him.

Casa Grandes

The chief reason for calling in at **Casas Grandes**, four hours north of Chihuahua, is to visit the ruins of **Paquime**, a former Indian settlement that thrived in this area between AD 1000 and 1200. The adobe structures are similar to those found in the American southwest and the town is noted for its canal network that was responsible for its development into an important agricultural center.

Although Paquime is in ruins, the region is still home to some of Mexico's finest potters who produce ceramics with distinctive black and white or earth-colored geometric patterns. No potter's wheel is used; instead every item is fashioned by hand and you can test the authenticity of each piece by placing your hand inside and feeling the fingerprint molds.

Durango

At first glance, **Durango**, the capital of Durango state, does not impress. But once you get into its center dominated by the Plaza de Armas, you will find that this the city of 340,000 – three times the size of Hidalgo del Parral – has delightful colonial architecture which makes a visit worthwhile.

Durango derives much of its wealth from the mining of iron, timber and agriculture. Its wild west appearance has also made it a favorite backdrop of many a Hollywood western, dating back to the days of John Wayne. The specially created movie sets, located 14 km (9 miles) out of town, can be easily visited by travelling on Highway 45 or by taking a bus from the Central Camionera bus station on the city's outskirts.

Other attractions in Durango include a twin-domed baroque **Cathedral** built from 1695 to 1750, the lovely 19th-century **Teatro Principal** and the wonderful murals of the Palacio Gobierno, which was originally the mansion of a mine owner.

Zacatecas

But the jewel to visit is the pink hued city of **Zacatecas**, the capital of the state of Zacatecas. It's a pity that the city does not figure on the top list of most travellers to Mexico for it certainly has much to offer.

For one thing, it has a picturesque setting, 2,459 m (8,068 ft) high in a ravine, surrounded by the slopes of Cerro de la Bufa, so named because their shape resembles a *orbufa* (leather wineskin). For another, the town is steeped in history and played a major part in Pancho Villa's revolutionary struggle when he made it his stronghold in 1914.

Zacatecas is the first of Mexico's silver cities encountered as you travel from the north. The capital of Zacatecas state, the key to the city's wealth was – and still is – silver. The story goes that a Zacateco Indian, whose people had been mining silver in the area long before the Spanish Conquistadores had arrived, gave one of them a silver trinket, sparking off a rush.

The Spanish overcame the Indians, set up a settlement in 1529 and went on to strip the hills of tons of silver that filled the coffers of Mexico City and Spain. So rich were the veins around Zacatecas that silver is still being mined today, at **Real de Angeles**.

The silver barons gave back to Zacatecas the riches they took from it by building a city that stands out as one of Mexico's architectural beauties. They constructed stunning churches of pink sandstone and filled them with artistic treasures. They generously supported the arts and built for themselves fine

Panoramic view of Zacatecas.

colonial mansions that line Zacatecas' downtown streets. Many shady parks and gardens are sprinkled throughout the city, enhancing its attractiveness. Silver mining went into decline briefly in the 19th and 20th centuries as a result of political turmoil.

In 1871, Benito Juarez managed to subdue local rebels and mining for the metal picked up again. Then in 1914, Pancho Villa took over the city when he defeated 12,000 government soldiers. He is remembered by a huge statue of him on horseback flanked by two of his generals on the summit of the city's highest point, **Cerro de la Bufa**. After the Revolution, silver mining resumed and continues to be an important source of the city's wealth.

The city is built on inclines and the steep streets with houses towering over one another give it a distinctive stamp. Some of the inclines are so vertical that steps had to be cut into them. You will find in Zacatecas many streets in the form of such stairways. The city is small and compact and everything of interest is within walking distance but you adopt a slower pace when sightseeing because of the steep hills.

Zacatecas' magnificent **cathedral** on Plaza Hidalgo was the first object of the silver barons' largesse. Sculpted from pink sandstone taken from nearby quarries, it took more than a century to build from 1612 to 1752 and thus sports three architectural styles.

Its northern facade is a riot in

The pink-hued city of Zacatecas has many parks and elegant buildings.

Churrisgueresque detail; its southern facade is European baroque while on its western side is a carving of the Eucharist in Mexican baroque. The cathedral's towers are also rich in carved detail.

To the side of the Cathedral on Plaza Hidalgo is the grand **Palacio de Gobierno** that was originally built in 1727 as a private home for one of the silver barons. Its iron-laced doorway leads into a courtyard overlooked by pink arches on an upper floor.

On the stairway leading upstairs is an intriguing 1970 mural by Antonio Pintor Rodriguez tracing the history and development of Zacatecas. The center panel almost leaps out – it depicts a series of roots representing a tree with the faces of prominent Zacatecans painted above each root.

Leaving the Cathedral, walk a few steps south on Avenida Hidalgo and you will come across the wonderfully ornate 19th century **Teatro Calderon**. Retrace your steps back to the Cathedral and walk one block west to arrive at the magnificent **Templo de Santo Domingo**, a Jesuit baroque church. Completed in 1746, it is in a less florid style than the Cathedral, but its interior is intact with eight beautifully gilded altars, a fine collection of religious paintings and an impressive 18th-century German pipe organ.

Next to the church is its former Jesuit college, now the **Museo Pedro Coronel**. Named after a well-known Zacatecan artist, it houses a treasure of artifacts and paintings from around the world that Dona Pedro had painstakingly collected over many years and which he willed to the city when he died in 1985. Among the precious exhibits are paintings by European masters such as Picasso, Chagall and Miro, artifacts from the pre-Hispanic era, India and Thailand, masks from Mexico and Guatemala, rare minority costumes from China and paper rice scroll paintings from Japan. The museum is open from Tuesday-Sunday, 10am-5pm, with an admission fee: N$3.

From the museum walk three blocks south along Calle Dr Hierro to the restored massive 18th-century **San Augustin Church** with its unusual Plateresque door. The church is now an arts exhibition center.

Atop the Cerro de la Bufa is a concentration of Zacatecas' historic monuments. It is possible to get there by car but the teleferico or cable car, which offers a breathtaking view of the city, is a more exciting way to reach the hill. You can reach the cable car station by walking up several flights of steps behind the Santo Domingo Church.

Dominating the Cerro de la Bufa is the **Museo de la Toma de Zacatecas** which documents the 1914 victory of Pancho Villa and his revolutionaries over the federal troops. Statues of Pancho Villa and two of his generals grace the square outside the museum which is open daily from 10am-6 pm, with an admission fee of N$3.

Next door to the museum is **La**

Capilla (church) **de la Virgen de Patrocinio**, the patron saint of miners and Zacatecas who is revered for curing the sick. The side of the church is decorated with arches from which you can enjoy panoramic views of the city.

For an insight into the terrible conditions many Indians were forced into when they were recruited to work in the city's mines, take a tour of **La Mina El Eden** for a glimpse of its mining shafts, subterranean pools and passageways spread over nine levels. The mine, which functions as a disco at night, is at the end of the road west of the cable car station. It is open from Tuesday-Sunday, 12.30pm-7.30pm.

Guadalupe

A 20-minute bus ride east of Zacatecas will take you to the religious site of **Guadalupe** where the church and ex-convent are the main sights to see. The beautiful tiled dome of the 18th-century **Church of Guadalupe** dominates the small town. The ex-convent is now a museum of religious art, housing some of the best from Mexico's colonial period. It is open daily from 9am-1pm and 3pm -5pm.

If you are shopping for *serapes*, Guadalupe is a good place to buy them. A couple of blocks from the Church of Guadalupe is the workshop of the Ruelas family who turn out very fine *serapes* of acrylic and wool. Ask directions to *"Sarapes Ruelas"*.

The Baja California peninsula is a world apart from the rest of Mexico – geographically, climatically, socially, in almost every way. Due to its aridity and physical separation from the main body of the country, for centuries it attracted little interest until the expansion of the fishing industry and the coming of tourism in recent decades, and was only linked to the mainstream of national development in 1973 when a highway was completed which ran the length of the 1,400 km (870 miles) finger of land.

Washed on the west by the Pacific Ocean and in the east by the Gulf of California (also known as the Sea of Cortes), it is a land of desert and semi-desert with a backbone of mountains, one of which surpasses 3,000 m (984 ft).

Averaging about 100 km (62 miles) in width, the terrain harbors desert species like cactus, lizards and rattlesnakes. Its extensive waters teem with humpback and gray whales, dolphins, sea lions and manta rays, and with

Cultural Center in Tijuana.

Baja Califorina

263

Whale Watching

Whale skull exhibit.

Baja California is famed for its whale watching opportunities. The mammal in question is the gray whale. Several thousands make an annual winter migration from the icy waters of the Bering Sea around Alaska down to the Baja Peninsula for calving.

They start arriving as early as December and some don't leave until May, but the high season is from early January to mid-March.

They can be seen passing close to the shore at the northern Baja town of Rosarito, and from Ensenada boat trips are organized for watchers to go out and "meet" them, even transferring into rubber dinghies so as to sidle up and pat their great shiny rumps and backs if possible. The gray whales' destination is further south – some lagoons which lie along the coast of Baja California Sur provide sheltered and warm waters in which the females can bear their calves and easily care for them in their first few weeks of life.

The principal calving lagoon is just south of Guerrero Negro at **Laguna Ojo de Liebre** which means "Hare's Eye Lagoon" but is actually called Scammon's Lagoon in English after an American whaling captain who "discovered" it in 1857. Subsequently the gray whale was hunted almost to extinction, until whaling was forbidden in 1937. Since then, numbers have steadily risen to possibly 15,000 now. Measuring up to 15 m (49 ft) in length, the gray whale is slender and lithe-looking and often encrusted with barnacles. The lagoon is protected as part of the Parque Natural de la Ballena Gris (Grey Whale Natural Park) and has a designated shoreside whale watching area with observation tower.

In the lagoon the whales often cavort, spout water and sound off. It is not that easy to approach them but well worth the effort. Boating in the lagoon is restricted so as to allow the birthing process to occur relatively undisturbed but licensed operators can sometimes get you

gamefish like marlin, sailfish and dorado. The skies are alive with booby and frigate birds, pelicans and osprey.

Magnet for nature lovers

Often unkindly described as a moon-scape, Baja has for most of this century been a magnet for nature lovers and sports enthusiasts undeterred by the physical difficulties of access. With its new highway, the peninsula became much more accessible and very popular with Californian motorists.

With almost 3,000 km (1,864 miles) of coastline and many offshore islands,

close enough to pat the leviathans, to thrill at their size and to ponder on what they might think of us.

The whales also gather in the Guerrero Negro Lagoon next to the town. About 150 km (93 miles) further south at Laguna San Ignacio lies another whale watching site. Boating is less restricted here and watchers can go out and even get nuzzled by the great beasts and their young. Further south again, at Puerto Adolfo Lopez Mateos and at Bahia Magdalena are other calving lagoons which are convenient viewing places for vacationers staying at Loreto, La Paz and Los Cabos.

The whales even cavort around the Cape (Cabo San Lucas) in the high season, as if they were on a winter holiday like the tourists who love to see them. But to be less anthropomorphic and more scientific, here's some solid gray whale data. Calves are born about 5 m (16 ft) in length and 500 kgs in weight. They guzzle 190 liters of milk daily and are weaned after 9 months. Gray whales (*Eschrichtius gibbosus*) are filter feeders who live off plankton and small fish ingested through baleens. They grow to about 15 m in length and about 40 tonnes in weight. Gestation takes 13 months and the cows calve every two years.

About half the stock migrates to Baja, the others wintering on the Asian side of the Pacific around Korea. On the way back up north to the Bering Sea, the whales take a track far from the shore. It's a mighty 5,000 km(3,109 miles) swim each way, but for such a massive beast, it's like water off a duck's back, you might say.

there is a tremendous variety of unspoilt beaches (as well as many packed with motorhomes) and seasport opportunities like surfing, sailing, diving and gamefishing. The climate is of a dry Mediterranean type; only the southern tip lies within the tropics.

Baja (Ba-ha), as it's usually called by English speakers, especially the

Americans who constitute the vast majority of its visitors, was originally settled by Indians, an estimated 40,000 when Spanish expeditions arrived in the 1530s. The Jesuits followed in the late 17th century to set up missions, teaching the Indians to farm vineyards, olive groves and date palms, before European contact decimated them with smallpox and syphilis.

For centuries small groups of Indians lived in isolation, in remote villages, practising subsistence farming and fishing. Now only a few hundred purebloods still inhabit the peninsula, in the north, and cave paintings in the south are about all that remains of this old Indian culture.

Outsiders have long been making inroads into Baja. Pirates, pearlers and miners came seeking their fortunes, and tourism operators in recent years, such that Baja's modern population is formed overwhelmingly from these settlers and their descendants.

History and geography have combined to give Baja a schizophrenic demography and economy. Because of the contiguousness with the United States, indeed with one of the biggest conurbations on the planet – the San Diego/Los Angeles area, the very north of Baja is populated with Mexico's biggest cities, Tijuana and Mexicali, both very industrial and commercial.

But as you go south down the peninsula, these urban messes rapidly fade in the memory to be replaced by the desert and mountainscapes which are

Typical desert scenery in Baja California.

Baja's true and dominant nature.

Tijuana

Tijuana is where most tourists enter Baja, and where most tourists get no further than, but unless you revel in tacky tourist traps and tawdry nightlife, skip it. If you're coming from the north, drive on down the often spectacular coast road with its high lookout points over the ocean waves crashing against the cliffs, to **Ensenada**.

Situated on Todos Santos Bay, this relaxed town of 250,000 is known for its sport and commercial fishing. Calling itself "The Yellowtail Capital of the World", it also hosts Mexico's premier winery, **Bodegas de Santo Tomas**. It has a pleasant seafront promenade, the **Malecon**, and a fishmarket that caters to every taste.

Just outside of town is **La Bufadora**, a big sea cave into which the ocean waters surge and spout upwards high into the air through a blowhole. Good lobster is served in local restaurants, fish tacos are a popular snack, and there's a lively nightlife too.

Picacho del Diablo

The Carretera Transpeninsular Benito Juarez heads south, close to the coast. At Vicente Guerrero, a road leads east through San Pedro Martir National Park up through forests into the **Sierra San Pedro Martir** to vantage points near Baja's highest peak, **Picacho del Diablo**. The views are some of the best in the continent: east to the Sea of Cortes, west to the Pacific and south to the granite peak. An old Jesuit mission still stands in the park and some Indians still live in the area.

The highway runs close to the coast from Vicente Guerrero through San Quintin to Rosario, with access roads to delightful beaches. It then cuts inland through the **Desierto Central Natural Park** with its many intriguing varieties of cactus – stately *cardones,* twisted *cirios* (or "boojums") among them.

A side road goes east to **Bahia de los Angeles** on the Gulf, a fishing town, boating place and beauty spot in a

Ocotillo plant, an intriguing variety of cactus.

sheltered bay, whilst the highway goes on south to reach the Pacific again at Baja's halfway mark and one of its highlights, **Guerrero Negro**, famous for whale watching [see box].

The rugged and remote Vizcaino Peninsula points into the Pacific to the west and presents marvellous material for beachcombers. The little road south along the coast under the Sierra Vizcaino provides relatively easy access to the kind of deserted seashores for which Baja California is so prized.

The Transpeninsular then enters Baja California Sur (South) and cuts across the Desierto de Vizcaino to **San Ignacio**, a date palm oasis founded by the Jesuits in 1716, its beautifully preserved Dominican mission standing in

Shell fossils.

Cabo San Lucas, the very tip of Baja California.

a shady plaza. This attractive town has thatched-roof houses and pastel-painted commercial buildings.

From here the road runs east past the dramatic triple cones of the **Volcano de las Tres Virgenes**, Baja's most recently active (1857), over solidified dark brown lava to the Gulf of California at Santa Rosalia.

Santa Rosalia

Santa Rosalia is an old copper mining town with the oddity of a prefabricated iron church designed by Gustave Eiffel, he of the Parisian tower. Its neat woodframe houses are a legacy of the French mining company which built the town in the 1880s.

There are fine beaches to the north and south and there are Indian cave paintings at nearby **San Borjita**. At **Mulege** further south the River Santa Rosalia River enters the Gulf as a lushly vegetated lake and the long narrow bay of Bahia Concepcion has beautiful beaches and good diving and snorkeling.

Loreto

Loreto is one of Baja's most historic towns and formerly its capital. The **Mission of Nuestra Senora de Loreto** was founded in 1697, the peninsula's first. It still stands, very finely so, in the Zocalo and remains the town's largest build-

San Felipe is a popular fishing and beach resort.

ing. Next door, the **Museo de Misiones** has exhibits detailing the Spanish discovery and conquest of Baja.

Loreto's situation is picturesque, beneath the slopes of the Sierra Giganta and facing the Isla del Carmen. Fishing is good and the seashore southwards has been developed for tourism, especially at Nopolo, with yachting facilities at Puerto Escondido. From here the highway swings over to the Pacific coast through Llano de Magdalena's citrus groves and cotton farms watered from artesian wells and leads off to Baja's best boating place at Bahia Magdalena.

Known to gringos as "Mag Bay", Bahia Magdalena has a fine natural harbor and lots of sandspits, inlets and mangrove forests, plus all sorts of ma-rine life, from lobsters to gray whales.

La Paz

La Paz, Spanish for 'peace', nestled in the Bahia de la Paz on the Gulf, is where Europeans first set foot on Baja California, in Hernan Cortes's 1533 expedition. In the 17th century, pearlers came to harvest its oyster beds, in the 18th, the Jesuits founded a mission.

La Paz came into its own as state capital in 1830 after Loreto had been razed by a hurricane. Though it is now bustling towards a 200,000 population and prospering under free port status, it still retains many attractive colonial elements. La Paz was famous for its black and pink pearls until the beds died in the 1940s. Early Spanish expeditions were attracted by tales of Indian maidens dressed only in strings of pearls; John Steinbeck picked up the material for his story *The Pearl* in a La Paz bar.

Though its main business today is commercial and sport fishing, it remains a relaxed place from which the Sea of Cortes can always be spied upon, especially dramatically in the frequent bright red sunsets. Its heart is the **Plaza Constitucion** where the Cathedral of Nuestra Senora de la Paz is situated.

The Carretera Transpeninsular ends at the very tip of Baja California Sur, at **Cabo San Lucas**. Baja's fingertip has in recent years become a Gringolandia, full of resort hotels and holiday homes for North Americans. Cruise ships frequently stop off here and sports fishermen fly or sail in to enjoy the abundant fishing grounds.

But it's not yet a mega-resort and quiet beaches are still within reach. The big scenic attraction is **El Arco**, a natural arch in the large wave-lashed rock formations at Land's End where the Pacific Ocean meets the Sea of Cortes. This phenomenon often appears as the motif of Baja California in its many publicity brochures.

Sporting opportunities include scuba diving at the largest coral reef on the continent's Pacific Coast, surfing the big waves at Playa Costa Azul, and horseriding along the beaches. Nearby **San Jose del Cabo** is a quieter tourist town of the cape.

Seals and pelicans perch on rocks in the Gulf of California.

Yucatan Peninsula

exicans refer affectionately to the Yucatan as "The Neighboring Republic of Yucatan", as if it were a land apart. For centuries it was – there were no road or rail connections from the rest of the country and travellers from the capital would take a ship from Veracruz to the ports of Campeche or Sisal. Land of the northern Mayas, it was not subjugated by the Aztecs like most of ancient Mexico. Administered separately from New Spain in colonial times, after independence it actually seceded from the United States of Mexico for a while.

273

A guiding hand to Mexico's finest white-sand beaches.

Yet it was Yucatan, that thick thumb of land sticking up into the Caribbean, where the Spaniards first washed up in Mexico in a 1511 shipwreck, and where the first *mestizos* were then born.

Eventually, in 1542, Spanish dominion was achieved over the Mayan

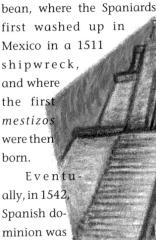

The Ball Game

Ball court and Nunnery Quadrangle in Uxmal.

The ball court is one of the most intriguing structures that stands out among the ancient monuments of temples in Mexico and Central America. Although the plumed serpent god-king Quetzalcoatl was attributed to have invented the ball game played in these courts, their real origin is shrouded in mystery and conjecture. The ball court was found in the ceremonial centers and played an important role in religious rites. The court apparently could vary in size but the shape was basically the same – in the form of the letter I. Each side of the elongated court slopes upwards to a high wall with stone rings placed at equal distances, the actual number depending on the court size.

On top of the walls are platforms – used, not for spectators, it seems, but for sacrificial rites which were performed at the end of the game.

With the tendency of pre-Hispanic Mexican cultures to inject symbolism in so many aspects of their lives, it is not surprising that the ball game was more than just a form of recreation. It was played as much for pleasure as for a more profound purpose. What that was, no one knows for sure but there have been suggestions that perhaps the result of the game served as an oracle for decision-making.

The sport is played with two teams using a hard rubber ball. The aim of the game is to shoot the ball through the stone rings with the players using any part of their anatomy except the hands, feet and arms. The players must have been masters of contortion indeed as they resorted to the use of knees, elbows, hips and thighs to hit the ball off the ground!

The game was considered a battle and like all battles there were consequences. In the ball game, there were rather gory endings with one or more players losing his head and having his heart freshly ripped out as an offering to the sun to feed its energy. Historians are divided as to

inhabitants, but they stayed true to themselves. Long isolated, the *yucatecos* – largely Hispanicized Mayas – developed a "national" character of their own, which has been well described by one observer as "bright, slightly nutty, and totally *simpatico*".

Physically and culturally they form a race apart. Short and stout, with broad faces and hooked noses, they traditionally wear white cotton, the men in *guayabera* tailored shirts with Panama hats, the women with floral embroidery on their shift-like *huipil* dresses.

But their amiable and courteous disposition of today belies a long history of rebellion against the Spanish and *ladino* dominion.

whether the player or players would be from the losing or winning team. But why the winning team, one may ask, when they were the ones that emerged victorious?

But it is precisely for this reason, some say, that the winning player is chosen, for his victory indicates his superior strength and his heart is presumably stronger and hence the better one to feed the sun with. Winner or loser, the chosen player is expected to accept this supreme sacrifice as an honor.

The best example of the ball court is to be found in the Mayan site of Chichen Itza in the Yucatan Peninsula. There are eight ball courts here in total but it is the main court – the biggest and finest of such courts in Mexico – that impresses, a sign perhaps of how important the game must have been. The walls of the main court rise high above the field and are topped by temples. Frieze sculptures on the walls show the ball game in sequence starting from the attire of the players – simple but with padding on the knees and elbows and a belt around the waist with a hook to hang the ball from – to the actual playing of the game and the final end when the captain of the losing (or is it winning?) team is decapitated and his heart taken out and held towards the sun.

It is believed that the rest of the team might also have suffered the same fate. Games played in this court were probably rather dramatic because of the court's great acoustic effects. If you stand in the middle of the field, for instance, and clap your hands, you will hear the sound reverberating clearly from within the walls.

Land of three Personalities

Having long been one state, the peninsula was eventually split into three: Campeche in the west, Yucatan in the north and Quintana Roo in the east. Geographically, this flat lowland territory sees rainforest in the south soon turn to dominant scrubland which receives little rain, even as it is lapped by the waters of the Gulf and the Caribbean on three sides. Dryness suits the *henequen* farmers who grow the agave cactus that provides sisal fiber, and the tourists who flock to the Caribbean beaches. The rainy season is brief, from mid-August to October. Successive Mayan city-states flourished here with the help of water reservoirs in large sinkholes called *cenotes*. Chichen Itza was the greatest city-state.

Roads are a recent development in Yucatan. In 1865, the Empress Carlota, wanting to see the Mayan ruins of Uxmal, had to ride by mule all the way from Merida. Now a network of paved roads leads everywhere. Travellers can drive from their beach hotel in Cancun to the Mayan ruins, of the seaside temple of Tulum perched on a cliff above the turquoise Caribbean. They can motor on south to the Guatemalan border or cut west across the jungles, bathing in the magical lagoons on the way or watching the chewing gum trees grow – most of the world's *chicle* comes from here.

Next would be the walled port city of Campeche on the Gulf and, if one so desires, the oil platforms of Ciudad del Carmen. From here travel north to Uxmal, the desolate and majestic ruins of the Puuc Mayas, and to the "White City" of Merida, one of Mexico's most pleasant state capitals. Turning eastward, tourers soon come to Chichen Itza, the most complete and impressive of Yucatan's Mayan cities. Another couple of hours' drive and they're back at the beach.

Always as much open to the world as to the rest of Mexico, Yucatan retains its traditional export sectors of *henequen* growing for rope-making and *chicle* production for chewing gum manufacture, and has recently added oil from Campeche's wells. But the biggest change in recent history has been the massive growth of the tourist industry: North Americans, Europeans, Asians and Latin Americans are all attracted to the sybaritic beach resorts of Cancun, Cozumel and Isla Mujeres and the tantaliszing mysteries of the Mayas.

The Beginning

The Mayas [see box] last flourished in the Yucatan. After the fall of the great cities in the southern lands, the Yucatan carried the Mayan torch with major centers of Late Classic civilisation at Uxmal, Kabah and Sayil in the Puuc region. Dominant from AD 900 to 1200 was the city of Chichen Itza, capital of the Putun Maya, seafaring traders who controlled the commerce of the whole of eastern Mesoamerica.

The last great Mayan center was Mayapan, but this fell in about 1440 and thereafter the Mayas built no more cities of stone, though they remained commercially powerful and retained their cultural traditions. Thus when the Spanish expeditions arrived in 1517,

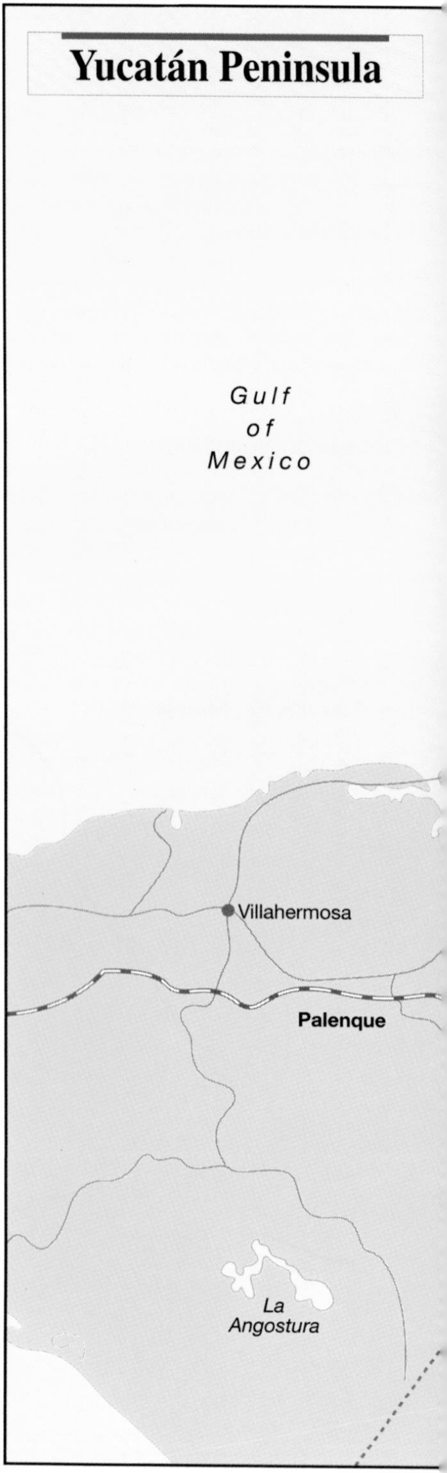

Yucatán Peninsula

Gulf of Mexico

●Villahermosa

Palenque

La Angostura

The cool and cobalt-blue waters of Xel-ha Lagoon.

they were impressed by cities larger than Seville, and thought they had reached China. When conquistadors attempted to take the peninsula, they found the Mayas fiercely resistant and only managed to establish a permanent settlement in 1542 after the Mayas had turned to internal strife. Merida was its name and Francisco de Montejo its founder. In 1562 their books were burned by Friar Landa, who later, as Bishop of Merida, made some amends by recording in Spanish some oral history gleaned from the Mayas.

Having no riches, Yucatan was largely ignored by the Spanish. A territory of the Spanish crown and not of New Spain, Mexico City's viceroys paid little attention to it. Spaniards settled only in Merida and Campeche and nowhere else. The Mayan economic and social structure was destroyed and the Indians became peons on plantations. Serfs in a feudal system, they preserved what traditions they could, and rebelled on several occasions.

As late as 1847 came the bloodiest revolt of all, the War of the Castes, in which the rural Mayas almost threw the *ladinos* into the sea, but were eventually crushed with help from Mexico City. At this point Yucatan gave up its attempts at independence which it had been mulling over for two decades. After joining the Republic of Mexico in 1823, it actually seceded in 1839, so that for a few short years it truly was "The Neighboring Republic of Yucatan".

In the late 19th century, the territory rose to riches on the back of the sisal trade, and Merida became a wealthy and elegant city. The population rapidly recovered from the devastating losses of the War of the Castes, in part through the importation of Yaqui Indians from the northwest state of Sonora as slave labor on the *henequen* estates. A railway line reached all the way from Mexico City, and Yucatan was finally firmly joined to the rest of Mexico.

The Yucatan's two chief cities that remain to this day are Merida and Campeche. From the beginning, a bitter rivalry existed between the inland city and the fortified port. The *campechanos* resented the political domination of the northern city.

Being the doorway to the peninsula, Campeche had to withstand the constant attacks of pirates during colonial times and, after Independence, even an attack from Santa Anna's navy in 1842. After the War of the Castes, Campeche finally achieved statehood in 1858. Quintana Roo, on the eastern flank of the peninsula, was taken over by the federal government in 1902 in order to quell continued rebellions, and became a state in 1974.

In the late 20th century, the tables have been turned in the Yucatan. Merida and the state of Yucatan are almost the poor relations now, the scene of past glories in the *belle epoque* and colonial and Mayan times. Meanwhile Campeche got rich on oil revenues and Quintana Roo on tourist dollars.

Four and a half centuries after their overthrow, the Mayas are still the predominant ethnic group, and still the typical house of Yucatan is the one the ancient Mayas lived in. It is a single storey dwelling, with whitewashed wattle-and-daub walls, a thatched roof, no windows with straight sides, rounded ends. As in the past, the Mayan (mostly) sleep in hammocks and cook outdoors. The farmers grow maize, beans, squash and chili, collectively since the Revolution's land reforms, an activity which is again is a part of the ancient past.

Most strikingly of all, despite centuries of racial mixing, the typical *yucateco* profile seen in today's streets and fields is the same one seen carved on so many ancient Mayan monuments.

Merida

As with so many of Mexico's old cities, a visit to **Merida** should start in the **Zocalo**. Merida's central square is an airy tree-shaded place favored by the locals for meetings and assignations, for business or pleasure. With park benches in the middle and colonnades of cafes on two sides, it's fine for just passing the time of day. Courtship is well catered for by S-shaped "love seats". Historically significant, many of the city's most important edifices look out onto the Zocalo: the cathedral, the town hall, the governor's palace, the mansion of the Montejos.

Francisco de Montejo was the conquistador who finally succeeded in es-

The Convent of St Anthony, c. 1533, one of the oldest convents in the western hemisphere.

tablishing the first permanent colonial settlement in the Yucatan. In 1542, he defeated the Mayas at Tiho, razed the town and founded Merida on the site, using stones from the ruins. It quickly acquired the symbols of Spanish power: a governor in his palace, a bishop in his cathedral, and a general in his palace. Two of these still remain, the cathedral and Montejo's Palace.

The **cathedral**, constructed with deliberate symbolism out of the stones of a Mayan temple, was built between 1561-98. It is an austere structure both

and the worship of this statue show two historically strong faces of Mexico: fierce anti-Catholic feeling and intense religiosity. Another cathedral artifact well illustrates the way that the Spanish conquered Mexico, by alliances with indigenous peoples. A painting shows a local Mayan chief, Tutul Xiu, paying respect to his ally Francisco de Montejo. The Xiu Mayas still live around Merida.

Montejo built himself a **palace** on the south side of the zocalo which still stands today, after renovations in 1850, as a Banamex bank branch. From 1549 until the 1970s, the Montejos lived in it.

Its interior public areas such as the banking hall with a leafy patio are pleasing to visit but the exterior view is the most striking and historically resonant. It has a massive gatehouse with a stone facade on which are carved conquistadors stamping on the necks of Indian savages.

On the west side of the square stands the **Palacio Municipal** (Town Hall), a colonnaded Moorish style building. The first municipal offices were built on this spot atop a Mayan pyramid. It was not until the 1730s that this "obstacle" was removed and the current building constructed. Weekly Yucatecan cultural performances take place here.

The Zocalo's most recent monument is the **Palacio de Gobierno** of 1892. No longer the gubernatorial offices, this spacious building with a courtyard in white and lime green, now displays works depicting Yucatan history executed with great panache by local

without and within, devoid of exterior carving and stripped of its rich interior decoration by anti-clericalists during the Revolution. It contains Merida's most prized religious object, the huge *Christ of the Blisters*, carved from a lightning-struck tree which burned one whole night yet, miraculously, was not in the least charred in the morning. The attack on the church

The Mayas

Statue of an early Indian native.

Buried deep in the Central American jungle or protruding from the scrubland of arid Yucatan, the mysterious ruined cities of the Mayas were a source of wonder to the early explorers who stumbled upon them: were these extraordinary pyramids and palaces the work of gods or men?

For three long centuries the mystery only deepened, despite the records left to the Spanish by the Yucatan Mayas and their continued existence as a fragmented people in Yucatan, Chiapas and Guatemala. The mystery persisted until Victorian explorers took up the trail again in the mid-19th century.

Magnificent ruins at Chichen Itza.

Archeologists followed the explorers to unearth the ruins and disentangle them from the overgrowth; artists and photographers came to record the remains in pictures; historians, mathematicians and linguists labored over the evidence. Gradually romantic conjecture gave way to scientific fact – and the true inhabitants of these elaborate sites were progressively revealed. Theories and counter-theories jostled for acceptance, until by the mid-20th century it was generally believed that the Mayas were a uniquely peaceful people, devoted to the arts and sciences, as exemplary as the classical Greeks.

So firmly did this idyllic image imprint itself on our times that its recent demolition has yet to sink in. In 1946, an archeologist entered a ruin at Bonampak, lit a torch and was astounded to see an array of fine multi-coloured murals of ornately dressed Mayas. These were a major key, along with the more recent deciphering of Mayan writing, to the exposure of the Mayas as a people of warring city-states.

Discoveries are being made all the time, with one crucial revelation made very recently: satellite photography has shown that the Mayas had extensive irrigated farmlands around their cities and did not rely on slash-and-burn agriculture as previously believed.

Despite continuing mysteries, the picture by now seems fairly complete. The Mayas were in fundamentals like all the other high civilisations of Mesoamerica. They built pyramid temples, played a ritual ball game in special courts, made

Intricate stone carving at Uxmal.

press both his subjects and his rivals, each monarch aimed to live in the most sumptuous palace, to construct the most lavish temples in honor of his ancestors on top of the highest pyramids, and to mark his reign with the erection of the most impressive monuments.

It was in this context that the Maya made remarkable scientific and artistic achievements in their Classic period from Ad 300 to 900. Inheriting Olmec advances, they perfected the Olmec counting system using zero and units of 20, and devised a calendar more accurate than that used in Europe until the late 16th century. They developed a glyphic writing system to record religious and secular historical information. Only the Mayas, in Mesoamerica, built using arches to create large interior spaces and portals. Their sculpture was of unparalleled excellence, whether in reliefs on buildings, or in figures of stone or jade. They painted expert and lively frescos on walls and pottery.

But the rivalry system couldn't last. The struggle for supremacy absorbed increasing energies, weakened the economies and wearied the people. Towards AD 900, the crunch came for the Classic Mayan civilisation: it collapsed under the combined pressure of several factors. Climatic change brought agricultural decline. The land was overpopulated, the people were resentful of their burden and there were internal wars and barbarian invasions. And so the great Classic centers of the south, like Copan in Honduras, Tikal in Guatemala, and Palenque in Mexico, were abandoned and fell into ruin by the end of the 9th century.

Mayan civilisation continued in the Yucatan at major centers like Uxmal and Chichen Itza, under strong influence from Toltec culture, but was in decline when the Spanish dealt it the final blow with their military conquest and Christianizing zeal. The Mayas resisted until 1542, when the Spanish established Merida, and burnt nearly all the Mayan codices – the folding illustrated books which recorded their history. But several million Mayas continue to live in the Yucatan, Chiapas and Guatemala. They still speak Mayan dialects, and go on worshipping ancient deities along with the Christian trinity and saints.

elaborate calendrical observations, wrote in glyphs, had folding books of bark paper or deerskin, worshipped a pantheon of gods which included a rain god and the Feathered Serpent, performed self-mutilation and human sacrifice for religious purposes, were ruled by priest-kings until the militarist era, regularly engaged in war, used cocoa beans as money, lived on a staple diet of corn, beans and squash, and so on.

But if they shared a broadly similar culture with the other civilised peoples of ancient Mexico, despite not being the peace-loving utopia once believed, they had features which single them out as the most striking and advanced culture of them all.

The Mayas were a people organized into rival city-states, sharing the same civilisation whilst cultivating individual traits. It was an intensely competitive society whose history is replete with battles, annexations, alliances and tribute won or lost. In each large city, a king, like a god, was responsible before his people for the successful functioning of the universe. To im-

artist Fernando Castro Pacheco.

Though Merida is a walker's city which repays aimless strolling with a myriad of interesting sights – street vendors, tortilla-making shops, little cafes, colorfully painted facades, teeming markets – some of the principal sights are far-flung and best located on wheels. No option is better than horse-and-carriage, many of which wait close to the cathedral for this very purpose. One of the highlights of a visit to Merida is rolling around the city behind a coachman and trotting horses just like the *clase divina* of the *belle epoque*.

The tour should include two handsome whitewashed edifices which symbolise the 20th-century integration of Yucatan into Mexico: the **Correos** (Post Office) and the **Termino Ferrocarril** (Railway Station), a building resembling a wedding cake.

It should definitely take in the **Paseo de Montejo**, a Parisian-style boulevard where the turn-of-the-century *henequen* plantation owners lavished their wealth on elaborate mansions.

At the avenue's head, the carriage should bowl around the **Monumento a la Patria** (1956), dramatically carved with a circular Maya-inspired frieze, and double back to the **Museo de Antropologia e Historia** which occupies Merida's most splendid *belle epoque* mansion. This museum provides admirably detailed information on Mayan and Yucatan history, well worth absorbing before visiting the great archeological sites.

Uxmal

An hour's drive south of Merida lies one of the most extensive and complete Mayan sites, the city of **Uxmal** (oosh-MAL). Developed in the Classic Period (AD 600- AD 900) in the region of the Puuc Hills, Uxmal's ruins spread through bushy scrubland and contain some impressive and fairly complete structures to which latterday discoverers gave fascinatingly fanciful names.

There is a steep temple-topped stone mound called the **Pyramid of the Magician**, 40 m (131 ft) high. A large plaza surrounded by elaborately carved buildings goes by the name of the **Nunnery Quadrangle**, though it probably had some military or regal function. The rain god Chac is frequently depicted at Uxmal, understandably in such an arid region, which the Mayas eventually abandoned in about AD 900.

In another complex upon a low bluff stands the **Governor's Palace**, a long rectangular building whose facade features a long frieze of carved stone showing stylized faces and geometric designs. This is regarded as the finest achievement of the Puuc Mayas.

Next to it rises the **Great Pyramid**, 32 m (105 ft) high with the massive steps of the northern side fully restored and made more easy for climbing. There are many smaller structures like the House of the Pigeons and the Temple of the Phalli, and many more which are now overgrown mounds.

Sisal – The Rope that made Merida

Sisal is today a small sleepy fishing town on the northwest coast of Yucatan, but in the last century it was a thriving port. It bustled with the business of exporting to the world the fiber of the agave cactus. Consequently both plant and fiber gained the popular name "sisal" around the world and the cactus got the scientific name *Agave sisalana*, and eventually, a century ago, sisal became Merida's "green gold".

In Yucatan it is known by its Spanish name, *henequen* (from the Mayan *geniquen*), and the word is synonymous with the glory days of Merida. The tough fibers had first been extracted from the sharp-pointed leaves of the cactus by the Mayas to make ropes – ropes strong enough to haul and hoist great blocks of stone in monument building. The Spanish continued the manufacture but sisal really came into its own with the American invention of mechanical bailing machines for the wheat harvest in 1875.

Suddenly there was a huge demand for tough bailing twine and the Yucatan set to fulfilling it – and setting the price. Vast plantations spread throughout the peninsula, worked by Indians as virtual slave labor, with Merida as trading center. The immense wealth amassed among the one thousand plantation-owning families transformed Yucatan's capital by the turn of the century. The *clase divina* took France as its model and gave Merida the soubriquet of "the Paris of Mexico", laying out new avenues and boulevards, parks and squares, building themselves magnificent mansions and Art Nouveau villas to suit the image. Even the Bishop did well, riding in a jewel-encrusted carriage designed by a Parisian goldsmith.

But the 20th century brought a slump as

Sisal is derived from the fiber of the agave cactus.

sudden as the boom. First the US harvesters formed a trust to beat down the price, then the Revolution's reforms broke up. the plantation estates and freed the labourers, Finally, sisal rope was substituted by artificial fibers in the 1940s. Today the fiber is of secondary importance in the peninsula's economy but still supreme in Yucatan state. Visitors encounter it in the markets, where woven hammocks are offered for all needs, from single to family size!

Within an hour's drive south are further smaller Mayan sites: **Kabah** (Palace of Masks, with multiple images of the god Chac), **Sayil** (Gran Palacio with extensive colonnaded facade), **Xlapak** (well reconstructed palaces) and **Labna** (magnificent archway).

Chichen Itza

Located 120 km (75 miles) east of Merida, Chichen Itza is the major Maya site of Mexico, spanning over 5 sq km (2 sq miles) and containing several large struc-

The Pyramid of the Magician in Uxmal.

tures. Its history extends over the period AD 600-1200 but the details of its development are still very conjectural.

Reckoned to have been the dominant Mayan city from 900 to 1200, it latterly came under strong Toltec influence, perhaps through conquest, though maybe through trade.

Chichen Itza's supreme monument is often presented as a symbol of Yucatan, or even of Mexico – the **Castillo**, a square pyramid of symmetrical proportions, with a central stairway on each side and a flat-roofed temple on top. Given a fanciful name like so many Mayan monuments, it was not a castle but the ceremonial center of the city.

Within it, up interior steps, lies a chamber containing a stunning red jag-

uar throne, with jade eyes and flint fangs, perhaps the high priest's seat. The bases of the stairways are flanked by open-mouthed serpent heads, and the stairs are so aligned that during the equinoxes the setting sun shining on the adjacent steps sends a serpentine shadow snaking down the stairway walls. Much of Chichen Itza is concerned with calendrical and astronomical matters. It reflects the Mayan preoccupation with precise chronology for religious and historical.

The Castillo is a case in point. Almost every element of its construction has a calendrical meaning, e.g. there are four stairways of 91 steps plus one platform on top, adding up to 365, the number of days in the year; it has 52

Chichen Itza observatory.

panels on each facade, the number of years in the Mesoamerican "century".

Then there is *El Caracol*, The Snail, so called because of its spiral staircase. This was a domed observatory whose four doors face the cardinal directions and whose dome windows are aligned with the stars.

Another distinctive image of Chichen Itza is the **Chac-mool**, the strange reclining figure which holds a plate over its midriff, probably for offerings, perhaps even of human hearts. There is one at the top of the steps at the Temple of the Warriors.

Chichen Itza also sports the most complete and massive ball court ever found, which features finely carved reliefs, one of them showing the ritual decapitation of the losing captain (or was it the winner?).

Chichen Itza means the Mouth of the Well of the Itzas, who were the dominant Mayas of the region. One of the notable features of the Yucatan Mayan civilisation is the use of large sinkholes for collecting water, an essential organizational element given the dry climate. Some of these huge wells, called *cenotes,* served religious purposes. At Chichen Itza, a sacred way leads to the Cenote Sagrado, 60 m (197 ft) in diameter and 35 m (115 ft) deep, into which were thrown jade and gold propitiatory objects, as well as animal and human sacrifices.

Fifty km (31 miles) west from Chichen Itza stands the attractive colo-

Chac-mool sculpture, another distinctive image of Chichen Itza.

nial town of Valladolid which possesses Yucatan's earliest church, dating from 1552. The **Cenote Zaci** provides a scenic attraction set in a park. A road leads due north from Valladolid to Rio Lagartos National Park, a flamingo sanctuary in coastal lagoons.

It is best in the July-August breeding season. Egrets, herons and pelicans also reside here, besides a few alligators, after which the place is named (Alligator River).

Quintana Roo– The Beaches

The Spanish conquistadors' first sight of what is now Mexico was the coast of Yucatan. They saw white stone temples and thought they had reached Cathay, the land of the Great Khan, and they named the place 'the Great Cairo'. No such geographical confusion is made by today's travellers: they know that the great white temples they spy through the airplane windows are sun-worshippers' playgrounds, the resort hotels of Cancun and Cozumel.

Cancun

Eastern Yucatan presents its face to the Caribbean and here lie some of Mexico's best beaches and finest resorts, all of them developed almost totally since 1970. Selected by a computer, Cancun was a purpose-built, federal-controlled

Luxury living in Cancun.

project which has been fabulously successful, even overtaking Acapulco in revenue. Seeing a seven-shaped sandspit presenting 23 km (14 miles) of white sand beaches to a turquoise sea and its back to a calm lagoon, the planners set to designing a mega-resort for the international tourist.

Today Cancun's shores are lined with luxury hotels catering to the package tour, its swimming pools and sea beaches packed with sunbathers and swimmers, its lagoon skimmed by windsurfers and waterskiers, its malls milling with shoppers, its discos gyrating through the night.

If this is not your kind of escape, there are nearby islands and beaches where vacation life is less developed.

Isla Mujeres is the best known, so called because of the Mayan female fertility figures found there by the first Spaniards in 1517.

On this relaxed little offshore island, swimmers relish Playa Los Cocos (Coconut Beach) and snorkelers delight in the El Garrafon coral reef. Here the hotels are smaller and cheaper.

Playa del Carmen and Cozumel

Lying 70 km (43 miles) down the "Turquoise Coast" from Cancun, **Playa del Carmen** is a beautiful beach resort currently moving upmarket from its budget traveller origins, but it's still got a long

Cooling off in Cancun.

way to go before it reaches the popularity of **Cozumel** which it faces. A 50 km (31 mile) long island, Cozumel is well developed with hotels and tourist amenities, but is older and more laid back than Cancun.

Something of a poor relation, Cozumel is still big on shopping, especially for handicrafts, but less so on nightlife. Its offshore reefs are a major attraction for snorkelers and divers, offering varying levels of difficulty for viewing a wondrous array of tropical marine life.

Tulum

An hour's drive south brings you to

Tulum, surely Mexico's most romantically sited ancient ruins. Its temples perched on cliffs above the Caribbean, Tulum was an important port of late Mayan civilisation. Small scale and less refined than earlier sites, its beautiful location makes it a natural favorite for trippers from the beach resorts.

Inland, 50 km (31 miles) northwest of Tulum lies a very large Mayan site, **Coba**, probably the largest ever. Related more to Guatemala's classic Tikal culture than later Chichen Itza and without much excavation, Coba's extensive jungle ruins let you feel like an early explorer as you wander amongst mysterious overgrown structures listening to exuberant tropical birdsong and watching the beat of brilliant butterfly wings.

Tulum is laid back, but is also the site of one of the most important Pre-Columbian ruins.

Campeche

Campeche, the largest of Yucatan's three states, faces the Gulf of Mexico and was known historically mostly for buccaneers and precious wood. The city of Campeche, firmly founded in the 1540s as the peninsula's port of entry, was also the only other port on the Gulf Coast besides Veracruz allowed to export goods in colonial times. For a century and a half, it suffered the regular depredations of pirates, including a gruesome massacre in 1663, after which massive fortifications were built around it including a sea gate.

A backwater after Mexican independence, Campeche has revived since the first road connections in the 1950s and the oil discoveries of the 1970s, which have transformed the port city of Ciudad del Carmen in the south. Still relatively relaxed for a state capital, the city of Campeche is a fine place for tourists who don't like other tourists. It is full of old world sights yet devoid of tour buses. A fair part of the old ramparts have survived urban expansion, some of the forts and bulwarks being converted into museums of local history and artisanry. Walking the narrow streets of the old town from *baluarte* to *baluarte* brings the sense of the old citadel to life. Shrimping boats and timber freighters provide the major traffic in Campeche's port today. As to the beaches, leave them to the locals.

O a x a c a

"Before us lies the gleaming pinkish-ochre of the valley flat, wild and exalted with sunshine. On the left, quite near, bank the stiffly pleated mountains, all the foot-hills, that press savannah-coloured into the savannah of the valley. The mountains are clothed smokily with pine ... and they rear in a rich blue fume that is almost cornflower-blue in the clefts ... darkest blue at the top. Like some splendid lizard with a wavering, royal-blue crest down the ridge of his back, and pale belly, and soft, pinky-fawn claws ..."

Thus wrote D.H.Lawrence in 1927 in *Mornings In Mexico*. The pines have since thinned, but the colors remain, and thus it is today, the exalted valley of Oaxaca, 500 km (310 miles) southeast of Mexico City. Looking from Monte Alban, a lone table mountain in its midst, all human habitation seems inconsequential, almost invisible, in the

Guelaguetxza folkloric dancers of Oaxaca.

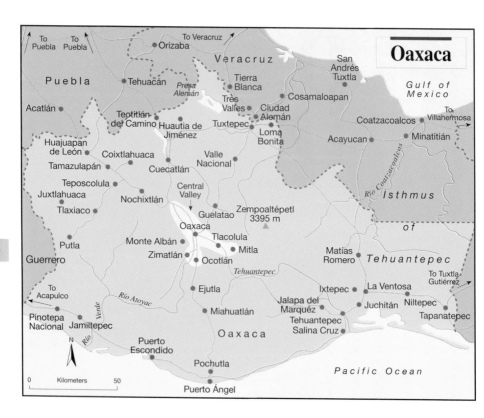

face of this parched splendor. Yet this valley is rich in history, rich in successive civilizations, indeed, rich in people.

Monument-studded Valley

Oaxaca (pronounced wa-HA-ka) combines richness of ethnicity, a sense of mystery, and a span of history, in a matchless setting. The grand central valley is studded with monuments of pre-Hispanic and colonial times.

As a synthesis of the finer elements in Mexico's past, it has no rival. In the diversity and strength of its present-day Indian population, it is unequalled as eighteen distinct ethnic groups live in the state. In direct touch with prehistoric times, it is renowned for its mystical nature healing.

And it even has a tree reputed to be the world's oldest living thing, the 2,000-year-old cypress of El Tule. Evidence of human habitation is far older at ten thousand years, while high civilisation dates from 500 BC, its revelation in the 1930s putting Oaxaca on the world stage. The archeologist Alfonso Caso was exploring a burial mound on flat-topped Monte Alban, overlooking Oaxaca city. There he unearthed a treasure of gold and silver jewelry, quartz vessels, jade and turquoise mosaics. The rich find captured the world's imagination.

Suddenly everyone wanted to know

Brightly colored traditional dressing in Oaxaca.

more about Monte Alban, about the Zapotecs who built it, and about the Mixtecs who made the exquisite jewelry. Oaxaca experienced its first tourist boom in recent years and has since become a national and international favorite for readily apparent reasons.

The Olmecs

Caso was instrumental in our current understanding of Oaxaca's history. He found that, as with practically everything in ancient Mexico, Monte Alban began with the Olmecs. Two thousand years before the Spanish conquest, around 500 BC, some Olmec groups left their steamy jungles on the Gulf coast,

moved south up through Mexico's mountainous backbone, and settled in the flat central valley of Oaxaca, at a brisk 1,500-m (4,921 ft) altitude.

Here they founded one of the three great classic civilizations of ancient Mexico, the others being the Maya, whose temple-cities remain even now in the east, and in neighboring Guatemala, and Teotihuacan, the latter marked to this day by massive pyramids near Mexico City. This is august company. All three were theocracies, ruled by a caste of astronomer-priests, but only at Monte Alban did the people go to the astonishing length of levelling a mountain top on which to build their ceremonial center so that it might be closer to the stars.

Monte Alban – ceremonial center atop a mountain.

The Zapotecs

The Zapotecs took the Monte Alban civilization to its height. Called the Cloud People, they perhaps originated in the cloud forest of Oaxaca's northern mountains. Coming down to the valley, upon the Olmecs' great foundations they built their temples "at the foot of heaven". Far above the fields and markets in the valley below, which stretches flat all around to a ring of enclosing blue mountains, Monte Alban itself is both physically and spiritually elevated.

A cosmic silence fills these heights. The immense rectangular plaza, some 750 m (2,461 ft) long and 250 m (820 ft) wide, is precisely oriented on the four points of the compass. Pyramids and platforms, temples and tombs, stairways and archways surround it in classical symmetry. One central building is irregular, its orientation and arrowhead-shape indicating an astronomical function, some historians even speculate that it was used as an observatory. Indeed, the structure is aligned such that the rising of a star indicates the zenith passage of the sun, that eerie day when at noon open spaces are filled with shadowless light and facades are contrastingly dark and obscured.

Thus the astronomer-priests make their ghostly presence felt whenever they keep their appointments with the stars. In the last moon before the spring equinox, at dusk, a visitor standing on the southern platform looking north receives a clear sign from these ancient sages. As the sun sets to the left, a full moon rises above the rim of the valley to the right.

For an instant, the heavenly bodies hang in a perfect balance of celestial mechanics, until the seesaw tilts to the west and the sun disappears in a horizon of liquid gold, leaving Monte Alban to receive the full silver flood of the moon's rays.

It is a magical place, whether in the dry air of winter, all vegetation parched yellow, life at a low ebb, the sun merciless, or in the lush green of the rainy season, or the moist still of night. It was all the more so in ancient times when maidens went calmly and serenely to the knife of the high priest in sacrifice to the Maize God, lord of life.

Or when, after the ceremonial ball game, both team captains (probably) lost their heads, the former for his unworthiness, the latter for his excellence. There's little doubt that the sacrificial victims' serenity was achieved not simply by cultural conviction but with the mystical aid of the hallucinogenic mushroom, peyote, centrally significant in Indian religion.

As with all classic civilizations, the Greco-Roman in Europe, for example, or the Khmer in Southeast Asia, decline and fall eventually occurred at Monte Alban, around 700 BC.

A period of warring states ensued and the Mixtec people eventually established themselves as lords of the Oaxaca Valley. It was the Mixtecs who named

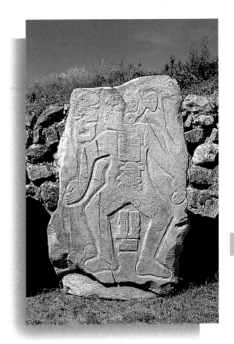

Gallery of Danzantes in Monte Alban.

Monte Alban, *Sahandevui*, "at the foot of heaven", and they made it a royal cemetery, hence Caso's gorgeous finds.

The Aztecs

Then came the Aztecs. They are by far the best known of the ancient Mexican peoples but what is little known is that they were very much late-comers, only founding their great capital of Tenochtitlan a mere 200 years before the Spanish conquistadors turned up and conquered them.

Only in 1486 did they establish hegemony over Oaxaca with the warriors being followed by the tax collectors. The resident Zapotecs and Mixtecs were sub-

500 BC astronomy tower in Monte Alban.

jected to outrageous taxes; one single province was required to pay 400 large cotton mantles, a warrior's quilted armor and shield, 20 gourds full of gold dust, 5 bags of cochineal and 400 bouquets of feathers from the quetzal, the local bird of paradise; all this every 80 days. Nevertheless, the records indicate a prosperous valley.

Many subject peoples suffered thus under the Aztec yoke, these nomad upstarts from the north who had rapidly come to lord it all over central Mexico. It is thus no surprise that, when Cortes led his conquistadors against the might of the Aztec Empire, he found keen allies, the Zapotecs amongst them. And soon below Monte Alban there arose a Spanish city.

Phoenix of Mexican Cities

Oaxaca is the phoenix of Mexican cities, rising from its ashes after each holocaust. First Zapotec, then Mixtec, next Aztec, then Spanish, twice over. The Aztec emperor Moctezuma I razed it in 1468 and built a fort that was in turn burned down by the Spaniards in 1521. Cortes, the conqueror of Mexico, was much taken with this valley. When he heard that some of his officers had founded a town there, he was enraged and ordered it to be torn down. He wanted Oaxaca for himself.

The reason was gold. He was evidently acquainted with the Aztec tax rolls and coveted the wealth of the province, which he parcelled out to his illegitimate children and closest friends and proceeded to plant with wheat. In 1528, King Charles V of Spain gave a royal charter to the city of Oaxaca and made Cortes, Marquess of the Oaxaca Valley.

So the conqueror of Mexico founded a great provincial capital, one which was to nurture two of independent Mexico's greatest leaders, Benito Juarez and Porfirio Diaz. What the visitor sees today is a jewel of Spanish colonial architecture, a spacious city of churches and squares, monasteries and colonnades, mansions and plazas, town houses and fine vistas, resplendent in crystal light and dry mountain air. Oaxaca city takes great pride in its colonial heritage, barring all construction that would mar its architectural integrity.

Touring Oaxaca

As is only fitting, the central square, always called the *zocalo* in every Mexican town, epitomises this heritage: a paved plaza, it is filled with pigeons, the great sandstone facade of the cathedral, colonnades of the Governor's Palace, and formal park with a circular bandstand. Through this pedestrian precinct wander townspeople and tourists and vendors of shawls, balloons, ponchos, pigeon feed and what-have-you. Around it cluster sidewalk cafes and restaurants, cosmopolitan in cuisine, as is much of the clientele. Here three worlds meet and mingle, Mexican provincial, indig-

enous Indian, and international tourist, in an incomparable atmosphere. Evenings are magical – cool, dry and sprinkled with *marimba* music from the bandstand, polyglot chatter filling the air, the sandstone facades bathed in yellow light.

By day, the straight colonial streets are deluged with sunlight in the crystalline air. North from the *zocalo* run two parallel streets, which are pedestrianised and prettified, spick and span, noble in ochre and white, leading the eye along their brilliant vistas to the blue mountain backdrop. One of these streets contains buildings extant since the 16th century, including a Castilian mansion of the Cortes family, fine and grave, its heavy stone mellowed with age, with carved stone portals and wrought-iron balconies. Only the lady in the mantilla is missing.

Monastery of Santo Domingo

The jewel of Oaxaca's Spanish heritage lies at this street's end, for the seemingly endless vista does reach a finale at the **Church** and **Monastery of Santo Domingo**. The church is celebrated for its exuberant gold and white stucco decoration, especially the ornate and elaborate genealogical tree, supposedly St. Dominic's, that flourishes resplendently over the entranceway. Many a visitor has cricked a neck here in cock-eyed wonder, attempting to stand up and see

Resplendent interiors in the
Monastery of Santo Domingo.

it all simultaneously. Quite how the Virgin Mary got into St. Dominic's ancestry we had better not ask!

The monastery, extensive and twin-towered, topped by blue-glazed domes, filled with cool cloisters, is now a museum. Its prize exhibits are the Mixtec art and jewelry from the tombs of Monte Alban such as obsidian ear ornaments, translucent alabaster vessels, a jade quetzal-bird lip plug and the gold mask of the god Xipe Totec. In other parts of the many-cloistered, tall-ceilinged building, there are exhibits of Indian costumes and religious art from the former Dominican monastery.

The Dominican Order had a profound influence on Oaxaca. Arriving early, it was instrumental in mediating between conquistadors and natives, then among the diverse Indian peoples, each fiercely individualistic.

The friars eased conversion to Christianity by co-opting local rituals and beliefs: Cocijo, the Zapotec rain god, became St. Peter, the Christian sprinkler, and so on. Thus the Indians converted quickly, and soon set to building Santo Domingo, probably the most magnificent example of Dominican architecture in Mexico. They also broke the missionaries' hearts by getting gloriously drunk at every festival. In pre-Hispanic times, anti-drunkenness laws were truly severe, to the extent of capital punishment. In this respect at least, the Spanish were not harsh, and so it was that the very first Christian wedding of Indians ended in a drunken brawl.

The conquerors introduced distillation to Mexico; it was unknown to the Indians. Their tipple was *pulque*, a kind of milky beer fermented from the *maguey* cactus, a huge plant with many thick, long, pointed leaves spreading from ground level. The Spanish discovered that some species of the *maguey* produced through distillation were quite acceptable and produced a potent liquor which they called *mezcal*. The world-famous *tequila* is actually a specific variant of *mezcal*, distilled from one particular species of *maguey*.

The *mezcal* cactus likes neither tropical lowland nor chilly highland, so the warm yet elevated valleys of Oaxaca are prime production areas. At harvest time, mounds of *maguey* hearts lie eve-

Dances of Oaxaca

Oaxaca's folk dances date to the Zapotec civilization.

Oaxaca is famed for its folk dances whose origins date back to the days when the ancient Zapotec civilisation ruled this land. The best time to see them is the annual Guelaguetza festival held on the two Mondays following at 16 July.

Also known as the *Lunes del Cerro* (Mondays on the Hill), the festival has its origins in an ancient fertility rite in honor of the maize gods. The Spanish Catholic priests diplomatically rejigged it as the feast of the Virgen del Carmen, but then banned it in 1882 as being too pagan.

Revived in the 1930s as a dance festival, its popularity surged until a special amphitheater was built for it on the Cerro del Fortin, a hill outside the city of Oaxaca.

Today the Guelagetza is a major folklore festival which draws Mexicans and foreigners alike to witness the amazing variety and vibrancy of Oaxaca's dance traditions. The city fills up in the preceding days and a delightful festive atmosphere overtakes it.

Up on the hill in the morning sun, splendidly costumed dancers, descendants of Zapotecs and Mixtecs from seven Oaxacan regions, perform their traditional dances to live music, the women sporting over 350 different colorful *huipils* and dresses. In the *Jarabe Tlacolula*, barefoot girls swirl in long lace petticoats overlaid with short, brightly colored skirts and ribbons as their male partners, all in white with colorful handkerchiefs, dance opposite with hands behind their backs. The independent women of Tehuantepec dance, without men, the slow and stately *Zandunga*, in long full velvet-topped dresses that are gorgeously embroidered.

Guelaguetza is Zapotec for "gift". After each performance, the dancers exchange presents and throw offerings of their local produce to the appreciative crowd – oranges from the Sierra Juarez, palm hats from the Mixtecs, pineapples from Papaloapan. The climax comes with the dignified, high-stepping Zapotec Feather Dance (*Danza de las Plumas*) precisely performed by men wearing glorious feather headdresses – a symbolic re-enactment of the Spanish conquest of Mexico.

rywhere like huge forty-kilo pineapples. From these come the drink that Oaxaquenos sup saying *"para todo mal, mezcal; para todo bien, tambien"* – for everything bad, *mezcal*; for everything good, as well.

The Oaxaquenos may solve and create problems with that liquor, Mexico's national drink, but their sustenance comes from a varied and tasty cuisine which is particularly famed for its *mole*, the nearest thing Mexico has to a national dish. *Mole* is of pre-Hispanic origins, and consists of baked turkey in a rich chocolate brown sauce compounded of many spices and foods, especially chilis and cocoa, and Oaxaca's variety is renowned.

This is no doubt due to the strength of indigenous culture in Oaxaca. The state harbors one fifth of all Mexico's pure Indian population, over one million souls and eighteen different peoples; still the Zapotecs and Mixtecs predominate at 350,000 and 300,000 each. This depth and diversity gives rise to of Mexico's finest selection of Indian handicrafts: brilliant woven blouses, delicate cotton brocades, satiny black ceramics, thick woollen rugs and shawls, filigree gold jewelry and fine woodcarvings, which Oaxaca's street vendors, shops and markets happily hawk.

El Tule

Rich in history and culture, crafts and customs, peoples and produce, splendid scenery and local color, Oaxaca seems to be symbolized by the churchyard of **El Tule**, a village not far from the city. Before the mellow white colonial church, on a great flat plaza, Indian women sell cold drinks of age-old recipes.

Over it all rises the oldest living thing in Mexico, some say the world, a gargantuan cypress tree over 40 m (131 ft) tall with a girth exceeding 42 m (138 ft) and an estimated age of 2,000 years. The church of Santa Maria del Tule is by

Mexico's oldest living tree, aged 2,000 years.

no means small, but it seems a mere toy beneath this behemoth of the plant world. In the exalted valley of Oaxaca, where natural and human history is intertwined, the continuity of life is ever apparent and ever dramatic.

Take **Mitla** for another example. A 30-km (19-mile) drive further southeast from Tule brings you to Oaxaca's second greatest ancient ruins, where a colonial church abuts the walls of Mixtec ruins and a sprawling open-air crafts market presents today's indigenous skills inherited from a long past.

Mitla is another complex of ceremonial structures started by the Zapotecs but taken over and heavily influenced by the Mixtecs, with its name given by the Aztecs, from *mictlan* –

There are numerous ceremonial structures to explore in Mitla.

"place of the dead". The architecture here, mostly dating from after AD 1400, is quite different from that of any of Oaxaca's other ruins. The stone and mud walls are inlaid with small stones cut into geometric patterns, forming a mosaic that appears strangely Grecian. (One courtyard is named Patio de las Grecas). Unlike other ancient buildings in Mesoamerica, there are no human figures or mythological events represented – only abstract designs. Also uniquely, Mitla remained in ceremonial use after the Spanish conquest.

Wealth of craftwork

While Oaxaca's Indian cultures, such

Tlacolula is famous for its Sunday craft market.

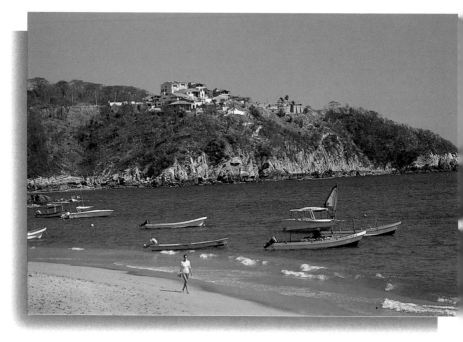

Huatulco, newly developed paradise on Oaxaca's coast.

as the Trique, necessarily survive most fully in remote mountain districts, the wealth and variety of craftwork which the state's peoples produce can easily be sampled by visiting the towns and villages near the city.

Atzompa makes fanciful clay dolls and **Arrazola** is famed for its wildly painted copal wood dragons and snakes. **Etla** sells famous cheeses and chocolate on Wednesdays and Ocotlan markets hawk woven baskets on Fridays.

The women of **Santo Tomas Jalietza** weave elaborate belts and the villagers of **San Bartolo Coyotepec** shape the famous glossy black pottery. **Teotitlan del Valle** has been renowned since pre-Hispanic days for its woollen rugs and ponchos.

The Pacific Coast

Oaxaca's 520-km (323-mile) Pacific Ocean coastline is Mexico's newest beach frontier. After Acapulco, Puerto Vallarta and Cancun have successively hit the headlines, ditching their fishing boats for fashion boutiques.

Watch out for **Huatulco**, the newest project of Fonatur, the Mexican government's tourism developers. Already the tiny settlement has the state's only international airport, albeit ever so humble, and a dozen classy hotels are up and running. **Bahias de Huatulco**, as it's been named, spreads along an extensive coastal stretch and its untouched mountainous hinterland.

Zicatela beach has been rated as having some of the world's best waves.

Puerto Escondido

But this might never have happened if those international trail-blazers, hippies and surfers, had not come upon Oaxaca's coast long ago. The whole stretch was wild and inaccessible until very recently, and perfectly symbolized by the name of the first beach to be "discovered", **Puerto Escondido** – "Hidden Port". This hideaway began drawing North American surfers decades ago for the Hawaii-standard waves that roll

Calm waters of Puerto Angel.

in much of the year, and it now pulls in board riders from all over the world, especially in August and November when competitions are held.

But you don't have to surf to enjoy Puerto Escondido, nor do you have to skimp these days. All kinds of hotels offer accommodations and expensive restaurants vie with the old taco stalls – Puerto Escondido is being discovered by all kinds of people attracted to the combination of a Pacific Ocean vacation with sightseeing around Oaxaca.

Yet still it's largely laid back – its main street was paved only in the 1980s. Though a town rather than a village now, fishermen still land their boats on its curving beach and sell their catch on the spot.

Fishing boats and town activities make the main beach somewhat messy but to the north there is good swimming at lovely **Puerto Angelito Beach** and the even more isolated **Carrizalillo**.

Both beaches lie at the foot of cliffs; walking or boating to them are definitely attractive options. A bit farther north is the long sandy stretch of **Bacocho** beach, but beware of the undertow there.

For surfers the mecca is **Zicatela** beach which has been rated as having some of the very best waves in the world, but its undertow is so fierce that only the very strongest swimmers should ever go out there. It is best to watch the "Mexican Pipeline" and its heroic riders from the beach.

Craft market in Oaxaca, where much of the famous black pottery may be found.

Puerto Angel

Further east lies **Puerto Angel**, still firmly a budget traveller's haunt, nestling in a small cove with rocky promontories blocking out the rough sea and protecting the two little beaches that form the focus of the town.

A few miles away by dirt road begins the long white stretch of **Zipolite** beach, a sleepy fishing village where beachfront restaurants offer cheap seafood feasts.

On the sands young tourists offer naked bodies to the sun, or swing lazily in hammocks slung between palm trees. But here again paradise has a hitch – a deadly undertow in the blue waters.

Bahias de Huatulco

Tomorrow Huatulco's nine bays will be filled with resort hotels and will be reached by road. Today Huatulco's beauty can best be seen from a boat, since most of the bays have no road access. **Tangolunda Bay** is the site of the first three major hotels (Club Med is one), and more hotels, condominiums and time-shares are on the way. The towns of **Santa Cruz** and **Crucecita** are also being developed. Santa Cruz has a waterfront pier, sightseeing boats, and a sprawling crafts market. But Bahias de Huatulco is mostly a coast in transition – where construction crews labor between sea and jungle.

The spectacular view of dawn breaking over the foothills of the inky blue accordion-like Sierra Madre de Chiapas is a perfect introduction to Chiapas, one of Mexico's most mountainous and colorful states with a myriad of attractions: Indian villages, Mayan ruins, cool waterfalls, a spectacular canyon and colonial architecture. The vista is glimpsed as you travel from Oaxaca on the Pan American Highway to **Tuxtla Gutierrez**, the Chiapas capital. Except for its *zocalo* and an excellent zoo – which appropriately includes among its exhibits jaguars, which are considered sacred in the folklore of the Indians of Chiapas – there is little in bustling commercial Tuxtla to detain you.

You should carry on instead for another 80 km (50 miles) to San Cristobal De Las Casas, the heart of southern Mexico's Indian country, an enchanting city bursting with color and vibrancy.

El Carmen Church in the Chiapas highlands.

Market day for the Indians in Zinacantan.

But first make a detour to the magnificent Sumidero Canyon into which many a Chiapa Indian made a death leap rather than submit to the Spanish Conquest. The canyon's near vertical walls plunge more than 914 m (3,000 ft) deep and the best means to appreciate the sheer majesty of the gorge is to take a boat trip down the dammed Rio Grijalva that flows north through it.

San Cristobal De Las Casas

San Cristobal enjoys a beautiful location in the Valley of Hueyzacatlan nestled in the range of mountains that skirts the border with Guatemala. At 2,134 m (7,000 ft) high, San Cristobal

enjoys crisp cool weather even in summer. The city of 120,000 is noted for its colonial architecture and Indian highland villages surrounding it. The Indians flock here daily to sell handicrafts or to buy from its market produce which is lacking in the highlands.

It is the presence of these Indians dressed in traditional costumes – men in woollen *serapes* or tunic tops teamed with calf-length loose trousers and sporting ribboned straw hats; women in thick woollen skirts and brightly colored embroidered *huipile* blouses – that lends a distinct charm to San Cristobal.

The capital of Chiapas until 1829 when it was moved to Tuxtla Gutierrez, San Cristobal has had a rather checkered past. There were always numerous

squabbles among the different Indian groups living in the area and a number of Indian rebellions against the unpopular Spanish. Indeed, when the Spanish first came to Chiapas in 1529, many Indians chose to throw themselves into the Sumidero Canyon rather than succumb to them.

Encomiendas

Five years after they established themselves in San Cristobal, the Spanish made the town the administrative center for there *encomiendas* or large plots of land that were given to the Spanish soldiers

Myth of Quetzalcoatl

Remnants of temples dedicated to Quetzalcoatl.

Mexico's pre-Hispanic cultures are steeped in myths and legends. Perhaps the best known among these is the myth of Quetzalcoatl, the omnipresent bird-serpent motif that appears on so many of its ancient monuments. It is a fable that is part fact, part fiction and part fairy tale. That Quetzalcoatl did exist has not been disputed. What is less clear is exactly who he was, when he lived and where he came from. He was highly revered and is represented as a feathered serpent in pyramids from Teotihuacan and Xochicalco in central Mexico to Chichen Itza in the Yucatan Peninsula.

It is a fearsome image showing a plumed snake's head with bulging eyes, an open jaw bearing sharp teeth, a bifid tongue and an articulated spinal column, a far cry from the gentle god-king that he was reputed to be.

Quetzalcoatl has been portrayed by historians as a serious, responsible lawgiver and compassionate ruler who was opposed to human sacrifices. He was thus assumed to have lived centuries before the Aztec period when sacrifices were practiced and even before Christ as it was he who had discovered corn.

So revered is the symbol of Quetzalcoatl that ancient pre-Hispanic civilizations at different times endowed the name on priests who had acquired the same virtues as the god-king. To qualify, they had to be virtuous, merciful, humble, friendly to all, god-fearing and be a fountain of knowledge.

The name Quetzalcoatl itself is wrapped in mystery. "Quetzal" is the name of a rare bird found in the highlands of Chiapas and Guatemala. Unlike other birds, it lacks claws and has only two front toes. "*Coatl*" means "snake" to the Nahua Indians, yet, if the word is broken up into two, "*co*" is "snake" in the Maya language and "*atl*" is "water" in the Nahuatl language.

While it is recognized that the Maya's Kukulcan was probably their answer to Quetzalcoatl, what has puzzled historians is: why did the Nahuas, who inhabit the high plateau, choose as a symbol of their god the quetzal bird that is only found in the highlands?

Whatever the reason, for the Maya and the Nahua, Quetzalcoatl was a transcendental figure that was both god and man, the embodiment of water, earth (depicted by the snake) and bird. Ancient myth has it that people came into being only when the gods had found them special human food. In the case of Quetzalcoatl, he discovered maize which made human life possible.

Although Quetzalcoatl was known as the wind god, he also represented all of man's foibles and strengths. He brought his own downfall by lusting (the plumed serpent); in repentance, he laid on his self-built funeral pyre to be consumed by fire. His heart rose to the heavens to become the planet Venus, an act that saves the universe from destruction, for by entering the solar world where he is swallowed by the sun he also becomes the sun, and hence becomes a source of light and life for Earth.

Symbol of a God

Hence, Quetzalcoatl's symbol is the morning star (Venus) while he has also been identified as the sun-god of the Aztecs, Huitzilopochtli, whose energy has to be fed constantly with the sacrifice of human hearts. However, these hearts had to be pure, deified through suffering, the way Quetzalcoatl's was.

Here's how one writer put it: "Quetzalcoatl is an embodiment of (the prophet) Mohammed's affirmation that God created the angels (stars, planets) and set reason in them, and He created the beasts (serpent) and set lust in them, and He created the sons of Adam (man, eater of maize) and set in them both reason and lust to war with one another until reason (Quetzalcoatl as king) prevails".

Quetzalcoatl has been described as tall, with a strong frame, wide brows, large eyes and sporting a beard. He is always seen in images wearing a conical hat, a seashell necklace and with a quetzal bird resting on his back.

According to legend, Quetzalcoatl was born of Coatlicue, goddess of the serpent petticoat, whose statue, found on the site of Tenochtitlan, can be seen in Mexico City's National Museum of Anthropology. (The word "*cue*" means petticoat and is used to denote a woman).

There are several versions of the story and of Quetzalcoatl's early life. One tells of how the goddess, a virgin, became pregnant after swallowing a piece of emerald. Another has it that it happened after she had placed a feather on her bosom while doing penance on a hill called Coatepec (Snake Hill).

Whatever the version, she bore a son who grew up virtuous and compassionate and was a ruler. Enemies tried to get him to perform human sacrifices but he refused. One day, his arch enemy Tezcatlipoca worked his magic on Quetzalcoatl by showing him a mirror in which the latter saw an image of his face that was hideously shrivelled, with sunken eyes and swollen eyelids. Alarmed, the poor young king went into hiding as he was afraid his people would

Motif of the Plumed Serpent.

... Myth of Quetzalcoatl

react violently if they saw him thus. Tezcatlipoca then closed in for the kill. First, he got Quetzalcoatl to don a wig, then dressed him in a coat of quetzal feathers, painted his lips and forehead and had him wear a beard of bright red and blue feathers of the guacamaya or macaw, and a turquoise mask. So impressed with his new image when he looked into the mirror, that was Quetzalcoatl was won over by Tezcatlipoca and agreed he emerge from his hiding place.

Tezcatlipoca and other evil magicians now saw their chance to destroy Quetzalcoatl. They first tempted him with wine which he at first refused. Then he decided to have a taste which was so good that he decided to have more. Soon his servants followed and became inebriated. Quetzalcoatl also called for his sister to

join in. Intoxicated, Quetzalcoatl then had sex with his sister. He only realized the horror of his deed when the effects of alcohol wore off. Feeling remorseful, Quetzalcoatl ordered his servants to build a casket in which he would lie in penance for four days. At the end of it, he constructed a funeral pyre, and dressed in a cloak of feathers and wearing his turquoise mask, he fell upon it and set himself alight.

His ashes turned into a flock of birds that flew into the sky carrying his heart which became the planet Venus. The legend goes that the morning star dipped below the horizon for four days for Quetzalcoatl to complete purgatory. When he rose again, it would be to sit on his throne in the sky forever. It was this act of repentance and self-sacrifice, so the myth goes, that has been the saving grace of humankind.

---

in lieu of pay. Each plot came with large groups of Indians who were literally enslaved, with many working to an early death. Although slavery was officially abolished in the 1550s through the efforts of a Dominican friar, Bartoleme de las Casas, the exploitation of Indians through forced labor continued through other forms.

In 1869, the Indians sank their differences to unite in a revolt against the Spanish, but it was quickly crushed. It was not until 1936 that the Indians were given a fair degree of autonomy over their own lands.

Harmony prevails these days among the Indians in San Cristobal's main square and marketplace where they flock to trade and do their shopping. Many of them belong to the Tzotzil and Tzeltal groups.

Touring the City

You can walk just about everywhere within the city on foot. The **Zocalo**, a 16th-century plaza built by the Spanish, is the center of activity. Ringed by colonial buildings, the garden-like *Zocalo* is a pleasant spot to spend evenings, especially on days when an orchestra strikes up in the band kiosk. One corner of the Zocalo is flanked by the city's 16th-century **Cathedral** which has an impressive. Baroque facade and a patterned wooden roof supported by Corinthian pillars.

From the Cathedral, walk left half a block into 16 de Septiembre, then right into Adelina de Flores and left again into 20 de Noviembre and continue northwards until you are in Lazaro

Mayan Indian market.

Cardenas. Midway you will find the **Iglesia de Santo Domingo** on whose grounds is a makeshift open-air bazaar where Indians spread out their colorful handicrafts to catch the eye of visitors on their way to the church.

You will spot Indian women weaving on looms tied to their backs in between tending to customers. The interior of Santo Domingo dazzles as the pulpit, walls and portraits are gilded with thin leaves of gold.

Its baroque facade is topped with twin towers from which rise black metalwork crosses. Opposite the facade is a statue of Diego de Mazariegos who founded San Cristobal.

Next door to Santo Domingo is its ex-convent, now converted into a religious museum and textile cooperative of **Sna Jolobil** (Weavers' House in the Tzotzil language) it is devoted to keeping the Mayan art of weaving alive. By providing the Indians with an outlet for their handwoven items, Sna Jolobil has helped to revitalize and save traditional weaving patterns in the San Cristobal area – patterns that have existed since the time of the Maya. The beautiful handmade articles are expensive but they make unique souvenirs.

On one wall of the cooperative is a mural painted by an unknown artist that traces the history of San Cristobal's Indian population, from their Mayan origins and the golden age of Mayan culture to slavery under the Spanish Conquistadors and eventual freedom.

La Reina De La Selva and the Lacandons

When a movie was made documenting her amazing life and work among the Lacandon Indians in the rainforests of eastern Chiapas, it was appropriately entitled *La Reina de la Selva* (Queen of the Forest).

The "queen" is Swiss born anthropologist Gertrude (Trudy) Blom, widow of Danish archeologist Franz Blom. The couple dedicated most of their lives to working among the fast disappearing community of the Lacandons in the Lacandon Rainforest near the Guatemalan border. Franz Blom also spent some of his time digging in Maya sites.

Although her husband died 25 years ago, Trudy, still sprightly and alert at 95, has continued to work as a crusader of the Lacandons. Indeed, the house where Trudy and her husband lived was given the name of Na Bolom by the Lacandons: "*Na*" meaning house and "*Bolom*" meaning jaguar, for them, a symbol of power and a play on the name "Blom."

Much of what is known of the 300 Lacandons now left in the jungles has been the result of the Bloms' research. The couple were active environmentalists and they campaigned for the Lacandon Rainforest to be saved so that the tiny Indian community, already faced with extinction, would not vanish forever.

The Lacandons are believed to be the direct descendants of the Maya. All of them have long hair and wear white tunics and they live in makeshift huts scattered in the rainforest. They live on maize, which since the days of the Maya, has been considered a sacred food.

Other crops such as banana, cassava, yam, squash, beans and tomatoes are cultivated to supplement their diet. And occasionally they hunt or fish from the rivers.

The Lacandons have lost the sophisticated concepts of mathematics and time for which the Maya were famous. However, like the Maya, the Lacandons' cosmos consists of 13 skies, nine inner worlds and many gods which show themselves in the form of a jaguar, the most sacred symbol for the Lacandons. The ancient Maya sites in the jungles are also sacred to them and they journey regularly to Yaxchilan to make offerings to them.

Trudy, who has won acclaim for her ethnographic work, still resides in Na Bolom. It was turned into a research center and a museum to contain archeological and religious artifacts – including those used by the Lacandons collected by the Bloms over a lifetime.

It also has an extensive library collection on Mexico and Central America and numerous periodicals and news clippings on environmental issues and on the work of the Bloms among the Lacandons. One room in the house is reserved specifically for the use of visiting Lacandons.

The museum is also a guest house with a small number of rooms to cater to travellers. It operates an artists-in-residence program as part of its contribution to the effort of keeping alive the art of textile weaving in San Cristobal. This ancient Maya craft is also explained in detail through exhibits in the museum.

Trudy also allows tours of her museum on Tuesdays to Sundays to promote her work and understanding of the Lacandons' way of life and that of other Indian communities around San Cristobal. There are also tours of nearby Indian villages conducted by volunteers working at the museum. The address: Na Bolom, Vicente Guerrero 33, tel: 814 18.

Walking east from the Cathedral on Real de Guadalupe are two other churches, the **Iglesia de Guadalupe** and the **Iglesia de San Cristobal de las Casas** located on top of two hills facing one other, about a mile from the *Zocalo*. There is a sweeping view of the sur-

rounding plains from the summits.

Perhaps the most colorful attraction of San Cristobal is its daily market on the northern outskirts of the city where many of the brightly-garbed Indian shoppers are as eye-catching as the exotic fruit and vegetables laid out for

Women of San Juan Chamula in traditional dress.

sale. Visiting the Indian villages ringing San Cristobal is an intriguing experience. The most accessible are San Juan Chamula and Zinacatan, 10 km (6 miles) from San Cristobal.

You can walk to the villages which are scattered across a vast meadow, or take a mini-bus from San Cristobal. However, the roads leading to the villages are potholed and travel is slow. Although the Indians are tolerant of visitors entering their villages, they are hostile about being photographed as they believe that the camera captures their soul.

They have been known to stone camera-clicking tourists, so it's best to put away the picture box before mingling in their midst. Photography of the villages from a distance is permissible so long as you do it on the quiet.

San Juan Chamula

A cemetery on a slope leads to the village of **San Juan Chamula** where women in bare feet scurry about tending to tasks, some carrying children in a shawl slung across their backs. There are some 40,000 Chamulans, representing one of the largest Tzotzil groups. Life centers around the main square which is the best place to glimpse the colorful costumes which the villagers typically wear. The Chiapenico highlands are one of the few remaining regions left in Mexico where traditional dress codes

The Practice of Faith Healing

The simple white-washed facade of the San Juan Bautista Church in San Juan Chamula is similar to that of many provincial Catholic churches in Mexico. But the similarity stops the moment one steps into the church.

Instead of pews, you will find devotees seated on the bare floor which is strewn with pine needles and leaves. Small groups sit cross-legged huddled over lighted candles and chanting prayers. Swirling incense smoke from burners fills the church with a fragrant scent, adding to the rather mystical atmosphere.

In the midst of each group is a faith-healer holding the hands of the sick person seeking healing, while the rest are relatives corralling around in moral support. Near the healer are bottles of Coca-cola or an egg. These mark, respectively, the first and second stage of faith healing.

The presence of Coca-cola bottles seems incongruous but for the faith-healers the effervescent drink is a convenient substitute for a time-consuming home-made brew used in the past. A distilled spirit is mixed with the Coca-cola and the "purifying" concoction is drunk by the patient to make him throw up, thus throwing out of the body the "toxins" that were causing the illness.

If the person does not recover, another ceremony is carried out three days later. An egg is passed around the patient several times after lengthy chants and prayer sessions; this is to draw the toxins out from the body and into the egg, thus cleansing and curing the patient.

If this again fails, a chicken is sacrificed a week later in yet another ceremony. The village's shamans claim this sacrifice is a sure cure. Such Chamulan healing practices date back to Mayan times.

The Faith Healers

Salvadore is a faith healer or shaman in San Juan Chamula. His home is very simple. The living room is dominated by an altar with a cross, around which are pine needles, animal figurines, flowers, plants and burning candles. Scented smoke rises from a nearby incense burner made from clay.

The Chamulans believe that when someone is born, a corresponding guardian animal is born in the mountains to protect him throughout life. Thus the mud floor of Salvadore's house is strewn with pine needles and leaves in the belief that this will bring him closer to nature and the spirits in the mountains.

Salvadore says he is training his 20-year-old daughter, Ros, to become a shaman.

Being a faith-healer is a calling, he says, received usually in a dream after which one would be "given" the power to heal which must be carefully nurtured by apprenticeship to an existing healer.

It's a metier that seems to run in families. Salvadore says her daughter received her calling when she was 16. Though already able to perform simple ceremonies, Salvadore reckons it would take her ten years to become a full-fledged healer.

are strictly observed and each Indian group has its own distinctive dress, patterns and colors which are vested with social meaning. The Chamulans are no exception.

Unmarried Chamulan women, for instance, are distinguished by the thin braided belts they wear round their waists, while married women sport wide belts. Both groups, however, take pride in brightening up their appearance by adorning their long braided hair with multi-colored woollen tassels. The men wear white or black wool *serapes* over their shirts, tied by thick belts. They often don "10-gallon" hats as well and if they are officials or village elders, their hats are draped with ribbons.

Not only do the Chamulans cling tenaciously to their own standards of dress, they have also developed their own form of spiritual worship blending Catholicism with folk practices of which the best known is faith healing. Like every church in Mexico, the Chamulan church of San Juan Bautista is decorated with *santos*.

However, in this Indian church, the *santos* wear mirrors around their necks since the Chamulans believe that saints are not infallible and that they need the mirrors to reflect the worshippers' faces so that the saints can remember who they are. The mirrors are also thought to frighten away devils lurking behind the devotees – when they see their own reflected images the devils flee, a belief that is similar to one held by the Chinese. In their efforts to retain their own form of spiritual worship, the Chamulans have continually rebuffed the Mexican religious authorities, allowing Catholic bishops to enter the church only to conduct baptism ceremonies.

Zinacantan

In contrast, the Indians in **Zinacantan** have fully absorbed the Catholic faith. Worship is conducted from pews similar to other Mexican churches and unlike those of Chamula, the faith-healers of Zinacantan are not allowed to conduct their ceremonies in church. However, the ceiling, walls and *santos* in the church are draped with long colorful ribbons

similar to the ones decorating the Zinacantan men's hats. The *santos* also sport mirrors around their necks.

Zinacantan is much smaller than San Juan Chamula, with a population of 15,000. The villagers here stand out in their shocking pink triangular *serapes*, worn by both sexes. In addition, the men wear broad-rimmed straw hats (reminiscent of English boarding school-girls') decorated with short-colored ribbons if they are bachelors, and long flowing ribbons if they are married.

During festivals, the Zinacantecos practise an ancient Maya custom when they sport leather sandals decorated with high heel guards.

Palenque

It's easy to imagine how American explorer John L. Stevens must have felt when he first stumbled across Palenque back in 1840 as you gaze at the exquisite Maya ruins entwined in the web of greenery that makes up the jade colored tropical jungles of Chiapas.

Palenque was a holy city of the Maya that reached its glory between AD 600 and AD 800 under the reigns of Pakal and his son Chan Balum. Archeologists have found similarities between Palenque and the great Angkor Wat temple of Cambodia and carvings in India, reinforcing the age old belief that the Maya were an ancient people who had migrated from Asia to the Americas. Palenque was, apart from Yaxchilan

The magnificent ruins of the palace in Palenque.

and Bonampak, the westernmost city established by the Maya; the rest are in neighboring Yucatan.

Among the rare finds in this ancient city of 65 sq km (25 sq miles) was the royal tomb of a priest king, believed to belong to Pakal, uncovered in 1949 after four years of excavation in the Temple of Inscriptions.

It is one of the few tombs ever to be found within Mexican pyramids and the first in a Mayan pyramid. The lid of the five ton sarcophagus is said to represent some of the finest carvings of ancient Mexico. The walls of Pakal's tomb depict the journey of death to the underworld, the nine gods of the underworld and the journey of rebirth.

The Mayas have been compared to the ancient Greeks for the prowess they possessed in engineering, astronomy, calendrical calculations and mathematics. Their civilization collapsed when the Mayas inexplicably abandoned their great city sometime between the 9th and 12th centuries.

Temple of the Inscriptions

Dense undergrowth has inhibited the excavation of all but 34 of Palenque's estimated 500 buildings. But what has been dug up so far is enough to keep you absorbed for hours. Excavations include temples, plazas, religious platforms, a palace and a ball court.

Standing above the ruins is the

Enchanting Agua Azul falls.

The base for visiting the Palenque ruins is the town of Palenque, 6 km (4 miles) from the national park that has been declared around the pyramids. The national park is open daily from 8 am-5 pm, with an admission fee of N$15. From Palenque town, arrangements can be made to visit Yaxchilan and Bonampak, two other sets of fascinating Maya ruins.

Getting to the two sites involves a long and arduous journey over pot-holed roads and a boat journey on Rio Usumacinta plus an overnight stay in the mosquito-infested Lacandon Rainforest. For this reason, the two archeological sites receive few visitors. For those who do make it, a hop by small plane from San Cristobal or Palenque is often

majestic **Temple of the Inscriptions** located atop an eight-stepped pyramid. The 23-m (75-ft) temple in which Pakal's tomb was found was dedicated to him and contains hieroglyphic texts tracing his rule and ascendance.

The **Group of the Cross** contains three temples – Temple of the Cross, Temple of the Foliate Cross and Temple of the Sun – built by Chan Balum in AD 692. They contain hieroglyphics of the sacred *ceiba* tree of the Maya and carvings depicting the mythical relationship of Chan Balum to three Palenque gods. But it is the **Palace** and its unique tower that knitted all of Palenque together. It was built over a 200-year period and it boasts some of Palenque's most striking carvings.

Stone bas-relief in Palenque.

Yaxchilan was used as a ceremonial center in Mayan times.

the preferred mode of transport.

However, if you are adventurous of spirit, have time to spare (three days at least) and are prepared to rough it, overland travel is a more exciting – and cheaper – option.

Travel agencies in Palenque offer good value for money with adventure tours to both ruins. A minimum of four people is required.

Yaxchilan

The road and river trip to **Yaxchilan** is a thrill in itself. As Yaxchilan is inaccessible by land, you transfer onto a *lancha* (boat) after a bumpy five-hour drive to travel across the Rio Usumacinta which forms a natural boundary between Mexico and Guatemala. It is high above this river in the lush rainforest that the spectacular ruins of Yaxchilan are perched. Yaxchilan was used mainly as a Mayan ceremonial center which took over three centuries to build from AD 514 to 807.

The temple ruins are spread over a wide area and seem to belong to one particular ruler known as *Escudo Jaguar* (Jaguar Shield) whose imprint, a jaguar in profile, appears in many of the glyphs and carvings in the complex.

The temples of Yaxchilan are adorned with a decorative roof comb and several round stones strewn in the area which are believed to have been used for human sacrifice.

Bonampak, where ancient Mayan murals were uncovered.

Bonampak

Unlike Yaxchilan, **Bonampak** has more of the appearance of a lost city as the ruins are still virtually hidden in the rainforest. The only way in is on foot and if it rains it can be a soggy 10 km (6 -mile) trek through mud and jungle to reach the ruins.

Bonampak was, like Yaxchilan, a ceremonial center, built during the Mayan Classical Period, from AD 200 to 900. Only a number of crumbling buildings have been rescued from the jungle but they are very precious as they house the few known painted Mayan murals ever uncovered. The frescoes are faded but the depiction of daily life in Mayan

times including ceremonies and festivals can be clearly discerned in the reddish paintings. Restoration of the murals, once almost completely obscured by calcium carbonate, is still on-going.

For a refreshing cap to visiting pyramid ruins in the jungles, a trip to two waterfalls near Palenque is recommended. The nearer falls, **Misol Ha**, is one long cascade descending 35 m (115 ft) into a small pool where swimming is possible. More impressive are the enchanting falls of **Agua Azul** in a jungle setting. Five hundred cascades plunge down a series of rocky terraces to create several pools. Strong currents make swimming dangerous – there have been drownings – but the spray from the falls is a wonderful freshener.

Leisure in Mexico is geared towards the great outdoors. In seaside resorts, there are opportunities for fishing, diving, snorkeling and for duck hunting, while in forests in the interior huntsmen seek out wild boar and deer. For those who can afford it, elitist recreation like golfing can be pursued in country clubs, and tennis in luxury city and resort hotels. Everywhere, national parks are inviting grounds on weekends for picnics with family and friends, while amusement parks and fairs offering joy rides are filled to the brim.

Mexicans enjoy playing the tourist on weekends and national holidays, travelling to a neighboring state to sightsee, sample local dishes and bring back souvenirs. It's a gregarious affair as not only do mom, dad and the kids go along, but grandparents, relatives and sometimes even the neighbors or office and factory colleagues as well. And if the car won't fit everybody

Turquoise clear waters in Xelha Lagoon.

Sports & Recreation

or if no one owns a *coche*, no problem; a *camionera* is hired and everyone piles aboard, chipping in to pay for their share of the cost.

For those who prefer to watch than to participate, there are several spectacles to choose from: dramatic bullfights, entertaining *charreadas*, exciting *jai alai*, nail biting horse-races, football, baseball and boxing.

Bullfights

The Spanish, who themselves were introduced to bullfighting via the Moors, brought the sport to Mexico. The story goes that the first bullfight in Mexico was staged in 1526 in honor of Spanish conquistador Hernan Cortes's successful expedition to Honduras.

As in Spain, bullfighting is more than a sport, it is an art; more precisely, it is a dance with death, a notion that fits well into the psyche of the macho Mexican male. It is not easy to be a matador. You need to be brave, you need to have the dexterity and the grace to execute the elegant movements that, by the very fact that they are a brush with mortality, make bullfighting so fascinating to watch.

A bullfight is not a spectacle for the squeamish; it is often gory and blood is spilled. As Ernest Hemingway points out, there are two types of spectators: those who identify with the bull and those who identify with the man. Those feeling more *simpatico* with the bull will

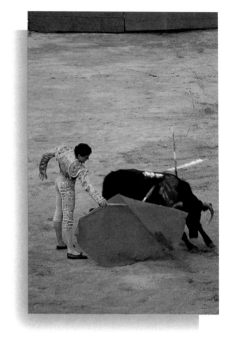

Matador and bull in a gruelling display of bravado.

wince in pain for the animal and will definitely not enjoy the drama.

But for those who succumb to the tragedy of the ritualistic art, and who enjoy the pageantry and the courage of the matador and the bull, a bullfight is a sensational spectacle which few others can match.

The *el toro* (fighting bull) is not an ordinary one; it is specially bred for its strength and spirit. It is four years old and weighs in at 900 pounds when it makes its debut in the bull ring.

The *fiesta brava* (bullfight) is usually held in the afternoon on Sundays at 4 pm, and for superstitious reasons, *aficionados* (passionate fans) of the sport make sure they arrive on time so that the fight can kick off as scheduled.

There are six fights with three matadors tackling two bulls each. Each fight has three *tercios* or acts lasting 15 minutes, with trumpet flourishes declaring the start of every *tercio*. It begins with *peones* with capes running the bull around so and that the matador can gauge its strength and spirit.

Then the matador takes over, using a golden silk cape to lead the bull in a series of passes to a *picador* on horseback who thrusts a *garrocha* (lance) into the bull's neck to weaken it.

The *picador* leaves and *anderilleros* enter the ring to weaken the bull further by piercing its hump with short decorated *banderillas*. The bull bleeds profusely. The *banderilleros* exit leaving only the matador.

Next comes the *faena* that brings the crowd on edge. The matador works close to the horns, making classic poses such as *naturales*, *veronicas* and *chicuelinas* with his scarlet *muleta* (cape) to dominate the bull. Oh how elegantly he executes his moves! But the spectators are critically assessing this display of skill as much as they are enjoying it.

Then, comes the high point of the man versus beast drama as the matador aligns himself for the kill. Positioning himself in front of the horns, he plunges his sword down the shoulder blades and punctures the heart. A perfect *estocador* will instantly kill the bull. Bravo! The crowd roars. *Toro, toro, toro!*

As they shout and applaud, the matador walks around the ring acknowledging the cheers. If the matador has been exceptional, he is sometimes awarded with an ear, or two, of the bull.

Hunting

Mexico is a favorite hunting ground for the sportsman in search of game, because of the variety available. The most popular game are duck, geese and wild turkey, found predominantly along the west coast, in central Mexico and on the Yucatan Peninsula.

Acapulco, Los Mochis, Mazatlan, Manzanillo, Zihuatenejo and Merida are best known for duck hunting. There are also geese and turkey in Zihuatenejo and quail in Merida and Mazatlan. The best white-winged dove hunting is offered in Guaymas.

Deer is concentrated in the northern border states: Sonora, Chihuahua and Coahuila. Mule deer are present in Tabasco and small jungle deer in Campeche and Yucatan. Wild boar are sought after in Nayarit, Campeche, Chiapas, Guerrero, Yucatan, Qintana Roo, Mazatlan and Manzanillo.

Puerto Vallarta has an abundance of doves, ducks, quail, wild turkey and pigeons in spring and winter, while its mountains are home to wild pigs, deer and mountain lions.

The jaguar and the black bear in the Yucatan Peninsula are now protected animals and cannot be hunted. The Mexican Wildlife Department has established hunting seasons and guidelines on the number of wildlife species that can be killed each day and the number allowed in possession. For a copy of the English language book on hunting regulations, write to the Secretaria de Desarrollo Urbano y Ecologia, Direccion de Flora y Fauna Silvestre, Calle de Elba 20, 8th Floor, Colonia Cuauhtemoc, Mexico DF 06500.

Since hunting permits are required whether or not you are bringing in your own firearms or renting them from an organizer, a hunting trip must be planned in advance. In addition, if you are importing your own firearms, a permit is also required. Contact the Mexican Hunting Association, 3302 Josie Ave, Long Beach, California 90808, tel: 310 421 1619 for applications.

Mexico's long coastline is a boon to windsurfers ...

Fishing

Mexico is an anglers' paradise. It has a long fishing season, an abundance of fish and plenty of spots where you can find them. Many resorts offer deep sea fishing trips and the charter boat operators will also apply for a fishing license for you at an additional charge. The license is obtainable from the local Fisheries Department. Fishing tackle is also provided or you can bring your own.

Acapulco, Cabo San Lucas, Guaymas, Ixtapa/Zihuatenejo, Mazatlan and Puerto Vallarta offer fishing year round. Among the many species that can be caught are barracuda, bonito, grouper, marlin, sailfish, yellowtail, mackerel,

... and parasailing.

A dive into Mexico's crystal clear waters reveal untold wonders.

needlefish, corvina and jack crevalle.

In Cancun, Cozumel and Manzanillo, you can fish for different species depending on the time of the year. Cancun, for example has marlin and bluefin tuna in April and May; wahoo and kingfish from May to September and dolphin and sailfish from March to July.

Many of the resorts organize annual deep sea fishing tournaments that attract anglers from around the world. The best known tournaments are in Acapulco, Cabo San Lucas, San Jose del Cabo, Mazatlan and Cozumel.

For more information on fishing, contact the Mexican Department of Fisheries, 1138 India St, Ste 125, San Diego, California, tel: (619) 233 6956.

Diving

Mexico's long coastline is a boon to scuba divers and skin divers. There is little need to bring your own gear as most beach resorts will have equipment for hire. They also usually offer diving courses as well as organized diving tours.

Skin divers will revel in the waters of Isla Mujeres, the Xcaret inlet of Cancun, Chancanab Lagoon in the island of Cozumel, Las Gatas Beach in Zihuatenejo, Los Arcos in Puerto Vallarta, Bahia San Carlos near Guaymas, Manzanillo and Xelha Lagoon in Akumal.

All of them have crystal clear waters teeming with coral gardens and

Los Charros

The art of the charros.

The *charro* is a Mexican institution and he practicses a sport that is most entertaining to watch. You can catch him in action on Sundays, in Mexico City, Guadalajara and several cities in the northern states, where *charros* gather in a ring, the *lienzo charro*, to exhibit their fine horsemanship and show off their skills with the rope in a rodeo called the *charreada*.

The *charro* has been likened to a cowboy, but there are differences between the two in the way they dress and perform. As with many things Mexican, the *charro* has its origins in Spain. The colonists brought along their horses but initially kept them exclusively for themselves. Only when cattle were introduced and men needed to work them, were Indians taught to ride horses. They soon became very adept in handling them and in using the lasso, developing their own brand of tricks with it.

The *charros* are elegantly dressed in well fitted trousers studded at the sides, an embroidered shirt, leather jacket, boots and spurs. They start their training from a tender age, sometimes as young as five years old.

Typically in a *charreada*, you will see a mix of teens, young men and veterans performing. There are women *charras* with their own version of the *charreada* called the *escaramuza* in which they perform in flouncy dresses and ride saddle. *Charros* run in the family and it's not unusual to have father and son or brothers competing in the same *charreada*.

For *charreadas* are as much a sport as a contest in which men pit their skills against one other, representing a club or association. Indeed, most *charreadas* are *jaripeos* or tournaments with teams competing; a panel of judges awards points.

Many *charros* travel all over the country to compete in *jaripeos*. Some even participate in tournaments in the United States and Europe.

A *charreada* is performed against the stirring background music of the *mariachis*. The three

multi-colored fish near the surface.

The same spots also offer excellent scuba diving for those who want to venture deeper. Other superb locations include: Roqueta Island in Acapulco, the Sea of Cortes or Gulf of California off Baja California, Cancun and Mazatlan.

The Palancar reef (the world's second largest) off Cozumel and the barrier reef skirting the 16-km (10-mile) beach of Akumal, are outstanding. Both have exquisitely clear warm waters with a visibility of 61 m (200 ft). For expert divers, the underwater formations of Los Moros de Potosi in Zihuatenejo/

hour show begins with a line up of splendidly costumed *charros* riding to take a bow before the judges and the spectators.

The first event is the *cala de caballo*, demonstrating horsemanship. The *charro* gallops at full speed across the ring then stops short within a chalked out rectangle. Then keeping within the box, he rides his horse in circles, first to the left and then to the right before ending the event by riding backwards out of the ring.

Next is the *coleadero*. A bull is let loose and it charges out of his pen down a corridor into the ring. The *charro* rides up to the bull to grab its tail to make it fall and roll over. The most skillful *charros* will grab the tail and pass it under his right leg, he then turn his horse around swiftly to bring the bull down to the delight of the crowd.

After each *charro* has gone through his paces, *bronco* riding and bull riding take place. It's then time to demonstrate the *charros's* mastery of the rope with a mesmerizing display. Groups of *charros* ride around the ring, pursuing a wild horse, trying to lasso it. Sometimes, a *charro* will break away to display his rope tricks while the rest gallop after the horse. Then, when the solo *charro* sees his chance, he throws his cord around the neck of the horse.

At times, the *charro* will dismount to play with his *lariat*, the routines getting faster and more complicated until suddenly the *charro* leaps into the air, and into a loop which he then tosses onto the ground which the horse's hoofs will run right into and be ensnared. If that is the epitome of skill, wait till you see the finale when a *charro* leaps off his galloping horse onto the back of a *bronco*!

Ixtapa provide a unique experience.

Golfing

Mexico offers all year round golfing and some of its courses are among the world's most challenging, designed by top names such as Robert Trent Jones and Joe Finger. Most golf clubs in Mexico City cater only to members while some of the newer ones may accept overseas players who are members of a US golf club. It's best to golf in resorts where the courses have been specially built for tourists. There are numerous resorts with golf courses. They include Acapulco, Guadalajara, Puerto Vallarta, Cancun, Manzanillo, Cuernavaca, Cuautla, Ixtapa, Merida and Mazatlan.

Acapulco's golf courses at the Princess and Pierre Marques rank as Mexico's finest. Equally outstanding is Ixtapa's Robert Trent Jones designed course with fairways ending right at the beach. There are also golf courses in Queretaro, Oaxaca and Morelia. Most golf courses have clubs and carts for hire as well as a caddy service.

It's best to check with the concierge of your hotel to find out where the golf courses are and to bring along your local golf club membership card and a letter of introduction from your club.

Jai alai

It's a ball game played in the Basque region and it was brought in by the early Spaniards. This very fast game, played in a long indoor court, is exciting to watch. It is similar to squash as players, wearing curved gloves made of basket material attached to the arm, try to score by hitting a small hard ball against a high wall.

Shopping

333

If there is such a thing as a shoppers' paradise, Mexico comes close to it. The broad array of beautifully handcrafted items is staggering; each is a work of art, the result of skills that have been honed for centuries and passed down from generation to generation.

Mexico's mountains served to isolate communities and thus helped to preserve age old traditions. It is thus not uncommon to find villages devoted to a particular craft or using motifs and designs that have remained unchanged for centuries.

Tulum handicrafts.

The Indians had been artisans long before the arrival of the Spanish, creating ceramic vessels to cook with, weaving clothes to wear, or making baskets to carry goods. From fashioning practical items purely for daily use, they progressed to making luxury items appreciated for their beauty: gold jewelry, fine woven cotton, vessels of lacquerware and

Hand-embroidered serapes are much sought-after items.

clay figures of deities. The crafts would be sold at outdoor Indian markets called *tianguis* along with fruit, vegetables and live animals.

Although the Spanish injected new ideas and introduced new techniques such as the potter's wheel and the use of metals, the exuberance of Indian design is still detected in many of Mexico's handicrafts. The fantastical trees of life and the effervescent sun faces made in Metepec, are a good example.

Because it was difficult to bring in certain bulky items like furniture or saddles, the Spanish later decided to have them made in Mexico, opening a crafts school in Mexico City and teaching Indians the necessary skills.

For the Tarascan or Purepeche Indi-

ans living around Lake Patzcuaro, they had the Bishop of Michoacan, Vasco de Quiroga, to thank for developing the arts and crafts that are so unique to Michoacan today: masks, copperware, straw handicrafts, guitars, embroidered textiles, lacquerware and pottery.

The bishop had, in 1540, encouraged the Tarascans to specialize in a craft which they could sell as a means of livelihood so that they could stop working under exploitative conditions for the Spanish in the mines. Some of the crafts were age-old traditions that had been in danger of dying out; others were introduced by the bishop.

Specialty craftsmen from Spain also played their part in imparting their knowledge to their Indian apprentices.

Soon the Indians became as good as their masters. However, locally made products took a while to gain recognition as made-in-Spain items were preferred. It was only upon independence that nationalistic fervor led Mexicans to spurn Spanish made products and turn to Indian crafted work. The crafts available in Mexico today embody the unique spirit of a rich Mexican culture that is a marriage of Indian and European design, skills and techniques.

Markets, craft shops and galleries throughout the country stock the tempting crafts in a bewildering array. The government-run Casa de Artesania usually found in each town, is a good place to see what's available in the region and to have an idea of prices. The Casa de Artesania is a good place to shop as you are assured of quality, though prices tend to be on the high side.

For lower prices, markets are the places to go. Bargaining is acceptable, although in some places, the prices are already low to begin with and it sometimes seems heartless to try to bring them down. In resorts however, most items are overpriced. Try to get them reduced by a third of the asking price. If you buy from beachside or roadside vendors, bargaining is *de rigueur*.

Pottery

Pottery making is deeply rooted in Mexican tradition and is widely practised throughout the country. Although the variety of pottery styles and design is amazing and is special to each region, they may be divided into two distinct types: brittle, unglazed ware made since pre-Columbian times and the sturdier, glazed and highly decorative pottery influenced by the Spanish.

Traditional Indian pottery is still produced by hand. The best example of this is Paquime pottery from Las Casas Grandes. These handsome creations are molded by hand without the use of the potter's wheel, employing special clay found only in the mountains of the Chihuahua Valley. Put your hand inside the vases to feel the fingerprint impressions left by the potters.

The pottery is dung fired and geometric patterns are painted with natu-

Traditional Indian pottery is still hand molded.

Motifs in Mayan Weaving

A Zapotec weaver at work.

The striking *huipiles* or brocaded blouses worn by Indian women vendors in the streets and markets of San Cristobal de las Casas are the first thing that wows the visitor to this highland town in Chiapas.

The *huipiles* are the expression of a weaving tradition that dates back to the early Maya period (around AD 300). Despite years of upheaval during the colonial era, the Tzotzil and Tzeltal Indian women descendants of the Maya living in the highlands of Chiapas have managed to preserve this precious skill, weaving

sacred designs that have long sustained the Mayan world. But they are designs that are the re-birth of ancient symbols. If you examine the images used in the ceremonial robes seen in the painted murals and carved stone reliefs of the Classic Mayan civilization, you will recognize their stylized forms in the contemporary textiles of Chiapas. For instance, the sacred toad, considered the musician of rain, woven on the robe of a woman in a Yaxchilan stone relief, is also a motif in the *huipil* worn by the Chiapas women.

These motifs, like the designs of the past, represent the dreams of the weaver, her concept of the world and her place in it. The brocaded *huipiles* which the Chiapas women wear, look like geometric patterns but they

ral pigment and brushes made from human hair. The beautiful black and white and earth colored creations are one of a kind and sought after by avid collectors of pottery.

Oaxaca also has its own distinctive pottery fashioned out of the black clay found in Coyopec that gives it its distinctive metallic black sheen. The pottery, startlingly attractive in its starkness and black color, a tradition inherited from the Zapotec Indians.

In contrast, Puebla produces a colorful, lavishly ornamental pottery

that recalls happy, summer days. The Talavera ware is a tradition imported by Spanish families who settled in Puebla from Toledo.

Tzintzuntzan's pottery produced by the Tarascans is more like stoneware – earthy and decorated with drawings of swans, fish and native fishermen. More primitive earthenware is available in San Cristobal de las Casas where clay jugs and vases are baked on an open fire while Tonala offers animal-shaped pieces, glazed with dull reds, browns and blue, on a cream background.

echo the Maya concepts of time, space, the mythological forces of nature and the Mayan view of the cosmos.

The designs are woven on white square necked cotton blouses or white blouses with red stripes. The area around the neck and shoulders is usually brocaded. Sometimes the entire blouse is brocaded. Four basic motifs are intertwined: diamonds, figures, undulating wave like patterns and vertical lines. The diamond represents the earth and the sky. In the diamond's center is a butterfly, emblem of the sun and the core of the Mayan universe. The diamond motifs appear on the main body of the *huipil* or they may form a border; half diamonds are also used to form the horizontal edge of the brocade.

Popular figures as motifs include the toad that sings for rain, patron saints who appeal for rain or family members working in the fields. The wave like motifs appear like a snake, feathered or crowned with flowers which transform into a cornfield. The vertical lines appear three in a row, signifying the foundation of the world, the community and its history. Past and present periods of the Mayan culture have thus fused in the Chiapas weavings for the new motifs reflect the same rhythms of life that once existed in the times of their ancestors and which still dominate the world of the Tzotzil and Tzeltal.

Baskets

As diverse as pottery in style, color and design are Mexican baskets. Natural materials used include reed, straw, palm and *henequen*. Merida in the Yucatan Peninsula is at the heart of Mexico's sisal industry.

Sisal is an extremely strong rope product of the pulp of the cactus. It is used to make the internationally renowned Yucatan hammocks, mats, bags and decorative wall hangings. Just as strong are Oaxaca's expandable string bags known as *bolsas* made from ixtle, a fiber of the maguey plant.

Puebla offers table mats, *sombreros* and other craft items from palm leaves. Tzintzuntzan's table mats, floor mats and figurines are fashioned from reed while you will find in Tuxtepec mule figurines made from the leaves of the maize plant and the trunk of the banana tree.

Weaving

Mexico produces the finest folk art of all in its weaving. Hand-crafted clothes and accessories, patterned rugs and blankets are among some exquisite examples. In many Indian communities, the spinning wheel is still used to produce yarn which is naturally colored in vegetable dyes.

The horizontal loom and back strap loom are widely employed for weaving. Indian women in Oaxaca's markets can be seen deftly using their looms while tending their stalls.

Jocotepec offers soft, woolen *serapes* and Zacatecas finely-woven *serapes* in acrylic wool. The Tarascan Indian women of Patzcuaro weave beautiful, traditional *serapes* on saddlebag looms. The *serape* is a Mexican blanket worn over the shoulders by men like the way a woman wears a shawl.

The women's equivalent of the *serape* is *quechqemet* made by the Totonac Indians in Veracruz. The delicate,

Vendor exhibiting his wares.

Taxco whose silver work is legendary. The range of bracelets, rings, necklaces and ear rings is dazzling. Many are of traditional design and all should bear the 0.925 stamp of silver authenticity.

Taxco is particularly noted for producing *milagros* which are silver pieces representing afflicted parts of the human anatomy such as the eyes, feet, an arm or leg. These silver pieces are pinned on the skirts of saints in churches as an appeal for healing.

Guanajuato is renowned too for its silver jewelry which is more contemporary in design and more so for its traditional gold jewelry, decorated with turquoise. Oaxaca offers gold pieces unusually adorned with pearls and coral.

Copperware in Mexico is a product

multicolored embroidery on cotton stands out against a white, black or blue background. Equally attractive is the *huipil*, a brocaded cotton blouse, and the *guayabera*, a cotton, front pleated, long-sleeved man's sports shirt, typical of the Yucatan Peninsula. Some very fine *huipiles* are available in Merida while the best traditional designs dating back to the days of the Maya can be found on the *huipiles* of Chiapas.

Silver and Gold Jewelry

Mexico was famous for silver and gold mining during the colonial period. "Silver cities" from this era still turn out fine jewelry. The best known among them is

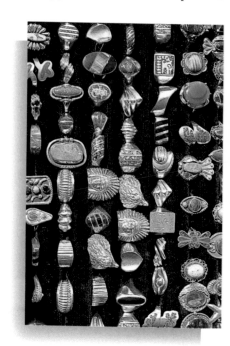

Silverware from Taxco and Guanajuato are particularly renown.

Colorfully painted wooden chest.

of the colonial occupation and Spanish influences are highly evident. Santa Clara del Cobre is the center of copper making, turning out finely wrought copper bowls, candlesticks, lamps, pots and pans. Its copper platters are embossed by hand hammering.

Woodwork

Woodcrafting in Mexico covers a wide gamut of products from fancy bird cages and hand-carved masks to colonial furniture. Guadalajara and the colonial cities of Queretaro, San Miguel de Allende and Cuernavaca are centers for the making of Mexican colonial furniture. Michoacan and Mexico City are best known for their masks used since pre-Columbian times for religious ceremonies. They are still widely used in traditional dances. Some are carved in plain wood, others are highly colorful and expressive. For hand made guitars, Paracho in Michoacan is the place to go.

Lacquerware

Michoacan is the center of lacquerware, a Mexican heritage that dates back to the Aztecs. Linaloa, a fragrant wood, is used and applied with lacquer coatings of contrasting colors. The floral designs are engraved with thorns. Uruapan is the best known town in Michoacan to hunt for lacquerware.

Ask any foreigner what he thinks of Mexican food, and chances are he will say it's hot and spicy. To be sure, the Mexicans have a penchant for chili and it is a penchant that is amply fed by a staggering variety of as many as at least 60 types of chilies found in the country, thanks to the favorable climate and productive soil.

341

The chilies, extensively used because of their abundant supply and their nutritional and medicinal value, range from the thin extremely hot thimblesized *pequin* to huge black dried peppers (*poblanos*) which look more like flattened aubergines.

Tortillas, a typical Mexican food of thin patties of corn paste.

Pequins and poblanos

Yet, Mexican food is not always hot. Neither are the chilies. The *pequin* may be very hot but the *poblanos* are *dulce* (sweet). And contrary to popular mis-

In a typical market stall can be found many exotic vegetables.

conception, Mexicans do not spice up all their dishes. Quite often, the *salsas piquantes* (hot sauces) made from the *pequin* chili are served on the side of the plate and it is up to the diner to make his palate as fiery as he so wishes.

Rich blend

Mexican cuisine is a rich blend of different influences. Indian cooking using corn and chilies are the base. Then came the Spanish whose cuisine was itself spiced by its Arab heritage and who brought with them sugar, garlic, cheese, beef, pork and chicken.

The French made inroads during the reign of Maximilian. A dessert that

certainly has been a product of those times is *flan*, the Mexican version of creme caramel.

But despite these influences, corn and chilies remain the main staples in the Mexican diet today. So important is corn that the ancient Indians called it *toconayo* – they performed religious ceremonies to their gods whom they believed made people from corn. For the isolated Indian mountain communities living in the deep south around Chiapas, corn is usually what they eat only. *Pozole* for instance, a stew of vegetables, meat and corn is the daily diet of many Indians. The dried kernels of corn are ground to make *masa*, the dough used in making tortilla which is to Mexicans what the baguette is to the French.

Appetizing buffet spread in Acapulco.

Tortillas

In towns and cities, you will often come across small shops where queues line up to buy the *tortillas* or thin patties of corn paste which have just been rolled out of a grinder.

Frozen *tortillas* are available in plastic packets from supermarkets but the Mexican gourmet prefers his freshly made. In some households, the maid makes them each day for the daily meal. The versatile *tortilla*, said to be Aztec in origin, is lightly toasted on a griddle before it is served either as a bed for fillings or as a wrapping. These thin pancakes vary from three to 12 inches in diameter.

The smaller *tortillas* wrapped around beef, chicken or pork slices laced with a *salsa verde* (mild green sauce) or *salsa piquante* (hot sauce) are eaten as tacos. *Burritos* are similar to tacos except that a larger pancake is used and more ingredients are added. These may be beans or cheese thrown into the meat or seafood filling. *Enchiladas* are when the same stuffed *tortilla* is dipped in sauce and baked or fried.

Quesadilla, tostada and *tamal*

Then there is the *quesadilla* in which cheese is folded into a *tortilla* and heated in a pan until the cheese melts. When

The fine art of making tortillas.

toasted to a crisp and filled with meat or cheese and garnished with tomatoes, lettuce and beans, the *tortilla* is known as a *tostada*. Another Mexican favorite made from corn and prepared since pre-Hispanic times by the Indians is the delicious *tamal*. Traditionally, *tamales* are made from *masa* seasoned with honey, herbs and *moles* (a chocolate based sauce) and wrapped in corn husks for steaming.

When the Spaniards arrived bringing pigs with them, the Indians learnt to use lard to lighten the consistency of the *masa*. Nowadays, vegetable shortening is sometimes used to make the *masa*. Fillings for the *tamal* are left to the imagination. The strips, coconut or fruit such as pineapple and guava. The *tamal*

is then wrapped in corn husk or banana leaf and steamed. It is suitable for eating at any time of the day.

Chilies

The Aztecs and the Mayas used chilies liberally and the same goes today for most Mexicans. Chilies are served either as a meal in itself or as a condiment. A typical dish is *chilli relleno* (stuffed green pepper) filled with either cheese or minced beef and served with tomato-flavored red rice *(arroz Mexicano)*. The Mexicans also serve white rice, flavored with milk, and green rice to which *poblano chilies* and avocados are added.

Chili relleno is a seemingly simple

Festive Menus

Mexicans celebrate their traditional fiestas with special menus. During the *posadas* from 16 December until Christmas Eve, crisp *bunuelos* and *atoles* are served. For every bunuelo that is eaten, the plate in which it is made is broken to bring good luck.

On 6 January, Epiphany or Day of the Three Kings, coffee, *atole* or chocolate is served in the afternoon with traditional Three Kings' Bread stuffed with a porcelain or plastic doll representing the Infant Jesus. The person whose portion of bread contains the doll is required to throw a party on 2 February, the day the Infant Jesus is removed from the Nativity Scene. The special dish on this day is *tamales*.

During Easter or Holy Week, Mexicans abstain from eating meat so fish and shellfish feature mainly on the menu. Shrimp fritters are eaten; *tamales* are stuffed with *charrales* (a small anchovy like fish) or *nopales* while bean rolls are filled with sardines and tuna.

3 May, the Day of the Holy Cross coincides with Bricklayers' Day and bricklayers are treated to a special lunch given by architects and construction site owners. The menu includes *barbacoa* (lamb baked in an underground oven), with rice, *tortillas* and beans and *barbacoa* broth, washed down with *pulque* and beer.

15 September is the national day of independence and lunches and dinners in homes feature a wide variety of dishes that include richly garnished *pozole*, *birria* (baked lamb), various types of *mole* served with turkey, chicken or lamb, different kinds of rice, chili soup and flavored water. Candies and sweets abound. 20 November, the anniversary of the Mexican Revolution is similarly celebrated.

dish that is time consuming to prepare. It involves roasting the peppers until the skin is blackened, "sweating" them in a plastic bag, then deveining them and stuffing them with cheese or beef. The peppers are then dipped in an egg batter and fried before they are simmered in a lightly tangy tomato sauce.

As a condiment, perhaps the most popular are the familiar green and red sauces or *salsas* that are also used as zesty dips for corn chips called *nachos*. These colorful garnishes on Mexican tables are what you put on your food to give them zing. It's easy to go overboard with the green *salsa verde* and the red *salsa piquante*, specially if you are enjoying them as appetizers to go with a drink and you are likely to pile up more and more of the sauce on each *nacho* as you progress – they are that good! That's when you will find your tongue starts to burn. Rolling a piece of ice in your mouth may temporarily ease the pain, while some believe that drinking hot water or tea helps to counteract the hot sensation, but the most effective cure is to take time and go easy on the sauces and you will recover in ten minutes.

The milder *salsa verde* sauce is made from small green tomatoes which the Mexicans call "*tomatillos*" and fresh green chilies called *jalapenos* (pronounced halapenos) mixed in a blender. The *salsa piquante* is a blend of red *jalapenos* or *chipotle* and the red tomato which the Mexicans call "*jitomate*" (hee toma te). In some concoctions of the two *salsas*, garlic and onions are sometimes added to the blend.

Frijoles

Frijoles or beans are widely used in Mexican dishes. They are boiled, fried or refried (*frijoles refritos*) and used for stuffing into tortillas, they are mixed in to make *tamales* or sprinkled into soups. Speaking of soups, *sopa mariscos* (seafood soup) available in coastal towns and resorts is delicious. *Gazpacho*, a chilled, lightly spiced vegetable soup, is great on a hot day. And in Chiapas, ask for *sopa pollo con arroz*, a rice broth served with strips of chicken meat.

Breakfast

Breakfast (*desayuno*) in Mexico can be as light or as heavy as you wish. *Pan dulce* (sweet rolls) is served as a matter of course when you order coffee or tea. You are charged according to the number of rolls you eat.

Mexicans drink coffee rather than tea. However, despite being a coffee producing country, most Mexicans are not too fussy about how their coffee is made, so wherever you go you usually get instant coffee. If you prefer your coffee freshly brewed you have to specify and ask for *cafe de olla*. If you want milk to go with it, say *cafe con leche*. Regular black American coffee is *cafe americano* or *cafe negro*. As an alternative to *pan dulce,* you can order *pan tostada* (toast) with butter (*mantequilla*) and jam (*mermelada*) or a slice of fruit.

More Mexican breakfast items include *chilaquiles* which are strips of tortilla fried with chilies and eggs or *huevos rancheros* – fried eggs on *tortillas* with *frijoles* and chili sauce added. Given the size of Mexico, it is not surprising that

regional specialities exist. On the sea coast for example, the tortilla is wrapped around fish and known as fish tacos. And although *ceviche* is available almost everywhere, the best is to be had is in coastal towns where the fish and prawns are plentiful and fresh. This delightful dish makes a wonderful appetizer; it comprises either raw fish slices or prawns marinated in lime juice to which is added chopped onions, tomatoes and chilies.

Seafood

Fresh oysters and clams, seasoned with a dash of lemon juice, served in a half shell and on a bed of ice, are not to be missed. These can be enjoyed in the simplest of restaurants and even open air on sidewalks where they cost very little. Other cooked fish dishes along the coast are *huachinango a la veracruzana* – a red snapper served in a blend of tomato sauce, chili, olives, onions and capers. The fish is first barbecued or grilled before the sauce is poured over. The dish originated from Veracruz but you can find it on the menu of many restaurants in most coastal resorts. The same goes for the wonderful *caldo-largo*, a thick soup of fish and shellfish.

Northern Cuisine

Northern Mexico's cuisine contains more American influences. *Tortillas* are made from wheat flour rather than corn. Fewer chilies are used here and beef (cattle is raised in these parts) is more popular than pork.

An exquisite northern dish is the imaginatively called *sabana* (blanket) which consists of thin tenderized slices of beef marinated in an adobe sauce made from chilies and spices.

Another regional specialty is *pollo con mole* (chicken in *mole*) in Puebla, although Oaxaca has also put in a claim and it is available all over Mexico. The secret of the dish lies in the light spicy brown *mole* that is poured over the chicken. Over 30 types of ingredients, of which the most important is chocolate and the chili *poblano* – are known to have been blended in certain *moles*. The best sauce, *mole poblanois,* is said to come from Puebla. *Pollo* of course can also be enjoyed without *mole*, mainly grilled (*a la parilla*).

Mexicans love their pork and have come up with many ways to cook it. You can choose from *chuletas* (pork chops), *carnitas* (fried pork slices), *patas* (braised trotters) or simply ask for *cerdo* (pork) to be grilled.

No parts are wasted and even the skin of the pig is fried to a delicious crisp called *chicharrones* or pork rinds, that go so well with drinks.

Mexico also has its beefsteaks (*bistec de res*) and lamb (*cordero*). All these dishes are usually served with a complimentary basket of tortillas which you eat like bread. You can ask for bread (*pan*) instead or order a portion of red

Mexican rice (*arroz Mexicano*) which goes well with gravy based dishes. Except for salads (*ensaladas*), vegetables are significantly absent from Mexican menus. They are usually added to soups, mixed into sauces or use as garnishes for dishes. There is, however, *nopales* or cactus paddles, which are stripped of their needles, sliced and fried like vegetables.

Exotic dishes

Mexico also offers a number of exotic specialities which you would never imagine possible. They are more of an acquired taste and would appeal to the truly adventurous. The first dish you can try is *chapulines* or fried grasshoppers, served in dainty *tacos* or *taquitos* and topped with *guacamole*.

Then there are the *huevos de hormiga* or *escamoles*, which are specially cultivated ants' eggs. They look like fish roe and some say tastes like it, and are eaten fried. Aficionados believe they endow longevity.

Another delicacy is *maguey* worms which are fried and eaten wrapped in *taquitos*. The worms are the same ones that are usually found soaked in bottles of top quality *mezcal* to enhance the flavor. When eating out in Mexico, you are likely to be tasting these specialities only during the *comida* rather than at dinner, except in tourist towns where restaurants stay open till late in the evenings. The reason is simple. The *comida* is the biggest and most elaborate

The Chocolate War of Chiapas

The English traveller Thomas Gage tells us a lovely tale of 17th century colonial San Cristobal de las Casas – a "chocolate war" between the bishop and his flock that took place during his stay in 1626-27. So much had the *gachupin* and *creole* ladies taken to the ancient Mexican drink that they could not forgo it even for the length of a mass – with unwonted results.

"It was much used by them to make their maids bring them a cup of chocolate to church in the middle of Mass or sermon, which could not be done to all, or most of them, without great confusion and interrupting both Mass and sermon. Disturbed and offended, the bishop eventually gave a warning, but the ladies carried on regardless. The following sabbath they found a threat of excommunication nailed to the Cathedral door. Indignant, the ladies asked the Dominican Prior to intercede for them. When he did, the Bishop thundered that he preferred the honour of god and his house before his own life.

Some ladies then bowed to episcopal authority but others defied it and went on "drinking in iniquity in the church, as the fish doth water. One day this caused such an uproar in the Cathedral that many swords were drawn against the priests and the prebends, who attempted to take away from the maids the cups of chocolate which they brought unto their mistresses. So the citizens forsook the Cathedral

for the convent churches where the nuns and friars were more reasonable. The bishop shot back with a command that the whole citizenry attend Mass solely in the Cathedral, upon pain of excommunication. Rather than surrender, the *damas* of San Cristobal holed up in their houses.

In that time the bishop fell dangerously sick and desired to retire himself to the cloister of the Dominicans, for the great confidence he had [in them]. Physicians were sent for far and near, who all with joint opinion agreed that the bishop was poisoned, and he himself doubted not of it at his death ... He lay not above a week in the cloister, and as soon as he was dead, all his body, his head and face, did so swell that the least touch upon any part of him caused the skin to break and cast out white matter, which had corrupted and overflown all his body."

A certain gentlewoman "was commonly censured. She was said to have prescribed such a cup of chocolate [to poison] him who so rigorously had forbidden chocolate to be drunk in the church ... It became afterwards a proverb in that country, 'Beware of the chocolate of Chiapas', which made me so cautious that I would not drink it afterwards in any house where I had not very great satisfaction of the whole family." Nearly four centuries later, chocolate drinking is safe in San Cristobal de las Casas, and very welcome on chilly winter nights.

meal for Mexicans and many restaurants usually open only for this, from 12 noon to 6 pm.

Comida time

Do not be alarmed if you walk into a restaurant at 1 o'clock and find it's virtually deserted. The lunch time crowd does not stream in until 2 pm. That's when offices, banks, shops and even

travel agencies close until 4 pm or 5 pm when they re-open till 8 pm.

The two to three hour break allows the Mexicans to enjoy their *comida* at leisure and even perhaps to indulge in a little siesta. So important is the *comida* that many restaurants offer several types of fixed price menus to choose from with names such as *comida corrida* or *menu el dia*. The three to five course set meal is a bargain and costs less than a la carte selections. Many restaurants now also

Roasting corn in a Tlaquepaque market.

offer buffet spreads with about a dozen dishes to choose from at one price.

Although most Mexicans have their *comida* in the late afternoon, it is not uncommon to see some of them eating in the early evening and having their lunch and dinner at one go. In contrast to the *comida*, dinner (*cena*) in Mexico is a simple affair and is usually skipped in favor of a late supper. In most homes, the *cena* is eaten at about 8.30 pm and it's usually a simple dish of quesadilla or tacos washed down with a glass of milk. Unless you are in a tourist town, chances are you will not find many restaurants open for dinner. Those that do, offer light selections of *tacos*, *quesadillas*, soups and pastries and they often close by 9 pm. In contrast, restau-

rants offering supper stay open way past midnight as most of the patrons don't start to eat until 9 or 10 pm.

Fondas

Everywhere on Mexican streets and in the marketplace, you can find *fondas*, stalls or carts where people flock for a quick bite. Don't turn up your noses at them for many of the *fondas* serve delicious food such as *tamales* and tacos. How to distinguish the more hygienic ones from the rest? No problem, just make sure the food you are ordering is cooked on the spot rather than warmed up after it has sat for hours in oil that is slowly turning rancid.

Colorful aguas frescas – sweet fruit syrups.

In tourist destinations, restaurants catering to tourists are not difficult to find. But the trick in finding the good ones to dine in is to look for those with filled with Mexicans. It would help to know a little Spanish to understand the menu and communicate with the waiters who would speak limited English. But you will enjoy the ambience and it's a good opportunity to see how Mexicans have fun among themselves. There are also small restaurants without frills on most streets. Some of them are very good and they offer cheap *tacos* (look for *taquerias*) and other *antojitos* (snacks such as *burritos* and *enchiladas*). For most people, THE restaurant to dine at would be Las Mananitas in Cuernavaca, a 45-minute drive from Mexico City. The food is exquisite and the ambience is pure Mexicana. The restaurant is part of an old elegant hotel. You can enjoy an after dinner stroll amid strutting peacocks in the fountain filled manicured gardens.

Drinks

Drink stalls in streets and the marketplace are a treat for the eyes because they are so colorful. Jars of red, green, yellow and orange liquids are temptingly lined up in a row. These are *aguas frescas* which are sweet syrups made from fruit juices, mashed seeds or grains. A measure of the syrup is spooned into a glass and water added before serving.

Table set for drinking the famed tequila.

Behind the jars, you will usually find mountains of oranges, lemons, pineapples, apples, carrots, tomatoes and other assorted fruit and vegetables for pressing into jugos. Pick a flavor or a combination of flavors; the juices are served with ice (*con hielo*) or without (*sin hielo*).

Licuados are fruit juices blended with milk and flavored with cinnamon, vanilla or nutmeg. There is also freshly made *cerveza* (root beer) served from a barrel. If you are hesitant about buying a drink from a market or street stall, you can find fruit and ice cream parlors in every town and city where freshly squeezed fruit juices and root beer are available. You can drink it on the spot or take it away. *Atole* is a traditional drink made from the *masa* used for making tortillas and is flavored with vanilla, cinnamon, chocolate or strawberries. *Pulque* is another traditional pre-Hispanic drink made from thesap of the *maguey* plant. The sap which is naturally fermented has a low alcoholic content. It is often flavored with different kinds of fruit to which cinnamon, cloves and peppercorns are added.

When it comes to meals, Mexicans usually drink a *cerveza* (beer) with them; either a *cerveza clara* (light beer or lager) or a *cerveza*. Beer was introduced by German immigrants in the 19th century. Wine drinking is not a habit, even though Mexican wines (which are improving all the time) are available. In any case, a refreshing beer goes well with Mexican food and warm days.

Nightlife in Mexico is a matter of class and cash, as in most other places. If you don't have much of either, you'll just stay in and watch telly or go and get smashed in the local *pulqueria*. If you've got plenty of both, and you live in the capital, you'll go to the opera or ballet, and drink expensive imported liquor in a fancy nightclub.

In between those two extremes, the choices for banishing your cares for a night run the gamut through bars, discos, cinemas, theaters, cabarets, concerts, variety shows, folkloric performances, and so on – assuming you're in a big city or resort.

Nowhere, naturally, is there more variety than in the capital, Mexico City, which offers a wide range of artistic and cultural events in addition to lashings of popular entertainment.

Other nightlife centers are major tourist resorts like Acapulco and Cancun, large

There is a wide variety of nightlife in Mexico City.

Nighttime allure of Acapulco Bay.

cities like Guadalajara, big ports like Veracruz, and the notorious border town of Tijuana.

Mexico City

When night falls on Mexico City, there are some especially atmospheric places for seeing the lights come on, and then for seeking out what they promise. You could just stroll along the Paseo de la Reforma as the spotlights begin to illuminate the statues of Cuauhtemoc and Columbus, glowing in the middle of traffic roundabouts.

And then seek out the pleasures of the Zona Rosa and Polanco, the capital's nightlife centers which hug the great boulevard, with their theaters, discos and nightclubs.

Or you could ascend to the observation platform of the Torre Latinoamericano, which has long the city's tallest building, or sip a drink in El Miralto bar, and see the myraid of lights twinkling all across the Valley of Mexico, little interrupted by other high-rise buildings as yet.

And then proceed to the restaurants, cabarets and clubs of the old colonial center, or to a performance in the Palacio de Bellas Artes. And then make acquaintance with the *mariachis* in the Plaza Garibaldi.

Or you could sit on the rooftop bar of the Hotel Majestic and look down upon the floodlit splendor of the *Zocalo*

The Mexicans are a dance-loving nation with much to offer for evening entertainment.

– the Cathedral, the National Palace, the City Hall and then wander the streets of the historic centre which are bathed in the golden glow from distinctive triple-globed streetlamps, before choosing a venerable old restaurant to dine in, or slipping into the ornate Bar La Opera, the exquisite Cafe Tacuba, or the cavernous mural-decorated dining room within the House of Tiles.

Zona Rosa

Mexico City is not globally renowned for its nightlife like Rio, say, or Paris, but, as the biggest city in the world, as a center of Hispanic culture, and as the capital of a music and dance-loving nation, there is nevertheless plenty to do after dark.

The long-standing nightlife center is the "Pink Zone", the Zona Rosa, located to the south of the Paseo de la Reforma, long renowned for its cafe society, cabarets and restaurants, and more recently for its glitzy disco scene.

The Zona Rosa began early this century as a bohemian meeting place and has moved steadily upmarket ever since, so that today it is markedly commercial and often expensive, while mercifully still retaining some atmospheric cafes and clubs that won't empty the average wallet.

Its streets have a determinedly cosmopolitan air as much through their names as their contents: they are mostly

A folkdance performance is one of the best ways to enjoy Mexican culture.

named after prominent European cities.

The most animated spot these days is the pedestrianised area comprising of Copenhague, Oslo and Genova Streets, with Copenhague's pavement cafes being particularly favored. This is where a night out begins with a cocktail for many chic *capitalinos,* who generally dine late at around 10 pm and party into the small hours.

In the Zona Rosa, bars, nightclubs and discos sparkle most brightly and loudly along Niza and Florencia Streets. Another lively focus is around Insurgentes Sur metro station.

Old-style nightclubs still thrive like El Patio (Atenas Street, good for crooners) and El Gran Caruso (Londres Street, where you can get an impromptu aria from your waiter).

Well-established floorshow clubs are Gitanerias (Oaxaca Street) for flamenco, and Marrakesh (Florencia Street) which is four exotic spaces under one roof. High energy *chilangos* (Mexico City people) head for the disco floors of Cero Cero (Hotel Camino Real, very popular, live bands too), Rock Stock (Reforma at Niza Street, industrial chic), Le Chic (Hamburgo Street, fashionable) and many others.

Plaza Garibaldi

All roads meet at Plaza Garibaldi, the old square where the *mariachis* gather to serenade anyone with enough pesos ready. Rich, poor and middling Mexicans turn up here any time between dusk and dawn, but around midnight sees the Plaza Garibaldi at its most animated. Dozens of *mariachi* troupes gather here each night, probably all the ones in the capital who haven't already been booked to appear elsewhere – at a wedding (their name comes from the word "marriage"), a party, or whatever. So they make their own celebration, and their living, here.

Around the square stand nightclubs, cantinas, music halls and theaters, so that the Plaza Garibaldi provides a fine array of entertainment to suit many tastes – but be warned that there's nothing refined or intellectual around here! Keep your hands on your wallet or purse and leave any sensitive ears behind - this is a spot where pickpockets abound and you're likely to be listening to five or six different serenades simultaneously.

With that in mind, don't miss this phenomenon and be sure to have at least one shot of tequila to get yourself in the true spirit.

Nowhere could there be a better place for this than Tenampa, a bar which looks like what a flamboyant old-style Hollywood director might have conjured up to represent the Mexican *cantina*, but which is actually a genuine old Mexican institution.

Push through the swinging doors and find yourself in a cavernous bar that has walls and plastered with huge mural scenes, the air is dense with to-

bacco fumes and seared by the blare of *mariachi* trumpets, whose tables are awash with tequila and *mezcal*, where a great hubbub of well-lubricated chatter issues from a packed house. All it needs, besides period costumes, is for someone to pull a pistol and start shooting at the ceiling and the movie set is complete.

Amongst the wide variety of establishments around the square is a *pulqueria familiar*, which means it's a respectable place to quaff the *maguey* juice, and a large nightclub offering salsa music, sometimes by famous foreign names like Oscar D'Leon.

Across the Avenida Lazaro Cardenas are two variety theaters, which may offer traditional music hall acts or sex acts of an outrageous nature, so make sure you've got the right one before laying out your pesos. Cantinflas, Mexico's greatest comedian, used to pack them in here in their mid-century heyday; the old mambo king, Perez Prado, was still jazzing them here only recently.

There are several theaters and revue clubs in the area of Plaza Garibaldi and Avenida Lazaro Cardenas, but the one that is in a class of its own is the Palacio de Bellas Artes. This *Belle Epoque* structure with an Art Deco interior is Mexico's pre-eminent theater where the best of the performing arts are presented, whether local or foreign.

This is where the most important opera, ballet and drama performances take place, and where the celebrated Ballet Folklorico de Mexico is based, usually giving three performances

The neon lights of Cancun.

weekly. Not to be missed!

Coyoacan

If the Zona Rosa represents upmarket popular entertainment and the Plaza Garibaldi district the more downmarket and traditional sorts, the more intellectual arts are most fully represented in the southern suburbs of Coyoacan and San Angel, the favored residential area of the intelligentsia and media people. Here you find many small theaters, cinemas and performance spaces. Details are published in *Tiempo Libre*, the listings magazine, and *The News*, the capital's English language newspaper, which cover all significant entertainment in town and are well worth your pesos.

Mexico's biggest tourist cities, especially Acapulco and Tijuana, are full of bright lights, including red ones, most frequently offering pulsating discotheques for your own dancing pleasure and colorful folk dance performances for spectator appreciation. The variety of Mexican musical entertainment is enormous – *marimba* bands in the southeast, guitar and harp trios on the Gulf Coast, *norteno* bands in the north, *mariachis* everywhere but especially in Jalisco. Veracruz and Merida are very good for open air music. One of the pleasures of visiting the colonial cities are their historic theaters which present all kinds of performing arts, for instance, at Puebla and Oaxaca, Guanajuato and Queretaro.

TRAVEL TIPS

AIRPORT DEPARTURE TAX

A tax of N$36 is payable for every international flight you take out of Mexico City while domestic flights are taxed at N$20 a person.

BUSINESS HOURS

Most banks are open from 9 am to 1.30 pm. In the bigger cities, the opening hours may be extended to 3 pm. Travel agencies, tour operators and other businesses tend to open from 9 am to 1 pm or 2 pm and then from 4 pm till 7 pm or 8 pm. The work week is from Monday to Friday. It's usually the supermarkets and tourist shops that are open all week.

CUSTOMS

When entering Mexico, visitors are allowed to bring in two bottles of liquor, one carton of cigarettes, 50 cigars, electrical appliances such as camera, videocamera, typewriter and notebook computer for personal use.

US residents returning home are usually entitled to a duty free exemption of US$400 on those items accompanying them. Expect to pay a flat 10 percent tax on the first US$1,000 exceeding the duty free amount.

Generally, the duty free exemption includes one liter of liquor, a carton of cigarettes and 100 cigars but each state has its own regulations so do check before you leave.

DOMESTIC TRAVEL

Getting Around in Mexico
By Air

Mexicana and Aeromexico are the two main carriers offering domestic flights. Smaller airlines offering flights to specific areas include Aero California and Inter. Flights within Mexico are expensive as the authorities seem to feel that those who can afford to fly should pay a premium price. Hence, there may be situations when you

may find it costs less to fly from say, Los Angeles to Mexico City than to fly from one city to another within Mexico itself.

By Rail

Mexico has over 16,000 miles of railways. Trains are a slow way to travel but you can overcome the long hours by travelling overnight. They are also prone to delays. The other disadvantage is not being able to make advance reservations through travel agents as they do not earn commissions from the government-run Mexican National Railways. You thus have to go to the train station a day ahead – more if you are travelling during a festive period – to buy your ticket. First class train travel is recommended. There are two types: the cheaper non-airconditioned *primera clase* and the more expensive airconditioned *primera especial,* which has better seats and needs advance reservations. A sleeping car for overnight journeys can be booked in conjunction with first class travel. Second class trains are usually overcrowded, dirty and unsafe because of pickpocketing. In Mexico City, call at Buenavista Central Passenger Station on Insurgentes Norte between 7 am and 9.30 pm for tickets (tel: 5471084).

By Bus

Mexico has an extensive network of buses serving even the smallest town and village. There are numerous bus lines, many specializing in a particular region. If you are considering travelling economically in Mexico, bus travel is the way to go. It's convenient, comfortable, safe and quicker than rail travel.

There are different kinds of service. The deluxe *Ejecutivoclase* or executive class and *primera plus* (first class plus) are the most expensive. Both usually have baggage check in at ticket counters prior to boarding; their own waiting room; toilets on board, airconditioning, video movies, refreshments and even a stewardess to welcome you on board. They are usually non stop. First class (*primera clase*) buses are slightly cheaper and just as good but without the waiting room, stewardess and refreshments. Stops are made enroute at major cities.

Second class (*segunda clase*) buses are without frills but their fares are cheap. They stop frequently to pick up passengers along the way or to let them off. They also call at bus stations en route where you get a chance to use the restroom or to buy food and drink. Tickets for the three kinds of buses can be bought on the spot just before travelling. During Mexican holidays and peak seasons of travel, it's advisable to book your ticket in advance, at least a day ahead.

ELECTRICITY

The power supply is 110 volts just as in the United States. All American plugs fit into Mexican sockets. If you need to use adapters, just use the same ones as for the US.

GETTING THERE

By Air

Mexico is well connected by air to many cities in the United States, Canada, Europe, Central and South America.

Direct flights from the United States on scheduled and chartered carriers originate from major cities and they fly to the main cities in Mexico and most of its resorts. The principal points of departure are Los Angeles, Miami, Dallas/Fort Worth and Chicago.

By Sea

Cruising to Mexico is a more leisurely way to get there. Cruise ships sail the Caribbean or along the Pacific Coast. Departures from the US are usually Los Angeles or San Diego calling at ports such as Cabo San Lucas, Mazatlan, Manzanillo, Puerto Vallarta, Ixtapa/Zihuatenejo and Acapulco on the Mexican west coast for longer cruises. Shorter trips take in only Ensenada.

Miami and Fort Lauderdale are the usual ports of departure from the US east coast for cruise ships sailing the Caribbean route, calling at Cancun, Cozumel and Playa del Carmen.

By Car

Driving to Mexico is a popular option for many Americans especially those who live in states bordering Mexico or who are travelling in a group.

There are over 20 official crossing points in the four states along the US Mexican border: California, Arizona, New Mexico and Texas.

To get across, you will need a car permit available at the Mexican customs office at the port of entry, a valid driver's license and as proof of ownership, the original current registration or a notarized bill of sale for the car. If the car is borrowed, say, from a friend, you will need to show a notarized letter signed by your friend stating you had permission to drive the car.

The car permit is free and is valid for 90 days; extensions for another 90 days can be made at the Temporary Importation Department of the Mexican Customs. You need to have the permit cancelled when you leave the country and the car exported by the expiry date of your permit.

As US automobile insurance is not valid in Mexico, it's wise to buy a comprehensive policy to cover your trip in Mexico. It can be done at any border town or at AAA (American Automobile Association) offices in Southern California, Arizona, Texas, Louisana and new Mexico.

By Bus

The extensive network of bus routes in Mexico makes travelling by bus across the border an attractive – and cheap – alternative. However, because of the distances, unless you are limiting your travels in Mexico to the northern states, travelling by bus all the way to Mexico City or points farther south can be an exhausting experience. The main US border towns served by Greyhound buses are Brownsville, Calexico, San Diego, Laredo and El Paso. Other border crossings are served by smaller lines. Once you reach the border, you have to transfer to a Mexican bus.

By Rail

You can travel by train into Mexico from the United States but you have to transfer to the Mexican national railroad system at the border. Also, you can only buy your train ticket to wherever you wish to go once you arrive at the Mexican rail station as it is not possible to make reservations on Mexican trains in advance – travel agents are not keen on selling tickets for the state-run Mexican trains as no commission is paid. This applies at all stations throughout Mexico (except Los Mochis). On Mexican national holidays, it is advisable to arrive a few days in advance at the railroad station to purchase your ticket way ahead of your date of travel to assure yourself of a seat.

HEALTH

Adopt a few precautions and you will avoid serious health problems. Water from the tap in Mexico is not potable. You can drink mineral water or agua mineral which is widely available. The better restaurants will serve purified water (*agua purificada*).

Ice is supposedly made from purified water. If in doubt, you can ask for your drink to be served *sin hielo* (without ice) or make sure they are *frio* (cold) in the first place.

It's safe to eat from street or market *fondas*. Just look for the cleaner stalls and make sure the food has been cooked on the spot and not left sitting for hours. Vaccinations against cholera and typhoid may be taken before arriving in Mexico and if you are travelling to the hot and humid jungle areas, you might wish to take anti malaria medication.

If you spend more than a few days in Mexico City, you may feel your eyes smarting; it's just the pollution in the air. It may also be wise to take it easy the first couple of days in Mexico City or in other cities at high altitudes as the higher elevations can easily cause exhaustion if you are tearing around sightseeing at a frenetic pace.

MEDICAL SERVICES

If you are ill and need to consult a doctor, you could ask your hotel, or the tourist office, for a referral. If you are in Mexico City, you could call your embassy for assistance. As it may not be possible to find an English speaking doctor, have someone go along as an interpreter. In an emergency, you could always go to the local hospital.

MONEY & CURRENCY

Mexico adopted a new monetary unit – the Nuevo Peso or New Peso, "old" Peso, the present currency, will be legal tender. The change was done to simplify transactions. Thus, one thousand "old" Pesos are equal to one New Peso. All figures quoted in "old" Pesos are simply converted to New Pesos by moving the decimal point three digits to the left. While old Peso coins and bills will continue to be in circulation together with the new ones, all monetary operations and prices in hotels, restaurants and department stores will be expressed in New Pesos. If in doubt, look for the N$ symbol.

The new centavo (cent) coins which are different in value and appearance and not marked Nuevo Peso will not be changed. With the change in currency, the centavo, which had almost gone

into oblivion, has regained its value.

The following table is a useful conversion of old to New Pesos:

	Old Pesos	New Pesos
Coins	50	5 centavos
	100	10 centavos
	200	20 centavos
	500	50 centavos
	1,000	1 New Peso
	2,000	2 New Pesos
Coins and bills	5.000	5 New Pesos
	10,000	10 New Pesos
	20,000	20 New Pesos
Bills	50,000	50 New Pesos
	100,000	100 New Pesos

The rate of exchange for one US dollar is 3.05 Pesos. Commission is usually not charged at the banks but they have shorter opening hours from 9 am to 3 pm in Mexico City and up to 1 pm in the smaller towns, while the Casa de Cambio operates longer hours. In Mexico City, they open from 9 am to 6 pm and in some resorts, they remain open till even 8 pm.

NATIONAL HOLIDAYS

The official holidays in Mexico are as follows:

January	New Year's Day
February 5	Anniversary of the Publishing of the Constitutions (1857 & 1917)
March 21	Anniversary of the Birth of Benito Juarez
May 1	Labor Day
May 5	Anniversary of the Battle of Puebla (Cinco de Mayo)
September 16	Anniversary of the Independence of Mexico
October 12	Dia de la Raza (Columbus Day)
November 20	Anniversary of the Beginning of the Mexican Revolution
December 12	Fiesta de Nuestra Senora de Guadalupe (Celebratio of the feast of Our Lady of Guadalupe)
December 25	Christmas Day

NEWSPAPERS AND MAGAZINES

The News is an English language daily tabloid that is available at newsstands in cities and bigger towns. Periodicals such as *Time* and *Newsweek* are also widely sold. If you read Spanish, you will find a large variety of newspapers and periodicals to choose from. Each city has its own newspapers but among the national dailies are *Excelsior, El Dia, Uno Mas Uno, La Jornado* and *La Prensa*. News magazines in Spanish include the weekly *Proceso* and the monthly *El Tiempo Libre* and *Siempre*. An excellent monthly color magazine, *Mexico Desconocido* (Unknown Mexico), is like an insider's guide to Mexico, with well researched travel articles on many off the beaten track places, festivals and customs. Each magazine comes with an English language supplement.

PASSPORTS & VISAS

All nationalities require a valid passport and a tourist card (*tarjeta de turista*) or immigration form to enter Mexico. The tourist card is available free on commercial flights to Mexico, Mexican consulates, embassies and tourist offices. Depending on which country you are from, you are given a period of stay of 30 days to six months upon entry.

POSTAL SERVICES

The post office is known as the officina de correos. Postal rates are often changed and the current rates are posted next to the stamp counters. Air mail letters to the US and Canada takes from six days to two weeks, up to three weeks to Europe and a month to Asia. Envelopes or post cards should be marked "Por Avion" (air mail).

There is free poste restante service in Mexico; it is known as lista de correos. Letters sent to you should have your name clearly marked, c/o Lista de Correos with the name of the city where you will be picking it up, the state, and postal code. To look up your mail, check under all your names, not just the last name. Bring along a passport or ID for identification. Uncollected mail is returned to the sender after 10 days.

RADIO AND TELEVISION

Mexico has over a thousand radio stations, broadcasting in Spanish, on FM and AM. There are two English language stations, Radio VIP (AM1560) and Stereo Best (FM105) which are affiliated to CBS and NBC respectively. There are over 560 television stations in Mexico and the national network is connected to other countries. You can improve your Spanish by listening to television news broadcasts or watch the popular *tele novellas* (soap operas) and talk shows. Some hotels

receive US stations such as UNO, the Spanish language network beamed from Miami. The more upmarket hotels offer CNN.

TELEPHONE

Local calls are cheap, costing one (new) centavo. Sometimes, tokens or *fichas* have to be used in place of coins; coins can be exchanged for fichas at wherever you are making the call from.

On the other hand, international calls are very expensive because of the heavy taxes levied. You can place calls wherever you see the sign "Lada" (for *larga distancia* or long distance). These are counters located within pharmacies or shops and the calls are placed through operators. You pay after the call has been made.

Or you can place calls through Latadel which are telephone offices located within airports, bus terminals and railway stations. The calls are cheaper as they can be dialled direct. You can use coins, *fichas* or credit cards. Discounted rates apply on weekends.

WHAT TO WEAR

Mexicans as a whole are still a fairly conservative lot although attitudes have relaxed in the past few years. For instance, it used to be taboo for women to wear shorts in towns and cities. Now it's become acceptable. In resorts, shorts have long been an accepted norm.

Still, when visiting churches, it is advisable for women not to wear skimpy tops or shorts. The dress code for dining is casual unless it is in the more upmarket restaurants in Mexico City and the major cities when a jacket and tie for men may be required. The hot and humid regions in Mexico do not require warm clothing but if you are venturing into areas of high altitude be aware that the night time temperatures may fall drastically even in summer so be prepared and bring along a sweater, at least. In winter, places such as Creel, where it snows, are extremely cold and you should have adequate warm clothing.

DIRECTORY

AIRLINES

American Airlines
Paseo de la Reforma 314
Tel: 533 5446

Aero California
Paseo de la Reforma 332
Tel: 514 6678

Aeromar
Tel: 574 9211

Aeromexico Airport
Paseo de la Reforma 445
Tel: 207 8233

Continental Airlines
Maria Isabel Sheraton
Paseo de la Reforma
Tel: 203 1148

Delta Airlines
Paseo de la Reforma
Tel: 533 2000

Mexicana Airlines
Tel: 660 4444
Xola 535
Juarez & Balderas
Reforma & Amberes
Camino Real Hotel
Presidente Chapultepec Hotel

United Airlines
Tel: 531 8344

BANKS & CASAS DE CAMBIO

American Express
Paseo de la Reforma 234
Tel: 533 0380

Banamex
Calle Isabel de Catholica 44
Tel: 203 1094

Bancomer
Aeropuerto International
Internacional Sala "D"
Tel: 571 7236

Barclay's Bank
Paseo de la Reforma 390
Tel: 525 1870

Casa De Cambio Atlantico
Paseo de la Reforma 342
Tel: 514 5666

Casa De Cambio Forex
Av. Universidad 1200
Tel: 621 3340

Casa De Cambio Cel Paseo
Paseo de la Reforma 208
Tel: 514 5953

FOREIGN MISSIONS EMBASSIES

Australia
Jaime Balmes 11
10th Floor
Tel: 395 9998

Austria
Campos Eliseos 305
Tel: 280 6919

Canada
Schiller 529
Tel: 254 3288

Denmark
Tres Picos 43
Tel: 255 3405

France
Havre 15
Tel: 533 1360

Germany
Lord Byron 737
Tel: 280 5409

Japan
Paseo de la Reforma 395
Tel: 211 0028

Switzerland
Hamburgo 66, 4th Floor
Tel: 207 4820

Spain
Parque Via Reforma 2105
Tel: 596 1833

United States
Paseo de la Reforma 305
Tel: 211 0042

United Kingdom
Rio Lerma 71
Tel: 207 2089

HANDICRAFTS
FONART
Av Patriotismo 691
Tel: 598 1666

Mercado de Artesenias Insurgentes
Londres 164
Tel: 525 5716

Galeria Reforma
Fco Gonzalez Bocanegra 44
Tel: 526 6800

Centro Artesanal Buenavista
Aldama 187
Tel: 529 7744

CASART
Av Revolucion 955 957
Tel: 598 5931

LIBRARIES/
BOOKSHOPS
American Bookstore
Av. Madero 25
Tel: 512 0306

Libreria Britannica
Serapio Rendon 125
Tel: 535 8408

Libreria De Cristal
5 De Mayo
Tel: 512 6869

Libreria Misrachi
Av. Juarez 4
Tel: 510 4231

Benjamin Franklin Library
(U.S. Information Agency)
Paseo de la Reforma 295
Tel: 211 0042

MUSEUMS
Museo Nacional De Historia
Chapultepec
Tel: 553 6202

Museo Del Arte Moderno
Chapultepec
Tel: 553 6211

Nacional De Antropologia
Chapultepec
Tel: 553 6266

Museo Rufino Tamayo
Corner of Paseo de la Reforma
and Gandhi
Tel: 286 5839

Museo Diego Rivera
Corner Altavista San Angel
Tel: 677 2984

Museo Frida Kahlo
Londres 127 Coyoacan
Tel: 554 5999

TOURIST
INFORMATION
MEXICO CITY
TOURIST BUREAU
Amberes 54 Corner Londres,
Zona Rosa
Tel: INFOTUR 525 9380 to 84

TOURIST POLICE
Av. Florencia 20
Tel: 625 8761

Calle de Argentinia
Tel: 789 0833

TRAVEL AGENCIES
(in Mexico City)
Grey Line Tours
Calle Londres 166
Tel: 533 1542/533 1666

Viajes Americanos
Paseo del la Reforma 87
Tel: 566 7711/566 4038

Viajes Alce S.A. Av.
Insurgentes Sur 598
Tel: 536 6675/687 4288

Viajes Liberacion
Mariano Escobedo 454
Tel: 255 2344/255 2489

HOTELS
*** Expensive
** Moderate
Acapulco
Villa Vera***
Lomas del Mar
Tel: (74) 840333

Acapulco Princess***
Playa Revolcadero
Tel: (74) 843100

Hotel Las Brisas***
Carr. Clemente Meji 5255
Tel: (74) 841580

Romano Palace Hotel**
La Costera 130
Tel: (74) 847730

Maralisa***
Calle Alemania
Tel: (74) 856677

Casablanca**
Cerro de la Pinzona 195
Tel: (74) 821212

Campeche
Ramada Inn Campeche***
Avda. Ruiz Cortinez 51
Tel: (98) 162233

Fiesta Americana Cancun***
Lt.3 Sec A
Tel: (98) 831400

Hotel Beach Club***
Punta Cancun
Tel: (98) 841643

Hotel Antillano**
Claveles y Tulum
Tel: (98) 841532

Camino Real Cancun***
Punta Cancun km 14
Tel: (98) 830100

Villas Plaza Cancun***
Zona Hotelera
Tel: (98) 831022

Chichen Itza
Villa Arqueologica***
near ruins
Tel: (98) 562513

Hotel Mayaland***
near ruins
Tel: (99) 252342

Chihuahua
Castel Sicomoro**
Blvd Ortiz Mena, 411
Tel: (14) 169217

Posada Tierra Blanca**
Av. Ninos Heroes 100
Tel: (14) 150000

Cholula
Villa Arqueologica***
2 Poniente 601
Tel: (22) 471966

Hotel Calli Quetzalcoat**
Portal Guerrero 11
Tel: (22) 471515

Cozumel
Stouffer Presidente***
Carretera a Chankanab
Tel: (987) 20322

F. Americana Sol Caribe***
Playa Paraiso
Tel: (987) 20700

Hotel Vista del Mar **
Avda. R. Melgar 45
Tel: (987) 20545

Creel
Parador de la Montana**
Calle Principal
Tel: (145) 60075

Cuautla
Hotel de Cuautla**
Batalla 19 de Febrero
Tel: (735) 27233

Las Mananitas**
Rocardo Linares 107
Tel: (73) 141466

Hotel Papagayo**
Motolinia 13
Tel: (73) 141711

Casino de la Selva***
Av. V. Guerrero
Tel: (73) 124700

Hosteria Las Quintas***
Av. Diaz Ordaz 107
Tel: (73) 183949

Hotel de Mendoza**
Venustiano Carranza 16
Tel: (36) 134646

Hotel Frances**
Maestranza 35
Tel: (36) 131190

Hotel Lafayette***
Avenida de la Paz 2055
Tel: (36) 150252

Guanajatuo
Real de Minas***
Nejayote 17
Tel: (473) 21460

Parador San Javier ***
Plaza Aldama No. 92
Tel: (473) 20626

Castillo de Santa Cecilia***
Camino a la Valenciana
Tel: (473) 20485

Huatulco
Club Med***
Tangolunda Bay
Tel: (958) 10033

Sheraton Huatalco Resort***
Tangolunda Bay
Tel: (958) 10055

Isla Mujeres
Hotel Perla del Caribe**
Madero 2
Tel: (988) 20444

Hotel del Prado***
Islote del Yunque
Tel: (988) 20029

Ixtapa
Club Med***
Playa Qieta
Tel: (753) 30924

Westin Ixtapa***
Playa Vista Hermosa
Tel: (753) 32121

Hotel Santa Anita***
Gabriel Leyva e Hidalgo
Tel: (681) 57046

Manzanillo
Las Hadas Resort***
Av. de los Riscos
Tel: (333) 30000

Puerto Las Hadas**
Access Hotel Las Hadas
Tel: (333) 32350

El Rancho***
Av. Camaron Sabalo
Tel: (69) 141266

Camino Real***
Playa Sabado
Tel: (69) 131111

Merida
Hotel Dolores Alba **
Calle 63 No. 464
Tel: (99) 213745

Mision Merida Park Inn***
Calle 60 No. 491
Tel: (99) 239500

Hotel Caribe**
Calle 59 No. 500
Tel: (99) 249022

Hotel Los Aluxes***
Calle 60 No. 444
Tel: (99) 242199

Posada Toledo**
Calle 58 No. 487
Tel: (99) 232256

Mexico City

Gran H.Ciudad de Mexico**
Av. 16 Septiembre 82
Tel: (5) 5129275 ·

Hotel Marquis Reforma***
Paseo de la Reforma 465
Tel: (5) 2113600
Hotel Geneve **
Londres 130
Tel: (5) 2110071

Hotel Bamer**
Av. Juarez 52
Tel: (5) 5219060

Maria Isabel Sheraton***
Paseo de la Reforma 325
Tel: (5) 2073933

Hotel Maria Cristina**
Rio Lerma 31
Tel: (5) 546 9880

Hotel Vasco de Quiroga**
Londres 15
Tel: (5) 5462614

Westin Galeria Plaza***
Hamburgo 195
Tel: (5) 2110014 R

Morelia

Posada de la Soledad **
Ignacio Zaragosa 90
Tel: (451) 21888

Villa Montana**
Patzimba 201
Tel: (451) 40231

Hotel Virrey de Mendoza**
Portal Matamoros 16
Tel: (451) 20633

Oaxaca

Mision de los Angeles***
Calz. Porfirio Diaz 102
Tel: (951) 51500

Victoria***
Lomas del Fortin 1
Tel: (951) 52633

Calesa Real**
Garcia Vigil 306
Tel: (951) 65544

Meson del Rey**
Trujano 212
Tel: (951) 60033

Hotel Monte Alban**
Alameda de Leon 1
Tel: (951) 62777

Palenque

La Canada**
Calle Merle Green no. 13
Tel: (934) 50102

Mision Palenque**
Rancho S. Martin Porres
Tel: (934) 50300

Hotel Papantla**
Enriques 103
Tel: (784) 21645

Patzcuaro

Posada de Don Vasco**
Calz.de las Americas 450
Tel: (454) 20227

Puebla

El Meson del Angel***
Av.Hermanos Serdan 807
Tel: (22) 482168

Gran Hotel de Alba***
Av.Hermanos Serdan 141
Tel: (22) 486055

Hotel Imperial***
4 Oriente 212
Tel: (22) 424980

Hotel Lastra***
Calz.de los Fuertes 2633
Tel: (22) 351501

Posada San Pedro***
Av. 2 Oriente 202
Tel: (22) 465077

Puerto Escondido

Suites Villa Sol***
Loma Bonita 2
Tel: (958) 220382

Rincon del Pacifico**
Av. A.P. Gazca 900
Tel: (958) 20193

Posada Real***
Blvd. Benito Juarez
Tel: (958) 20133

Hotel Santa Fe**
Playa Zicatela
Tel: (958) 201 70

Puerto Vallarta

Hotel Molino de Agua**
Ignacio Vallarta 130
Tel: (322) 21957

Hotel Rosita**
Paseo Diaz Ordaz 901
Tel: (322) 21033

Camino Real***
Playa las Estacas
Tel: (322) 30123

La Jolla de Mismaloya***
Carr. Barra de Navidad
Tel: (322) 30660

Hotel Posada de Roger**
Basilio Badillo 237
Tel: (322) 20836

Queretaro

El Meson de Santa Rosa**
Pasteur Sur 17
Tel: (42) 145993

La Mansion Galindo***
Carr. Amealco
Tel: (42) 20000

Hotel Mirabel**
Av. Juarez 23 Nte.
Tel: (42) 143444

San Blas
Hotel Las Brisas**
Cuauhtemoc 106
Tel: (321) 50412

S. Cristobal de las Casas
Hotel Santa Clara**
Insurgentes no.14
Tel: (967) 81140

Posada Diego Mazariegos**
Ma.Adelina Flores no.2
Tel: (967) 81825

San Miguel de Allende
Mansion del Bosque**
Aldama 65
Tel: (465) 20277

Hotel El Atascadero***
Ancha de San ANtonio 30
Tel: (465) 20392

Hacienda de las Flores**
Hospicio 16
Tel: (465) 21808

Hotel Posada la Ermita**
Pedro Vargas 64
Tel: (465) 20715

Casa de Sierra Nevada***
Hospicio 35
Tel: (465) 20415

Taxco
Hacienda Solar***
Paraje El Solar
Tel: (762) 20323

Hotel Monte Taxco***
Lomas de Taxco
Tel : (762) 21300
Rooms: 158

Posada de la Mision**
Cerro de la Mision
Tel: (762) 20063

Teotihuacan
Villa Arqueologica**
Zona Arqueologica
Tel: (595) 60244

Tepoztlan
Posada del Tepozteco**
Calle de Paraiso no.3
Tel: (739) 50010

Toluca
Plaza las Fuentes***
Carr. Mexico/Toluca
Tel: (72) 160010

Uruapan
Mansion del Cupatitzio**
Parque Nacional
Tel: (452) 32100
Pie de la Sierra**
Carr. Uruapan/Carapan
Tel: (452) 42510

Uxmal
Hacienda Uxmal**
near ruins
Tel: (99) 247142

Villa Arquelogica**
near ruins
Tel: (992) 47053

Veracruz
Hotel Veracruz***
Independencia/Lerdo
Tel: (29) 313233

Hotel Villa del Mar**
Blvd. Avila Camacho 2707
Tel: (29) 313366

Hostal de Cortes**
Blvds. Camacho/Casas
Tel: (29) 320065

Hotel Colonial**
Miguel Lerdo 117
Tel: (29) 320193

Villahermosa
Hotel Miraflores**
moderate Reforma 304
Tel: (93) 120022

Hyatt Villahermosa***
Av. Juarez 106
Tel: (93) 134444211

Cencali**
Juarez y Paseo Tabasco
Tel: (93) 151996

Zacatecas
Gallery Best Western***
Blvd. Lopez Mateos
Tel: (492) 23311

Zihuatenejo
Hotel Sotovento***
Playa la Ropa
Tel: (743) 42032

Bungalows Allec**
Playa Madera
Tel: (753) 42002

Villas Miramar**
Playa la Madera
Tel: (753) 42106

Villa del Sol**
Playa la Ropa
Tel: (753) 42239

PHOTO CREDITS

Randa Bishop : Backend, x, xi, xiv (top & bottom), xv, 3, 9, 26, 29, **35**, 40, 45, 52, 58 (bottom), 64 (top & bottom), 66 (top & bottom), 69, 73, 80, 97, 110, 124, 128, 140, 158, 162/163, 164, 166, 168/169, 174/175, 179, 180, 181, 182, 187, 188, 190, 191, 198, 204/205, 206 (top), 207, 208, 214 (bottom), 215, 219, 224, 228, 236, 246, 250, 251, 253, 262, 272, 278, 282 (top), 288, 289, 292, 295, 298, 303 (top), 304, 305, 306, 326, 328 (top & bottom), 329, 330, 332, 338 (top & bottom), 340, 355, 358/359, 360

Greg Evans : 24/25

Cherie Glaser: 4, 58 (top), 65, 76, 83, 88, 93 (bottom), 98, 119, 125, 126, 170/177, 172, 173, 216, 248, 257, 339, 343, 344, 351, 384

Keith Mundy : xvi, 8, 11, 19, 20, 22, 23, 93 (top), 104, 308, xii (top & bottom), xiii

Odyssey/Robert Frerck : 2, 5, 6, 10, 12, 13, 14, 17, 42/43, 47, 48/49, 96, 99, 103, 107, 114, 116/117, 118, 122/123, 129, 131, 132, 141, 203, 214 (top), 226, 233, 238, 240, 274, 280/281, 303 (bottom), 307, 312, 315, 321 (top), 324, 336, 352, Backcover (top, left)

Ann Purcell : 50, 94

Carl Purcell : 34, 36, 44, 60, 70, 72, 74, 78, 84, 89, 91, 100, 101, 109, 176, 184, 185, 186, 188, 282 (bottom),283, 285, 286, 287, 290, 335, 342, 249, Backcover (top, right & bottom), Front end paper

Louisa Preston : 38/39, 51, 59, 61, 146, 264, 267 (top & bottom), 269, 270/271

Douglas Peebles : 54/55, 55, 64, 68/69, 266, 268, 296, 297, 300, 301

Morten Strange : 56 (top & bottom), 57 (top & bottom)

Life File/R Powers : 227

Tan Chung Lee : 46, 75, 77, 81, 90, 92, 136, 143, 144, 145, 148, 149, 150, 155, 157, 161, 165, 192, 196, 197, 199, 202, 206, 209, 210, 217, 221, 223, 234, 237, 241, 242, 243, 244, 245, 254, 256, 259, 260, 291, 302, 310, 313, 317, 320, 321 (bottom), 322, 323, 334, 350, 356

370

An acknowledgement of thanks is due to Francisco Mendez of The Embassy of Mexico in Singapore for helping with information.

INDEX